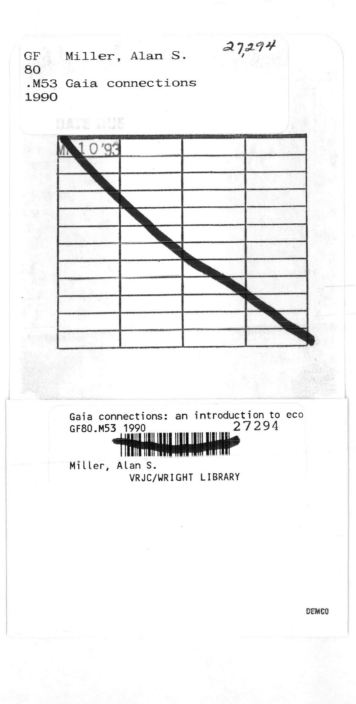

GAIA CONNECTIONS

Gaia Connections

An Introduction to Ecology, Ecoethics, and Economics

Alan S. Miller

Rowman & Littlefield Publishers, Inc.

ROWMAN & LITTLEFIELD PUBLISHERS, INC.

Published in the United States of America
by Rowman & Littlefield Publishers, Inc.
8705 Bollman Place, Savage, Maryland 20763

British Cataloging in Publication Information Available

Library of Congress Cataloging-in-Publication Data

Miller, Alan S.
  Gaia connections : an introduction to ecology, ecoethics,
economics / by Alan S. Miller.
    p.   cm.
Includes bibliographical references and index.
    1. Human ecology—Moral and ethical aspects.
2. Environmental policy.   3. Economic
development—Environmental aspects.   I. Title.
GF80.M53   1990
179'.1—dc20   90–20632 CIP

ISBN 0–8476–7655–2 (alk. paper)
ISBN 0–8476–7656–0 (pbk. alk. paper)

Printed in the United States of America

∞ ™ The paper used in this publication meets the minimum requirements of
   American National Standard for Information Sciences—Permanence of
   Paper for Printed Library Materials, ANSI Z39.48–1984.

This book is dedicated to the memory of
my mother,
Marjorie Miller Dahlberg,
and my sister,
Mary Lou Miller Hartley,
who together taught me much of what I know
about practical ethics.

Gaia, Mother of all, I sing, oldest of Gods.
Firm of foundation, who feeds all creatures
    living on earth.
As many as move on the radiant land and swim
    in the sea
And fly through the air—all these does she feed
    with her bounty.
Mistress, from you come our fine children
    and bountiful harvests.
Yours is the power to give mortals life and
    to take it away.

Homeric Hymn 30:1–7

In the beginning there was Te Kore, the Nothingness. Then came Te Po, the Night. Then Rangi-nui, the Sky Father, was joined with Papa-tu-a-nuku, the Earth Mother, and they had many children. Tane-Mahuta, their son, was growth. Tane-Mahuta took of the sacred red earth, and made the body of a woman. He breathed life into her nostrils and she became Hine-ahu-one, the Earth-formed maid.

And the earth burgeoned with trees and flowers, grass, flax and fruits, and in the forests beasts, birds, and insects found food and shelter. This is the realm of Tane-Mahuta, and in it men and women and children, whom Tane caused to be, find solace and refreshment and great delight, for the realm of Tane-Mahuta is beautiful above all else.

Maori Creation Myth

What man most passionately wants is his living wholeness and his living unison, not an isolated salvation of his soul. I am part of the sun as my eye is a part of me. That I am a part of the earth, my feet know perfectly well, and my blood is a part of the sea. There is no thing of me that is alone and absolute except my mind, and we shall find that the mind has no existence by itself. It is only the glitter of the sun on the surfaces of the waters.

D. H. Lawrence
The Apocalypse

Contents

Ecoethics. Four case studies. Shallow, deep, and deepest ecology. Ecofeminism: Women, men, and nature. Alternative approaches to environmental ethics.

General principles in ethics. Theories of justice in the past. Modern theories of justice.

World order and the environment. The poverty–ecology connection. Rights and just expectations. The nature of security in the modern world. The peace equation: Economic conversion equals job insurance. New politics and paradigms for the solar age.

The pros and cons of the sustainability debate. The two faces of scarcity. Biological ethics and thermodynamics.

Capitalism and socialism. Dilemmas of political economy.

List of Tables and Figures

Tables

Figure

Acknowledgments

Those of us involved in teaching are always indebted to a variety of
people who have provided us with different kinds of intellectual
stimulation. We read, discuss matters with friends and colleagues,
then lift up ideas and perspectives in our lectures and writings that
are—more than anything else—the consequence of what we have
absorbed from others. Surely that has been the case in preparing this
book, chapters of which are basically revisions of lectures delivered
over a ten-year period in my environmental issues, environmental
ethics, and bioethics classes in the Conservation and Resource Studies
(CRS) Department at the University of California, Berkeley. I am
keenly aware of how important the thinking and writing of others has
been in the formulation of my own perspectives. I hope I have
properly indicated within the text those books and people who have
frequently provided the primary stimulus for my own work. If I have
missed an acknowledgment here or there, I (at least) am comforted
by the fact that we all in turn stand on one another's shoulders. There
is, after all (as Ecclesiastes reminds us), not that much that is new
under the sun.

I need, however, to more formally acknowledge three different
groups of people who have made my life an ongoing learning process.
In 18 years on the Berkeley campus, more than 10,000 students have
enrolled in my classes and it is to these people—whose thousands of
papers and exams I have (often reluctantly) read—that I extend
primary thanks for their continuing insights into the real world, for
their instruction, and for their willingness to criticize their teacher.

I am also deeply indebted to friends and colleagues both within
and outside the university whose "uncommon wisdom" (as Fritjof
Capra might say) has regularly enriched my own understanding.
Within the CRS Department, I wish to offer special thanks to my
faculty colleagues: Miguel Altieri, Claudia Carr, Don Dahlsten, Dick

Garcia, Mike Maniates, Carolyn Merchant, and Arnold Schultz. My special non–U.C. Berkeley friendly mentors have included Fritjof Capra, J. Baird Callicott, and Frances and George Porter.

Persons (most of whom I have not known personally) whose writings or ideas have been enormously influential in shaping my own perspectives include Murray Bookchin, Herman Daly, Bill Devall, Brian Easlea, Richard Falk, Joseph Fletcher, Warwick Fox, Paulo Friere, Stephen Jay Gould, Hazel Henderson, Ivan Illich, Thomas Kuhn, Aldo Leopold, Richard Lewontin, James Lovelock, Arne Naess, Arnold Pacey, John Rawls, Jeremy Rifkin, E. F. Schumacher, Peter Singer, and Langdon Winner. I am deeply indebted to Patricia Merrill for her patient and competent copyediting. Finally, I am especially grateful to my best friend and lifetime companion, Barbara Miller, for her constant support, her affection, and her frequent reminders never to take myself too seriously.

Introduction

In Robert Heinlein's science fiction classic *The Green Hills of Earth*, the story is told of the poet-astronaut Rhysling who writes a ballad in which he yearns

> for one more landing on the globe that
> gave us birth. May we rest our eyes
> on the fleecy skies and the cool green
> hills of Earth.[1]

When musician Paul Winter was composing his *Missa Gaia: The Earth Mass* in 1981, he discussed the fresh and powerful whole Earth images now made possible by modern space exploration with his friend, astronaut Rusty Schweickart. Based on these new physical views of the planet, Winter sought in words and music to create a unique spiritual vision for the Mass:

> For the earth forever turning, for the skies, for every sea;
> To our God, we sing returning home, to our blue green hills of Earth.
>
> For the mountains, hills and pastures, in their silent majesty,
> For all of life, for all of nature, sing we our joyful praise to you.[2]

Most of us, in whatever way we express our own subjective praise and thanksgiving for the natural world, have sensed that the Earth is indeed like a vast, living organism. In its turn, it blesses and protects and provides for the creatures of the planet. It also brings privation and pain and sorrow in separate measure. The worship of Earth—its creatures and its creative force—is a theme common to us all.

In 1975, British atmospheric chemist James E. Lovelock, reflecting on the photos of Earth from outer space and on his own earlier

1

scientific efforts to understand the workings of the planet, described his own realization of the Earth's vitality this way:

> It appeared to us that the Earth's biosphere is able to control at least the temperature of the Earth's surface and the composition of the atmosphere. Prima facie, the atmosphere looked like a contrivance put together cooperatively by the totality of living systems to carry out certain necessary control functions. This led to the formulation of the proposition that living matter, the air, the oceans, the land surface were parts of a giant system which was able to control temperature, the composition of the air and sea, the pH of the soil and so on as to be optimum for survival of the biosphere. The system seemed to exhibit the behavior of a single organism, even a living creature. One having such formidable powers deserved a name to match it; William Golding, the novelist, suggested Gaia—the name given by the ancient Greeks to their Earth Goddess.[3]

In the past ten years, this so-called Gaia hypothesis has developed an enormous following, particularly within the activist and "deep ecology" segments of the environmental movement. And whether or not the Gaia concept—Earth as a single, self-regulating organism—holds up within the formal boundaries of the earth sciences, it is metaphysically correct. Until we do come to think of the Earth as organism—complex, fecund, self-sustaining, connected in all its parts—we will have difficulty moving beyond the shallowest levels of ecology.

Metaphors can also, however, be pushed to a point where they become a hindrance rather than a help to proper understanding. Too many environmentalists, in singing praise to Mother Earth's powers, fail to reckon adequately with the utter truth that it is today humankind that has the power to determine Gaia's future. We, with our science and technology, have the whole world in our hands. The theme of this book is that, although there is a spiritual dimension to Earth's functioning (whether from an internal or some external pulse), there is a danger in overly romanticized Gaia imagery if it ignores the overall context of ecology, the strictures of economics, and the imperatives of ethics in the quest for planetary healing.

In his *Guide for the Perplexed*, environmental economist E. F. Schumacher noted that people who acknowledge or describe things as they really are in life are commonly denounced as doomsayers and pessimists.[4] In similar vein, Theodore Roszak stressed the inadequacy of even the wisest comment on life when it does not begin by squarely confronting the outrage and horror Earth's inhabitants have let loose on the planet in this century. We all prefer to avoid the facts of the holocausts we have created, hoping that either the prophets are wrong or that the crisis such as it is will simply go away.[5]

The urge to bypass reality is perhaps even more real and understandable today. Things, we sense, are falling apart. The social-psychological glue that has for so long bound us to our primary institutions now seems to be fast dissolving. Our biological systems are increasingly stressed. Neither of the great political-economic systems really work. The arrogance of political power is overwhelming, and we rightly distrust politicians quite as much as we fear the motives of lawyers, car salesmen, and oil companies.

But we can no longer avoid facing up to the environmental crisis. Only a decade ago, people criticized my book *A Planet to Choose: Value Studies in Political Ecology* for its moderate pessimism as it assessed the then dominant environmental crises: outmoded economic systems, environmental mismanagement, pollution, resource scarcity, patterns of exploitation and alienation, and ethical backwardness.[6] Now most of us know more surely than I did then that our lives and the lives of our children have been placed at risk by political and economic decision-makers who have discounted the survival risk for our species from their short-range, profit-oriented planning. The problems have not gone away.

Unhappily, the crisis has in fact accelerated rapidly during this period. What seemed ten years ago to be pessimism is now recognized as current reality. But there are also new hopes. In an effort to stimulate governments to more clearly recognize the environmental threat hanging over the planet, the United Nations established the World Commission on Environment and Development (WCED) in 1983 to assess and report on long-term environmental strategies. The report of the commission was published in 1987 under the title *Our Common Future*.[7] Assessing the ultimate nature of the current environmental crisis and the likelihood that civilization as we know it cannot last long without a new emphasis on steady-state economic development, the WCED study—also known as the Brundtland report, after its editor—intersected an increasing popular concern about environmental quality.

Focusing on the importance of "sustainable development," by which the Brundtland authors mean "development that meets the needs of the present without compromising the ability of future generations to meet their own needs," the study arrived at precisely the moment when the realities of global warming, ozone layer thinning, and a host of other ecological problems were receiving global recognition. Although the Brundtland data are not new, the study spells out in clear fashion the nature of the present ecological dilemma and suggests new directions to those who are concerned for planetary healing.

Brundtland begins its assessment of the environmental state of the world with an essentially economic rather than an ecological analysis. Top priority in assuring our common future must be given to meeting the basic needs of the poverty-stricken majority of the world's population. If this is to happen, the priorities for truly sustainable development must be to revive and change the character and quality of economic growth and development; to conserve and if possible enhance the resource base; to move toward population stabilization; to reorient science and technology; to integrate responsible, sustainable economic planning into our ongoing environmental assessment and analysis; and to work toward the reformation of the global economic and resource management systems. We will review many of these concerns in this book.

Once again, however, some will protest that things are not so bad as the gloomier prophets claim. Perhaps we do at times take ourselves too seriously. Generational arrogance is not unusual. Our age, like every other in humankind's history, considers its own time to be unique. But in a fashion qualitatively different from that in any preceding period, we have now created both a set of socio-economic-environmental-ethical problems and a science and technology that together pose the real possibility of unimaginable chaos in the near-term future. In an altogether fascinating but frightening manner, our physicists, chemists, and molecular biologists have all developed schema with the potential to provoke such an apocalypse. Nuclear wars and mutant bugs are futurist scenarios familiar to us all. Social scientists and policymakers alike seem helpless to redirect our priorities or control the technological drift.

Many of our ancestors would have coveted our modern prowess in multiplying the possibilities of mortality. The pogroms, crusades, and social injustices of the preceding two millenia give ample evidence of the fact that our current ethical myopia is hardly new. In no century but our own, however, has the possibility of a massive Gaian disaster, occasioned by both social and scientific malfeasance, been so immediate and so indiscriminately directed.

Accordingly, the Promethean legends hold more import for human beings today. With our ancestors, we increasingly learn more about the arts and the sciences. We have gained relative mastery over the forces that will determine our destiny. In the Greek legends, however, hope always remained as a possibility for the present and as a moral linchpin to the future. Whether or not our political and industrial leaders—whose conscious decisions to maximize short-range benefits have largely created the conditions of environmental decay we all now experience, and who seem intent on engineering what for them seems to be a better future for the rest of us—will long permit such hope to remain is a primary subject of this book. Analyzing the major problems that today confound both environmentalists and ethicists, the book should also help construct an analytical framework for assessing how it is that we can go about making ecoethical decisions in our time.

Ironically, the growing severity of the human assault on nature has had its positive side. We now understand that ethics is broader and deeper than simply the concern we have for our fellow human beings. Many of us now realize that any viable modern ethic must also include a consciousness of our duty to and our moral responsibility for nature itself. Indeed, a major change in moral philosophy is now under way as we come to better understand our biological interdependence— our connectedness—with the rest of the created orders and our consequently broadened sphere of ethical responsibility. The primary question I pose in the book is simple. If we are in fact in the process of defining a new ethic, how does this understanding relate to ecology, economics, science, medical practice, the conduct of war, the rights of nonhuman parts of the creation, and the social responsibility of human beings who understand the necessity of organizing for change within the structures of society? Long-term resolution of the more visible environmental problems will be impossible until we begin to think through and reassess the substance of our moral and ethical valuation of nature. This study has many origins. More generally, it emerges from three concerns: (1) the actual state of the global environment today, and the imperative for the development of sustainable economic and resource systems; (2) my apprehension over the nature and direction of molecular biology and its frightening promise, in the words of a Berkeley colleague, "to genetically redetermine the nature of our species within this generation"; and (3) the equally important and disturbing movement within science toward biological determinism and the attempt to reduce all of life to a set of physical and chemical equations. Teaching as I do in the College of Natural Resources at the University of California in Berkeley, I know only too well that the one-dimensionality of the new biology in its movement toward the microscopic and away from the analysis of whole systems manifests a new and quite frightening scientific reductionism.

More particularly, this little book is the result of some reflection on questions posed to me over the years by students in my Berkeley classes. What are the social sources of environmental values? Does our class, race, sex, or geographical origin affect the way in which we relate to the natural world? How and why does this happen, and what are the environmental policy consequences of such accidental circumstances? What is the nature of normality? Are there not dangers in even beginning to think about establishing biological norms for human beings? What's all this about ecological restoration? Is it possible to begin to restore the damage we've already done? Again, analysis of such questions will recur regularly throughout this text. While it is usually best to start a book at the beginning, readers can begin at the point where they have most interest. Common threads do tie the book together, but chapters are relatively independent and focus on quite particular subject matter.

I present this study in part as an acknowledgment of the good ethical sense and honesty of almost all the thousands of men and women who have taken my political ecology and bioethics classes in the past 17 years at Berkeley and who have contributed far more to my education than I to theirs. Accordingly, my hope is that this book will be helpful to those lay ethicists of the common life who, with the writer, know very few answers but continue to be concerned about human values, the nature of science, and the politics of biology. Together, perhaps, we can take the psychological risk of facing the world as it really is, tilting an increasingly critical eye at those who—in the name of scientific and industrial progress—seek not only to control but perhaps also to determine our destinies.

Notes

1. Robert A. Heinlein, "The Green Hills of Earth," in *The Past through Tomorrow* (New York: G. P. Putnam's Sons, 1967).

2. "The Blue Green Hills of Earth," words and music by Paul Winter and Kim Oler, in *Missa Gaia: The Earth Mass*, copyright by Living Music Records, Sausalito, California, 1982.

3. James E. Lovelock and Sidney Epton, "The Quest for Gaia," *New Scientist* 65 (1975), p. 304.

4. E. F. Schumacher, *A Guide for the Perplexed* (New York: Harper and Row, 1977).

5. As noted in Peter Horsley, "Environmental Ethics and the Dominant World View: Cultural Change and Individual Action," Department of Geography White Paper, Massey University, Palmerston North, New Zealand, 1989.

6. Alan S. Miller, *A Planet to Choose: Value Studies in Political Ecology* (New York: Pilgrim Press, 1978).

7. Gro Harlem Brundtland, ed., *Our Common Future*, report of the UN World Commission on Environment and Development (Oxford, U.K.: Oxford University Press, 1987).

1

Environmental Ethics

As this chapter is being written, the cleanup of the March 24 (Good Friday), 1989, Exxon Valdez oil tanker spill is under way. This largest oil spill in U.S. history had long been predicted by environmentalists, who opposed both the production and export of petroleum in the fragile Alaskan environment. An accident, the spill was nevertheless statistically inevitable. Reckoning with the risk, the oil companies had been promising that their response to such a crisis would be immediate and thorough. Unhappily, as environmentalists had also feared, the response was in fact slow and marginal. The oil slick has now covered thousands of square miles and done perhaps irreparable damage to the Alaskan ecology.

Although the incident will not be mentioned again, this is, indirectly, a book about the ecological catastrophe occasioned by the crack-up of the tanker. The Valdez event symbolizes the two primary dimensions of the current environmental crisis: the terrible reality of the planetary ecological and environmental breakdown that we shall soon be describing; and the moral crisis symbolized by the penny-pinching, defensive response of Exxon and the U.S. government to this threat to nature. In a time of unprecedented environmental peril, the bankruptcy of traditional ethics (concerned only for the relationship of person to person and largely ignoring the human–nature connection) reflected in the official management of the Valdez crisis is increasingly evident. Neither traditional politics nor our best science and technology seem able to cope with these ever more common threats to the planet.

Ecoethics

The overall theme of *Gaia Connections* is the relationship of ecoethics to the environmental struggle. Ecoethics is not a complicated concept.

It suggests simply that the categories of ethical and moral reflection (which form a significant portion of our Western intellectual traditions) must today be broadened to encompass nature itself. When Aldo Leopold suggested in 1949 that a new requirement for any relevant contemporary ethic must include a "land ethic," he was talking about ecoethics.[1] When Rachel Carson pointed out the inevitability of some future "silent spring" if we do not contain our production and use of pesticides, she was talking ecoethics.[2] When E. F. Schumacher suggested for development theory the possibility that "small is beautiful" and that we need to develop a new "Buddhist economics"—an economics that would in fact function "as if people mattered"—he was focusing on ecoethical concerns.[3] When Christopher Stone posed the question "Should trees have standing?" it was clear that new ecoethical formulations were in process.[4]

There is an ancient myth describing how the king of the Persians applied a basic rule in evaluating the work of his regional governors.[5] He would simply observe the condition of the land and the forests within particular jurisdictions. If the land and the forests were well cared for, he automatically rewarded his governors. If the land was ill-tended and restoration efforts to repair damage delayed, the king replaced the caretakers. He evaluated the overall governing ability of his subordinates by their care for the natural world. The political principle is clear and as applicable today as it was in the mythical past. Those who genuinely care for the Earth, who are sensitive to the effects of human impacts on the environment, can be trusted to govern well generally. The final assessment of the integrity of any political system may be judged on two primary concerns: (1) the respect the system shows for nature; and (2) the care it provides for the least advantaged in the society. Today, as the Brundtland report (see the Introduction to this book) suggests, both concerns are prerequisite for planetary survival.

One of our current dilemmas is that we are all products of philosophical systems that suggest humankind can infinitely progress toward the goal of perfection. We are all, in a sense, direct descendents of the Age of Enlightenment, decrying limits of any kind, and confident in our ability to plan properly and manage well. Our dominant ecoethic has been essentially instrumental. We see nature as little more than the colorful background for working out our own little dramas of fulfillment and salvation. Essentially, as Woody Allen once remarked, "We are at two with nature."

While many traditionalists have argued that such an instrumental view of the human–nature connection is adequate, increasing numbers of people understand intuitively that nature has intrinsic value, in and of itself. We acknowledge the wisdom in Chief Seattle's response to President Franklin Pierce in 1855 when he questioned the intentions of the U.S. government's interest in Indian lands and suggested an ethic to govern the relationship between rulers and resources:

> How can you buy or sell the sky, the warmth of the land? The idea is strange to us. If we do not own the freshness of the air and the sparkle of the water, how can you buy them?
>
> Every part of this earth is sacred to my people. Every shining pine needle, every sandy shore, every mist in the deep woods, every clearing and humming insect is holy in the memory and experience of my people. The sap which courses through the trees carries the memory of the red man.
>
> All things are connected. Whatever befalls the earth, befalls the sons of the earth. One thing we know. Our God is the same. This earth is precious to Him. Even the white man cannot be exempt from this common destiny.[6]

The point here, to be explored in much more detail in later chapters, is that there is a kind of linearity between the spiritual values of much of human civilization and the prescriptions we must develop for environmental healing. Without sensitivity, for example, to the spiritual values of native peoples around the world, there will be little hope even of ecological restoration. The recently formed Maori Secretariat of New Zealand's Ministry of the Environment, for example, selected for its organizational title the Maori word *maruwhenua*, which reflects the historic land ethic of the Maori people. *Maru* refers to a general shielding power and authority. *Whenua* is the Maori word for land. *Maruwhenua*, then, is an ecoethical word, referring to the shielding power over all of the land that is the responsibility of its human inhabitants.

Generically, ecoethics belongs within the disciplines of ecology and philosophy. Ecology, more than any other subdiscipline of biology, is concerned about wholeness, about relationships between particular organisms within larger ecosystems, and about the healthy interaction of all components of those systems. In a very real sense, the moral/environmental dilemmas facing humankind today are the result of atomistic and antiecological thinking. Any ethic—especially an ecoethic—will both encourage us to think holistically and place some form of limit on our scope of action. We do not have the freedom to get drunk and crash oil tankers on Alaskan reefs! The ethical actor no longer has the option of pursuing the kind of unenlightened self-interest that even today too often programs our individualism and defines our understandings of responsibility. Ecoethics, then, suggests the need for the development of both an instinct and a concern for cooperation and for community well-being.

Methodologically, ecoethics applies the insights and disciplines of philosophy to the quest for ecological health. At base, ethics is simply the philosophical study of morality, a study that enables us to arrive at a basis for conduct and action. Ecoethics, as a new discipline within ethical philosophy, attempts to create a conceptual framework for human interaction with the environment, a framework that can assist us in holding our own lives together and enable us to act with discipline, understanding, and reverence toward the natural world.

Four Case Studies

Since ethics is also the case-study branch of philosophy (albeit much more than this), it is worthwhile at the outset to look specifically at four of the longer range environmental problems. Many others could have been selected. Although most readers are by now aware of the extensive ecological damage being revealed daily around the world, these specific references may help to illustrate and to focus the ecoethical perspective. Moreover, each of the following instances of environmental disruption is particularly significant because of being directly or potentially implicated in the frightening scenarios of climate change that now threaten our traditional modes of living and perhaps our very existence.

Ozone Depletion

The ozone layer, produced in geological antiquity and situated some 15–25 miles above the Earth's surface, screened out enough solar ultraviolet (UV) radiation to have allowed life as we know it to establish itself and thrive on the Planet Earth. When ultraviolet light penetrates human tissue, it is preferentially absorbed by proteins and nucleic acids like deoxyribonucleic acid, DNA, the genetic material that codes our inheritable characteristics. As it is absorbed, the UV radiation breaks the chemical bonds in these molecules and leads to a variety of forms of cellular disorganization. Both germ (reproductive) cells and somatic (regular tissue) cells can be affected, leading to a variety of human diseases including cancer.

Happily, 99 percent of this UV radiation was, in the past, absorbed by the ozone in the thin stratospheric shell surrounding the Earth. Unhappily, a combination of advanced industrial impacts—nuclear tests in the atmosphere; high-flying jets; and, of most importance, the worldwide use of chloroflourocarbons (CFCs)—has now begun to break down the ozone layer. Since CFCs have an atmospheric lifetime of more than 100 years and proliferate through chemical reactions over time, the measurements of ozone concentration today reflect most directly emissions that occurred in the past. The impact of today's vastly accelerated emissions will not be measurable for many years as they meantime slowly but surely go about their deadly business of destroying ozone.

Beginning in 1983, scientists started noticing a distinct thinning of the ozone layer—as much as a 40 percent reduction over the south polar regions. This "hole in the ozone doughnut" is now also being seen in the north polar regions. The U.S. Environmental Protection Agency (EPA) estimates that, for every 5 percent reduction in ozone concentration, we can expect at least an additional 1 million cases of skin cancer per year. The National Aeronautics and Space Administration officially predicts hundreds of thousands of new cases of skin cancer in the United States by the year 2000 and a minimum 10-percent further reduction in the ozone concentration by 2050. Although these predictions are to some degree guesswork, it is clear that skin cancer will be a much more common human disease in the future.

Eighty-one nations within the UN umbrella have now agreed to ban all CFC production and use by the year 2000. Many U.S. cities are drafting legislation to outlaw products containing CFCs. Sadly, however, the impact of the free hand with CFCs in the past half-century will not really be felt for years to come. Banning CFC-laden products is now ecologically, ethically, and economically sensible. But the diseases occasioned by their use will be with us long after the polluting products have been taken off the market.

Greenhouse Gasses

For decades, scientists have been predicting that we would someday pay a heavy survival price for our constantly increased burning of fossil fuels and the consequent buildup of carbon dioxide (CO_2) and

other "greenhouse gasses" (methane, nitrous oxide, chloroflourocarbons) in the atmosphere. In 1800, air contained some 260 parts per
million (ppm) of CO_2. Today we have measured levels of more than
340 ppm. Jessica Tuchman Matthews of the World Resources Institute
(and a former earth-sciences adviser to the National Security Council)
estimates that CO_2 levels will increase to 600 ppm by the year 2025.[7]
Methane—originating in its biospheric excess from forest fires, coal
mining, landfills, termite colonies, and the digestive tracts of billions
of animals—is perhaps 20–30 times more effective than CO_2 at
trapping heat close to the Earth. In the past 300 years it has more
than doubled its concentration in the atmosphere, from 650 parts
per trillion (ppt) to 1,700 ppt today. Methane is now estimated to be
responsible for 20–25 percent of overall greenhouse warming; CO_2
and the chloroflourocarbons are considered responsible for 50–55
percent and 20–25 percent, respectively.

This accumulation of so-called greenhouse gasses (because of their
function in blocking the reradiation of solar heat from the Earth's
surface and out through the atmosphere) will lead to a global temperature increase of at least 1.5–4.5 degrees Celsius by the year 2025.
Because such temperature increases will slowly melt the polar ice
caps, Tuchman predicts a rise in sea levels around the world of several
inches to a foot or more during the next quarter-century. In May
1990, the United Nations' Panel on Climate Change predicted minimum temperature increases of 5.4 degrees Fahrenheit and a 25.6-
inch rise in sea level before the end of the twenty-first century. At
current rates of CO_2 buildup, rainfall is expected to decrease as much
as 40 percent in the north temperate zones by the year 2040, with
corresponding increases in other parts of the world. Already, glaciers
and sea ice formations are everywhere receding. The California
coastline, for example, has been dramatically resculptured in the past
five years by a combination of rising sea levels, unusual winds, and
the effects of El Niño (the cyclical change in Pacific Ocean temperatures and currents that typically causes severe but short-term weather
changes). Marin County, California—just north of San Francisco—is
already making plans to dike one major shopping center within the
next decade. Policymakers in coastal cities worldwide are having to
think out the implications of these sea-level increases. Whether or not
the worst effects of the greenhouse scenario happen on schedule or
are delayed, major transformations in climate are now clearly in the
forecast and are certain to be an item on planning agendas in the
future.

Tropical Rainforest Destruction

The tropical forests of Planet Earth are being destroyed at the incomprehensible rate of 100 acres each minute of every day. According to the United Nations' Food and Agriculture Organization (FAO), this amounts to a total of at least 40,000 square miles per year. Other scientists estimate the annual rate of destruction at 80,000 square miles.[8] If current rates of rainforest eradication continue, the child born in 1990 will inherit a planet totally stripped of rainforest by the time she is 50 years old.

Biologists estimate that tropical rainforests—which cover only 6 percent of the surface of the planet—contain at least 50 percent of all the plant and animal species that have come into being throughout our evolutionary history.

> Indeed, the importance of tropical forests as a habitat for wildlife cannot be understated. 90% of the world's non-human primates are found in tropical rainforests, along with two-thirds of all known plants, 40% of birds of prey and 80% of the world's insects. The Amazon basin alone contains an estimated 1 million animal and plant species, including 2,500 species of tree, 1,800 species of birds and 2,000 species of fish. A single hectare may contain 400 trees, every other one a different species. By contrast a typical temperate forest contains a mere 10–15 trees per hectare. One river in Brazil has been found to contain more species of fish than all the rivers in the United States.[9]

In addition to the loss of genetic resources, tropical forest destruction has also led to an intensification of the drought and flood cycles now becoming commonplace throughout the developing world. Although tropical forest soils are usually poor, the vast network of root systems acts as a sponge to hold rainfall for release into streams and lakes. When forests are destroyed, the soil can no longer retain water. This leads to massive flooding during rainy seasons, with subsequent droughts in the dry periods. Similarly, climatologists have long known that rainforests play a critical role in the regulation of biospheric climate patterns. As the rainforests disappear, tropical regions will become hotter and drier, and temperate regions cooler. Without the forest mantle to absorb vast quantities of carbon dioxide, the greenhouse effect with its global temperature increase will be accelerated.

Other biological effects are also inevitable from rainforest destruction. In 1989, there were some 140 million human beings living within the world's tropical forests. The entire life-support system for these people comes from the forest around them, including the rich cultural inheritance of native societies. The forest is the home of their deities and the resting place of their ancestors. It is the provider of all that is necessary for life. But on an ever-increasing scale, forest dwellers are being robbed of their lands, forcibly resettled in non-forest areas, and compelled by unsympathetic governments to become assimilated into poverty-stricken urban slum areas. Formal attempts by governments to rid themselves permanently of native populations are all too common—the withholding of medical services to colonists who wish to locate in the forest, the harassing of native peoples by police and military sectors, and even the outright introduction of infectious diseases among indigenous populations. The old practice of the U.S. government in distributing smallpox-infected blankets to American Indians may have been resurrected by developers in sections of South America.

And inevitably, the poor people of the forest—native as well as immigrant—are being scapegoated as the main actors in the rainforest debacle. Forest destruction is *not* the result of peasant action, but of the commercial development schemes visible everywhere in the Third World. The clearing of rainforests to make way for cattle raising, cotton and sugarcane plantations, and road building is the direct consequence of industrial and commercial planning seconded by local government structures. As one critic noted with regard to rainforest destruction in Central America, "To blame colonising peasants for burning the rainforests is tantamount to blaming soldiers for causing wars. Peasant colonists carry out much of the work of deforestation in Central America, but they are mere pawns in a General's game."[10]

Unhappily, the negative lessons of unrestricted and unregulated development that we should know by heart are being ignored. Rainforest destruction is accelerating everywhere in the tropics, with Brazil alone increasing its cutting by one-third every year. The same pattern can be seen in India, Nepal (which has lost 90 percent of its trees since 1945), Ethiopia, sections of West Africa, and many areas of tropical America and Southeast Asia. Once again, short-term profit for the few is shortening the life span of Planet Earth.

The Nuclear Winter

Nuclear winter has been a well-publicized scenario since the first "TTAPS" study (its authors being Turco, Toon, Ackerman, Pollack, and Sagan) in the magazine *Science* in 1983.[11] The basic formula is as follows: If 30–40 percent of the current strategic nuclear arsenals of the United States and the Soviet Union were used in the first exchange of a nuclear war, the diminution of sunlight due to smoke and particulate matter released into the atmosphere would cause a reduction in sunlight of 95–99 percent in the northern hemisphere, with an accompanying temperature decline varying between 10 and 40 degrees Celsius. Photosynthesis would largely stop in many portions of the world for varying lengths of time. Although climate-change estimates have been adjusted in the past five years to accord with new data, even the U.S. Department of Defense now agrees essentially with the predictions of TTAPS and other scientists.

Although the southern hemisphere would not be so severely impacted by the nuclear winter, there is little cause for solace down under. Three-dimensional computer projections recently developed by astrophysicist Carl Sagan track the probable drift of smoke and haze from such an exchange. The clouds would be blackest over the northern hemisphere; but as the days and weeks go by, the soot and atmospheric debris would drift inexorably south. Studies in New Zealand have recently predicted massive agricultural and social impacts on that nation ensuing from such a catastrophe.

It is not the purpose of this study to document or describe in detail the other major elements in the global environmental crisis: generalized pollution; declining air quality; toxic waste management; groundwater poisoning; increasing use of herbicides and pesticides; health threats from nuclear radiation; the pollution of space with nuclear and other waste materials; the threats posed by new genetically modified organisms and other new life forms created in the laboratories; the depletion of both renewable natural resources (forests, fisheries, grasslands, croplands) and nonrenewables (coal, petroleum, natural gas, minerals); and the ongoing extinction of thousands of plant and animal species. The data are reasonably clear on all of these issues. Each poses an enormous threat to all life forms on Earth. Whether or not and why and how we begin to make the political and economic and ethical decisions to change the quality of our environment in time to do any actual good is the real issue, anyway.

Shallow, Deep, and Deepest Ecology

A new chapter in the environmental ethics debate was opened in 1972 by ecologist Arne Naess of the University of Oslo. Writing in *Inquiry*, Naess stated,

Ecologically responsible policies are concerned only in part with pollution and resource depletion. There are deeper concerns which touch upon principles of diversity, complexity, autonomy, decentralization, symbiosis, egalitarianism, and classlessness.

The emergence of ecologists from their former relative obscurity marks a turning point in our scientific communities. But their message is twisted and misused. A shallow, but presently rather powerful movement, and a deep, but less influential movement, compete for our attention.[12]

Naess then compares the "shallow" with the "deep" ecology movement. Shallow ecology is establishment ecology—the ecology of government, industry, and university—limiting its concern at the very most to the fight against pollution and resource depletion. Its central objective is the maintenance of the status quo, attempting to do a bit better environmental biology and working for the health and affluence of people at home. Deep ecology, on the contrary, moves beyond formal reductionist biology and concerns itself with whole-system values and with the well-being of people in the poorer and developing countries. It rejects the "man in the environment" concern of most popular ecology and raises questions about the possibility of there being intrinsic values within nature.

California scholars Bill Devall and George Sessions became the most popular supporters of deep ecology following Naess's work. Both agree that the primary task of the environmental philosopher is not simply to search for a formal, precise traditional kind of environmental ethic so much as to develop an ecological consciousness. Deep ecology is a process leading to a sense of self-realization and interaction with the natural world. As George Sessions puts it, "As we discover our ecological self we will joyfully defend and interact with that with which we identify; and instead of imposing environmental ethics on people, we will naturally respect, love, honor and protect that which is of our self."[13]

Deep ecology is concerned not simply with the articulation of alternative ideologies, but even more with stimulating the development of the kind of character and conduct in people that can contribute to the healing of a broken planet. It posits unambiguously the groundwork for a normative ethic (an ethic of "oughts") directing us to develop our own ecological sensibilities so that we may more closely connect with the natural world. As we recognize the infinite complexity of ecological systems, certain ethical imperatives emerge that will condition our future responses. As Aldo Leopold long ago suggested,

> The land ethic changes the role of Homo sapiens from the conqueror of the land-community to plain member and citizen of it. It implies respect for his fellow members, and also respect for the community as such.
>
> In human history, we have learned (I hope) that the conqueror role is eventually self-defeating. Why? Because it is implicit in such a role that the conqueror knows, *ex cathedra,* just what makes the community clock tick, and just what and who is valuable, and what and who is worthless, in community life. It always turns out that he knows neither, and this is why his conquests eventually defeat themselves.[14]

Deep ecology, then, is a process of deepening our self-understanding, challenging the assumptions we make about the world, and reshaping the paradigms that have so prompted us to attempt to control the world around us. The deep ecologist understands that technological society contributes to the ever-widening alienation of people from themselves, from one another, and from nature itself. Deep ecology sees the world not as a collection of entities—of individually separated objects—but, in the words of philosopher-physicist Fritjof Capra, "as a network of phenomena fundamentally interconnected and interdependent. Deep ecological awareness is spiritual awareness and it is thus not surprising that the emerging vision of reality is consistent with the 'perennial philosophy' of spiritual traditions."[15]

While a few critics have faulted the deep ecology movement for failing to "define new values," not attempting to "provide hard guidelines for ecological living," and becoming "befuddled by mysticism,"[16] ideological founder Arne Naess suggests that deep ecology's intentions have in fact always been modest. It aims simply to work toward the conservation of what is left of the richness and diversity of Earth's biological and cultural systems. Naess has formulated "a platform for the deep ecology movement" that suggests its direct, simple affirmations and intentions. Naess's major points include:

1. The flourishing of human and nonhuman life on Earth has inherent value. The value of nonhuman life forms is independent of the usefulness of the nonhuman world for human purposes.

2. The richness and diversity of life forms are also values in themselves and contribute to the flourishing of human and nonhuman life on Earth.

3. Humans have no right to reduce this richness and diversity except to satisfy vital needs.

4. Present human interference with the nonhuman world is excessive, and the situation is rapidly worsening.

5. The policies affecting basic economic, technological, and ideological structures must therefore be changed.

6. The ideological change required is mainly that of appreciating life quality, rather than adhering to an increasingly higher standard of living.

7. Those who subscribe to the foregoing points have an obligation to participate in the attempt to implement the necessary change.[17]

Perhaps the most telling criticism of deep ecology has been from advocates of "social ecology" like sociologist Murray Bookchin, whose neosocialist anarchism focuses on the social and historical bases of the present dilemma. These critics say that deep ecologists tend to overlook the socioeconomic roots beneath the environmental crisis.[18] While there has been an occasional tendency for certain deep ecologists to be apolitical and to overromanticize the potential of the independent environmental actor, those acquainted with the movement's regularly stated concerns for egalitarianism and classlessness as norms for the good society will not fault deep ecology in general for the political innocence of a few.

Australian philosopher Warwick Fox brings us back to a genuine concern for the Earth as he elegantly states the case for the ecoethical, genuinely deep ecology effort to enlarge the sphere of human concern for nonhuman elements of creation:

> Justice does not require equality. It does require that we share one another's fate. The lesson of ecology is that we do share one another's fate in the shallow sense since we all share the fate of the earth. The message of deep ecology is that we ought to care as deeply and as compassionately as possible about that fate—not because it *affects* us but because it is us.[19]

Ecofeminism: Women, Men, and Nature

Although widely understood as a significant new dimension of environmental ethics, ecofeminism (which establishes the connection between the oppression of women and the oppression of nature) is not precisely new. More than 40 years ago, Simone de Beauvoir sought to establish an ecofeminist connection.

> History has shown us that men have always kept in their hands all concrete powers: since the earliest days of the patriarchate they have thought best to keep women in a state of dependence: their codes of law have been set up against her. . . . This arrangement suited the economic interests of the males; but it conformed also to their ontological and moral pretensions. . . . Man expects something other than the assuagement of instinctive cravings from the possession of a woman: she is the privileged object through which he subdues Nature. . . . In women are incarnated the disturbing mysteries of Nature, and man escapes her hold when he frees himself from Nature.[20]

Throughout history, men have dominated both women and nature. The traditional social norms of most societies and the normative stability of economic-system functioning have required the formal subjugation of both feminine and earthly values. Woman has been confined (with modest changes only in quite recent times) to certain carefully defined roles in much the same fashion that the intrinsic values of nature have been carefully obscured by both philosophers and social planners in order that the formal "use-value" of each may be maximized. The theologian Rosemary Reuther notes that "Women simply cannot be persons within the present system of work and family, and they can only rise to liberated personhood by the most radical and fundamental reshaping of the entire human environment in a way that redefines the very nature of work, family and the institutional expressions of social relations."[21]

It is important to note, however, that women and nature have not been the only groupings oppressed by these "institutional expressions" of social reality. Neither men nor children subdued by powerful patriarchal and economic hierarchies have escaped the subjugation expected by those whose class and/or social expectations have been dominant. The physical and psychological trauma suffered by men who are forced into military service and/or alienating or unhealthy workplaces, and the loss of autonomy for children who are socialized into conformity with social and political priorities established by patriarchal leaderships, may not be all that different from the similar insults forced on women throughout the ages. Societies ideologically controlled by a hierarchy of male values have traditionally rewarded only the most aggressive behavior in the political, social, and economic realms. Since most women, children, and many men are neither psychologically nor socially adept at such behavior, they tend to end up as unwilling but often compliant victims of such externally imposed value systems.

Western religion (and most other religions) have similarly placed a great burden on women. The cult of the virgin in Christianity, for example—the idea that woman is redeemed only by destroying her female attributes—has tended both to define role expectations and to provoke socially constrictive feelings of guilt when the individual fails to fulfill the cultic expectation. Reuther explains the further irony of the situation:

> Classical Christianity attributed all the intellectual virtues to the male. Woman was therefore modeled after the rejected part of the psyche. [Thus] she is shallow, fickle-minded, irrational, carnal-minded, lacking all the true properties of knowing and willing and doing. Her inferiority and subjugation are thus rationalized. . . . This same model of social projection of psychic dualism has been extended to each of the other rejected, subjugated groups in society.[22]

A variety of women writers have more recently suggested that ecology is a particularly feminist issue. While the feminist movement and feminist concerns have been expressed in a number of ways that have incorporated within them other social values—liberal feminism with a dominant focus on gender-free equality of opportunity; Marxist feminism with an emphasis on class as well as sexual oppression; socialist feminism that critiques the interconnections between the dominant economic paradigms and the gender expectations; radical feminism that points to the primacy of biological distinctions and reproductive roles as the vehicles of oppression—most of these writers agree that "if eco-feminism is to be taken seriously, then a transformative feminism is needed that will move us beyond the four familiar feminist frameworks and make an eco-feminist perspective central to feminist theory and practice."[23]

Karen J. Warren has devised a minimal set of ecofeminist affirmations that can provide a basis of unity for all persons—male or female—seeking to redefine environmental values:

1. There are important connections between the oppression and exploitation of women and the oppression and exploitation of nature.

2. An understanding of the nature of these connections is neces-

sary to any adequate understanding of the double oppression of women and of nature.

3. All feminist theory and practice must include an ecological perspective.

4. Any solution to ecological problems must include a feminist perspective.[24]

In a similar vein, ecofeminists like Ariel Kay Salleh note that, while deep ecology does critique existing class relationships, it pays less attention to sexual oppression and the social differentiations occasioned by class society. According to this view, then, deep ecology ignores the psychosexual nature of the society and thus of its ecoethic. Because nonecological values have been the result of traditionally patriarchal perspectives, the deep ecology criticism of anthropocentrism (which includes women as part of the species) remains inadequate to define a full value theory. Ecofeminists suggest that the gender-neutral position falls short.

> Sadly, from the eco-feminist point of view, deep ecology is simply another self-congratulatory reformist move; the transvaluation of values it claims for itself is quite peripheral.
> The suppression of the feminine is truly an all pervasive human universal. The deep ecology movement is very much a spiritual search for people in a barren secular age; but . . . much of this quest for self-realization is driven by ego and will.[25]

More generous and perhaps more helpful in the critical task of coalition building between mainstream environmentalists and ecofeminists is the observation of Green movement activist Charlene Spretnak:

> Deep ecologists write that the well-being and flourishing human and non-human life on Earth has value in itself and that humans have no right to reduce the richness and diversity of life forms except to satisfy vital human needs. Eco-feminists agree, but wonder how much one's concept of "vital needs" is shaped by the aspirations of the patriarchal culture.[26]

Alternative Approaches to Environmental Ethics

Others have faulted the deep ecology movement for philosophical shortcomings. William Godfrey-Smith, an Australian biologist, expresses his concern that

Deep ecology has an unfortunate tendency to discuss everything at once. Thus, a social critique can be backed by such disparate authorities as Ginsberg, Castenada, Thoreau, Spinoza, Buddhist and Taoist physics. With a cast of *prima donnas* like these, it is very hard to follow the script.

In their zeal to effect this integration [of human beings and nature], deep ecologists have firmly coupled their central intuition of no boundaries within a field of biospherical egalitarianism.[27]

Unquestionably justified in many aspects of their criticism, both the traditional philosophers and the ecofeminists (in their zeal for ideological coherence) perhaps overlook the fact that the concept of deep ecology is, more than anything else, a metaphor for a new and necessary view of the deeper relationships that must obtain between human beings—male and female—and the natural world. Admittedly, there is more to environmental ethics than deep ecology. And it is important that ecoethicists not fall prey to a romanticized gender-neutral relativism in their attempts to resolve the ecological and economic dilemmas facing the planet. But the primary strength of the deep ecology movement—affirmed by even its harshest critics—is the fact that it lifts to a popular level the generalized philosophical, ecoethical, and usually ecofeminist concerns for a nonanthropocentric value theory that can move us beyond our traditional views of human and patriarchal dominance of the natural order. Environmental ethics is now universally accepted as a legitimate subdiscipline of moral philosophy. This new respectability is due in large part to those deep ecologists who have coupled environmental action to their philosophical theory. Environmental ethicist J. Baird Callicott has said,

As with anything new in philosophy or the sciences, there has been some controversy, not only about its legitimacy, but about its very identity or definition.

Environmental ethics is not an applied ethics similar to biomedical or business ethics; it constitutes nothing less than an incipient paradigm shift in moral philosophy.

An adequate value theory for non-anthropocentric environmental ethics must provide for the intrinsic value of both individual organisms [and] populations, species, biomes, and the biosphere [; it must recognize] intrinsic value for wild and domestic organisms and species. And it must provide for the intrinsic value of our present ecosystem, . . . not equal value for any ecosystem.

Environmental ethics is environmental because it concerns non-human entities . . . and ethical because it attempts to provide theoretical grounds for the moral standing of non-human entities.[28]

The basic deep ecology movement has contributed much to ecoethical thought—reminding us that, insofar as ecology focuses only on human beings and their place within ecosystems, it will be unable to solve environmental problems; and suggesting the possibility that there may in fact be a spiritual as well as a scientific basis for sound ecological thinking. The issues that deep ecology raises are important and worthy of study. Our operative assumptions regarding our place in the natural world have largely determined the ways in which our social and economic systems and our science and technology have developed. Ecofeminist philosopher Carolyn Merchant has developed a taxonomy that summarizes the assumptions made by human beings throughout history in regard to the natural world.[29] Tables 1.1, 1.2, and 1.3 incorporate perspectives from both Merchant and the deep ecology movement and schematically represent three different approaches to environmental ethics that can be used to describe major historical tendencies in the human–nature relationship:

1. the self-interest or *egocentric* approach—the dominant Western world view—where reality is always seen as how we human beings can maintain our separateness and dominance over the rest of creation (see Table 1.1);
2. the *homocentric* approach, which stresses an essentially human-centered but still socially responsible way of living (see Table 1.2);
3. the *ecocentric* approach emphasizing that, while human beings do have special characteristics distinguishing and to some degree setting them apart from the other animals, they are nevertheless interdependently involved with the global ecosystem (see Table 1.3).

Although we currently function in all of our relationships under the first and second approaches, we must at least be informed by the alternative world view reflected in the third mode. Whether or not the deep ecologists have been able to satisfy all the concerns of the environmental ethics movement, they have certainly suggested a clear, compelling, and workable alternative paradigm to the more traditional human–nature relationships. Whether derived from deep, deeper, or deepest ecology, the perceptions of these seminal thinkers now define the framework of ecoethics. Utilizing their insights, we will

Table 1.1   The Self-interest or Egocentric Approach to Environmental Ethics

Assumptions about:

The Nature of Human Beings: People are fundamentally different from all other creatures on Earth over which they are to exercise control.

Social Causation: People are masters of their own destiny; they can choose their goals and learn to do whatever is necessary to achieve them.

Human Society: The world is vast and provides unlimited opportunity for human beings. It is proper for humans to control and have "dominion" over the rest of nature.

Constraints on Human Behavior: Human history is a record of never-ending progress. For every problem there is always a solution. Progress need never cease.

Responsibilities and Duties:

The goal is the maximization of individual self-interest: What is good for the individual will ultimately benefit society as a whole. Within the Judeo-Christian tradition, appeals to the authority of the Wholly Other coupled with the primacy of the individualist salvation ethic minimize the need for social responsibility.

The Metaphysical Base:

The Mechanistic Paradigm:
1. Matter is composed of atomic parts and is to be so understood and viewed.
2. The whole is thus equal to the sum of the parts.
3. Causation is a matter of external action on inert/inactive parts.
4. Quantitative change is more important than qualitative change.
5. Dualistic: separation of mind/body; matter/spirit.

Exponents:

Plato, mainstream Christianity, Descartes, Hegel, George Berkeley, Hobbes, Locke, Adam Smith, Malthus, Garrett Hardin.

End Goals:

The knowledge of idealized "truth"; of "form" or "idea" (Plato); of "innate ideas" (Descartes); of "faith" rather than "works" (Christianity). "Conception" (generalizing principles prior to experience) as the way to knowledge.

Table 1.2   The Homocentric Approach to Environmental Ethics

Assumptions about:

The Nature of Human Beings: Humans have a cultural heritage in addition
to and distinct from their genetic inheritance and are thus qualitatively
different from all other animal species.

Social Causation: The primary determinants of human affairs are social
and cultural (including science and technology) rather than individual.

Human Society: Social and cultural environments are the crucial context
for human affairs. The biophysical environment is essentially irrelevant.

Constraints on Human Behavior: Culture is a matter of cumulative advance; thus technological and social progress can continue indefinitely.
All social problems are ultimately soluble.

Responsibilities and Duties:

Greatest good for the largest number of people. Social justice rather than
individual progress is the key value. Sense of responsibility to and for other
people important. In religion, some sense of responsibility toward nature,
of human stewardship over the creation.

The Metaphysical Base:

A combination of mechanism and organicism depending on the particular
approach. Philosophically, materialism and positivism fit in here. Major
subcategories would include most utilitarianism, consequentialism.

Exponents:

John S. Mill and Jeremy Bentham (utilitarian theorists); Barry Commoner
(socialist ecology); Karl Marx and Mao Tse Tung (political theory); Randers
and Meadows (limits-to-growth theorists).

End Goals:

Maximization of utility and the good of the greater number. Through the
study of the material, social conditions of society we can discover the truth
about human responsibility; sense perception within the historical process
can alone enable us to discover the "really real."

Table 1.3   The Ecocentric Approach to Environmental Ethics

Assumptions about:

The Nature of Human Beings: While humans have exceptional character-istics (culture, communication skills, technology), they remain one among many other species and are interdependently involved in the global ecosystem.

Social Causation: Human affairs are influenced not only by social and cultural factors, but also by intricate linkages of cause, effect, and feedback in the web of nature. Thus, purposive human actions can have unintended consequences.

Human Society: Humans live in and are dependent on a finite biophysical environment that imposes potent physical and biological restraints on human affairs.

Constraints on Human Behavior: Although human inventiveness and power may seem to exempt us from the constraints of biospheric limita-tions, ecological laws will always provide the primary context for human and other animal life.

Responsibilities and Duties:

A belief that all living and nonliving things have value. Duty is to the whole environment. Sometimes includes a rational, scientific, empiricist belief system based on the laws of ecology; sometimes a religious and/or mystical approach to the wonder of the natural world.

The Metaphysical Base:

The Organic or Holistic Paradigm:
  1. Everything is connected to everything else.
  2. The whole is far greater than the sum of the parts.
  3. The world is active and alive: internal causation.
  4. The primacy of change and ongoing process is always affirmed.
  5. Nondualistic unity of mind/body, matter/spirit, people/nature.

Exponents:

Taoism; Buddhism; Native American philosophy; Thoreau; Gary Snyder; Theodore Roszak and "right brain" analysis; Aldo Leopold; Rachel Carson; Fritjof Capra; political ecology; deep ecology; ecofeminism.

End Goals:

Unity, stability, diversity, self-sustaining systems, harmony and balance in nature and within competitive biological systems, survival of all organisms, democratic social systems, "less is more," soft energy systems, self-sustain-ing resource systems, sustainable development.

in succeeding chapters consider how to develop models for ecologically healthier systems of scientific and economic endeavor.

Notes

1. Aldo Leopold, *A Sand County Almanac* (New York: Oxford University Press, 1949).
2. Rachel Carson, *Silent Spring* (Boston: Houghton-Mifflin, 1962).
3. E. F. Schumacher, *Small Is Beautiful: Economics as if People Mattered* (New York: Harper and Row, 1973).
4. Christopher Stone, *Should Trees Have Standing? Legal Rights for Natural Objects* (Los Altos, Calif.: W. Kaufman Publishers, 1974).
5. Xenophon, *I Oeconomicus*, 4:8–9, as noted in J. D. Hughes, "Gaia: An Ancient View of Our Planet," *Environmental Review* 6, no. 2 (1982).
6. Chief Seattle, "The Great Chief Sends Word," in *Chief Seattle's Testament* (Leicester, U.K.: St. Bernard Press, 1977).
7. From "An Interview with Jessica Tuchman Matthews," Bill Moyers' *World of Ideas* Series, PBS Television, 1988.
8. Peter Bunyard and Edward Goldsmith, "Tropical Forests: A Plan for Action," *Ecologist* 17, nos. 4/5 (1987), pp. 129–33. Much of the data reported in this article appears throughout Chapter 1.
9. Ibid., p. 129.
10. Ibid., p. 131.
11. R. P. Turco, O. B. Toon, T. P. Ackerman, J. B. Pollack, and Carl Sagan, "Nuclear Winter: Global Consequences of Multiple Nuclear Explosions," *Science* (December 23, 1983).
12. Arne Naess, "The Shallow and the Deep, Long-range Ecology Movement," *Inquiry Magazine* 16 (1972), pp. 95–100.
13. A number of publications dealing with the deep ecology concept have been published by the authors. Of particular note is Bill Devall and George Sessions, *Deep Ecology; Living as if Nature Mattered* (Layton, Utah: Gibbs M. Smith Publishers, 1985). See also Bill Devall, *Simple in Means, Rich in Ends: Practicing Deep Ecology* (Salt Lake City, Utah: Peregrine Smith Books, 1988).
14. Leopold, *Sand County*, p. 240.
15. Fritjof Capra as quoted in Alan S. Miller, "Science and Ethics: An Interview with Fritjof Capra," *Pacific World* (May 1988).
16. See Grover Foley, "Deep Ecology and Subjectivity," and Henryk Skolimowski, "Eco-philosophy and Deep Ecology," *Ecologist* 18, nos. 4/5 (1988), pp. 119–27.
17. Arne Naess, "Deep Ecology and Ultimate Premises," *Ecologist* 18, nos. 4/5 (1988), pp. 128–31.
18. For good reviews of the social ecology/deep ecology perspectives, see

Brian Tokar, "Social Ecology, Deep Ecology, and the Future of Green Political Thought," *Ecologist* 18, nos. 4/5 (1988), pp. 132–35.

19. Warwick Fox, "Deep Ecology: A New Philosophy of Our Time," *Ecologist* 14, nos. 5/6 (1984), pp. 344–45; emphasis in original.

20. Simone de Beauvoir, *The Second Sex* (New York: Vintage Books, 1952), pp. 157, 177, 281.

21. Rosemary Reuther, *Liberation Theology* (New York: Paulist Press, 1972), p. 117.

22. Ibid., p. 20.

23. Karen J. Warren, "Feminism and Ecology: Making Connections," *Environmental Ethics* 11 (Spring 1989), p. 17.

24. For other perspectives on the deep ecology/ecofeminism debate, please note the following articles: Jim Cheney, "Ecofeminism and Deep Ecology," *Environmental Ethics* 9 (Summer 1987), pp. 115–45; Warwick Fox, "The Deep Ecology–Ecofeminist Debate and Its Parallels," *Environmental Ethics* 11 (Spring 1989); Marti Kheel, "The Liberation of Nature: A Circular Affair," *Environmental Ethics* 7 (Winter 1984), pp. 135–49; Ariel Kay Salleh, "Deeper than Deep Ecology: The Eco-feminist Connection," *Environmental Ethics* 7 (Winter 1984); and Michael E. Zimmerman, "Feminism, Deep Ecology, and Environmental Ethics," *Environmental Ethics* 9 (Spring 1987), pp. 21–44.

25. Salleh, "Deeper than Deep Ecology," pp. 344–45.

26. Charlene Spretnak, "Ecofeminism: Our Roots and Flowering," *Elmwood Newsletter* 4, no. 1 (Winter 1988), p. 8.

27. William Godfrey-Smith, "Environmental Philosophy," *Habitat* (June 1980), p. 24.

28. J. Baird Callicott, "Non-anthropocentric Value Theory and Environmental Ethics," *American Philosophical Quarterly* 21, no. 4 (October 1984), p. 304.

29. Carolyn Merchant, "Environmental Ethics and Political Conflict: A View from California," *Environmental Ethics* 12 (Spring 1990), pp. 45–68.

2

Theories of Justice

For most human beings, the practical questions involving ethical decision-making revolve around the everyday matters of living, relating to other people, problem-solving in the present and planning for the future. Ethics, then, may be regarded as the case-study branch of philosophy, relevant for most people mainly because of its application to particular human life situations. Although the other branches of classical philosophy (esthetics, logic, metaphysics, ontology, epistemology) tend to focus on the question of absolute truth and the means of gaining knowledge, ethics is more pragmatic. As much concerned as any other division of philosophy for thoughtful analysis, ethics tends to ask questions such as: What is the good life? How should human beings act in that life? Why should they act in certain ways and not in others? And although as a society we have lived in a relativistic age for a very long time, most people understand that questions of morality and ethics are by no means out of date. Because of the enormity of the survival issues facing the species, its questions are more relevant than ever before.

The ethicist faces the double task of clarifying abstract principles and then applying them to everyday problems. Accordingly, the ecoethicist carries certain primary responsibilities: to identify issues relating to the complex relationships of human beings and nature, develop frameworks for analysis, and contribute to good decision-making within the ecological, ethical, and economic communities. While the nature of truth and the problem of knowing how human beings attain wisdom can be subjects of systematic analysis, ethics is a more flexible discipline, changing as human beings and societies change. Much as we need and value consistency in moral conduct, it is impossible to formulate one particular ethical system that can answer the same problem the same way in every historical period. At the same time, ethics is valueless if it is absolutely relativistic. Some

31

things are more universally true than others. Standards of dress and patterns of sexual conduct may well vary "ethically" from one age to another. But simply because slavery, sexual discrimination, resource exploitation, or indiscriminate use of the means of war may be acceptable in some societies at certain times does not mean that such practices are ever ultimately justifiable—in those societies or in others. Throughout this chapter, the ethical tension that pulls between the desire for universality in the application of norms and the need for relevance in practice will be evident.

To give our examination of holistic justice some degree of consistency, and to illuminate the background of ecological ethics and political biology that together are the integrating focus of this book, this chapter has been sectioned into: (1) an introduction to the general principles of ethics; (2) an outline of the views of some premodern ethical thinkers; and (3) an overview of key figures in the contemporary ethical debate.

General Principles in Ethics

Although the words "ethics," "values," and "morals" are often used interchangeably (and sometimes appropriately so), there are certain practical differences in the words. *Ethics,* as has been noted, traditionally refers to the systematic framework of thought and analysis that deals with questions of right and wrong and the nature of the good and proper life. Thus, an ethical act would be an act that is consistent with such a framework. *Values* refers more particularly to factors that the individual prefers or feels strongly about and that might suggest or indicate a possible course for future action on an issue. *Morals* most generally refers to that natural working-out of a personally affirmed ethical or value system, which then becomes the conscious—and visible—basis for conduct and action. Morality is concerned more with how one acts than with the system providing the framework for action.

Various comparative methods of categorizing ethical systems have been employed. A *subjective* ethic, for example, will place primary emphasis on the act or feeling of the individual. Thus, to "do your own thing," without any particular concern for the consequences of that action to another person or group, becomes under a subjectivist approach a rational and proper approach to life. Subjectivist ethics are always *relative* ethics since they essentially reject any absolute apart from the self-interest of the individual—the ethical actor. To state that "I believe in capital punishment" is, from this perspective, as fully ethical a statement (and, for that individual, prompting quite as moral an action) as the opposite statement for another person operating under a different ethical framework.

There are a variety of problems with this kind of subjectivist, relativist thinking. In its extreme applications, it can lead to a kind of individualist moral chaos where responsibility to other people and to society is ignored. It can too easily minimize the important ethical distinctions between legal justice and moral justice—key constructs in any contemporary effort to effect social equity. When I was working as an organizer in the civil rights movement in the 1950s and in the anti–Vietnam War movement in the 1960s and 1970s, the distinction between moral and legal justice was an absolutely critical basis for psychological survival. In both instances, moral justice was far removed from the legal prescriptions. Practical ethics (even affirming that other systems of action and conduct can be philosophically viable)—insofar as such an ethic moves into the sphere of morality—must always go beyond self-interest. To the fullest extent possible, there needs to be a universality to ethical decision-making that extends beyond simple personal likes, dislikes, and/or preferences.

The opposite of subjectivist theory is *objectivist* ethics. Objectivist categories of thought are those that posit the need for an outside authority as the basis for each particular individual action. Many religious and political systems have utilized such objectivist theory. Certain Christian sects, for example, enforce stern codes of conduct on members, appealing for authority to any one of a number of external guides: the Bible, the church, past traditions, a charismatic leader. Marxist-Leninist political/ethical theory has often similarly enforced uniform behavior on its members by an appeal to the same kind of absolute, external authority: doctrines from the past, the party, the traditions of the formative era, obedience to the party leaders.

An even more serious tendency in an objective ethic is when the advocates of the ethic assert the absolute and objective goodness or badness of a certain state of affairs. Leaders of groups like the Moral Majority appeal for verification of the objective nature of their ethic not to the source of the political or social judgment—for most of us usually reason or empirical evidence—but rather to the compelling righteousness of the judgers or the judgment itself. Politician-theologians Jerry Falwell and Pat Robertson, in assaulting the virtue of liberals and Democrats in electoral campaigns, do so based not so much on the demonstrated inadequacies of the opponents so much as on the clarity of their own vision. Liberals are evil, foreigners are suspect, white people are racially superior, and choice for women is a corruption of nature. One comes to the truth of these professed realities not through the evidence but by one's readiness to trust and obey the leader because of the quality of his vision.

Thus, objectivist theory poses its own variety of rather apparent problems. It is characterized by rigidity in the application of the moral standard. It makes historical criticism almost impossible since critics are seen as enemies of the tradition. In a fast-changing world, such theory is doomed to general social irrelevance since it is unable to admit contemporary historical development.

Another helpful double category of practical ethics construction is that of *motivist* as opposed to *consequentialist* theory, which will be reviewed in more detail later in this chapter as the ethics of Immanuel Kant and John Stuart Mill are contrasted. For the moment, it is enough to note that the distinction between the two approaches provides a handy shorthand for describing primary trends in ethics. Motivist theories affirm that the motive or intention behind a particular action should be the basis for determining whether or not it is a right act. Consequentialism suggests, quite to the contrary, that motive is relatively unimportant and that the primary consideration in evaluating the merit of an action must be the consequences that result from it. The subtleties in these alternative viewpoints will be considered later.

Similarly, there are differing manners in which ethical principles can be applied to the problem of moral inquiry, one way being to contrast *normative* and *analytical* ethics. Normative ethics has as its primary concern the description of what is morally right or wrong in human social action and conduct. It attempts both to describe and often to prescribe the norms of conduct that should be generally applied in particular situations. More simply, normative ethics is concerned with determining whether or not there are absolute principles that can be applied in all similar situations. Analytical ethics (often called metaethics), at the other end of the methodological spectrum, attempts to provide a more systematic and holistic review of the broad moral and ethical questions of history. What is the meaning of duty? What is the contemporary meaning of justice? What does ethical responsibility mean for the scientist? Analytical ethics is primarily concerned with description and reflection and does not necessarily attempt to develop normative or authoritarian standards of conduct for individuals.

Two other concepts often referred to in ethical writing should be noted. A *teleological* approach to ethical inquiry, as the word suggests (i.e., *telos* in Greek meaning "end"), focuses on the longer range or ultimate results of actions and their end goals. Much like consequentialist or utilitarian ethics in some ways, but asking the larger questions as to the nature and purpose of life, the teleological approach emphasizes ends rather than means to ends in the actions of individuals or societies. Contrasted with this is the *deontological* approach. Deontology is basically the science of duty in philosophical thinking and the branch of human inquiry that deals with questions of moral obligation in both short and long range. Accordingly, deontologists (as we will see in reviewing the work of Kant) are concerned with the sense of duty or responsibility as the essential nature of the ethical act, rather than with its consequences.

Before moving on to a review of some of the primary figures in the history of ethics, it should be noted that the categories listed above are by no means mutually exclusive. They simply describe broad approaches to ethical analysis. Purity in the method of ethical inquiry is not always a plus, however. The utilitarian John Stuart Mill, for example, could be described as objectivist, analytical, consequentialist, and teleological. Of such syntheses is much good ethics composed!

Theories of Justice in the Past

To the philosopher in the Golden Age of Greece, ethics was the science of moral duty and involved the creation of a set of principles that could provide a framework for analysis of the worlds of matter and spirit. Although the classical approach always tended toward the abstract, there was nonetheless an acknowledgment on the part of the early philosophers of the necessary interplay between the theoretical side of ethics and the actual practice of those ethics in everyday life. Although it is not possible in this brief review to provide anything like a systematic overview of Greek thought, a short summary of its most influential voices will help us to evaluate later the formal and enduring problems in ecoethics.

For Plato (427–347 B.C.), the most obvious and essential characteristic of the visible world was the reality of change. Himself desirous of stability and certainty as he sought to understand the world, Plato saw then what we cannot help but see today. Everything visible to human beings seems to be in flux. The only constant quality is the spiral of motion—of growth and development and decay. The cosmos itself seemed to Plato to be forever tilted toward chaos. The senses on which we ordinarily depend for our perception of reality can show us only eternal change in which nothing seems stable or ultimately dependable. Plato reckoned that the world of change, the world of sense perception, must therefore somehow mask that which is "really real." Some other level of a more perfect reality must exist. Only that which is less conditioned by movement and transition can be finally good. Thus, Plato set out on a philosophical quest to understand that which is eternal and unchangeable and ultimately trustworthy. Since nature is visibly imperfect, the only way to find some approximation of absolute order must be to image it in the mind. So it was that Plato developed the concept of absolute Form or Idea, the archetypal images of a world as it might be in its purest form. Since such a perfect world could never encompass the disorder that reveals itself to the senses, the only way to know real order must be through the rational intellect. Only through the most disciplined exercise of the human mind can we thus impose a sense of order on the external world.

Humans, suggested Plato, are called on to bring order into nature: first, through the application of reason so that the perfection lurking behind reality can be more readily understood; and then, through the philosophical application of these rational conceptions to the imperfect world. Since the contemplation of Form and Idea and absolute Truth was considered the principal task of the superior human being, it should not be surprising that Platonists (and the Platonic tradition as expressed in other Western intellectual and religious traditions) have never been much concerned about the real, everyday problems that face suffering humanity. Our real task, suggests this early idealist tradition, is to overcome the imperfection of the real world by reflection on the "really real" that rests behind it.

For Plato, evil was always due essentially to lack of knowledge. If one could but discover the good, then one (at least the educated members of society's ruling class) would be able to do the good. The real and stable realm of existence was always situated within the realm of ideas. Plato was the archetypal idealist. From his point of view, there could be only one good life, the life involving the constant refinement of the intellect and the consequent search for absolute understanding. Truth and moral principle might indeed be known, but not so much from the practices of the common life as from the application of theory. When one understood the basis of good conduct and could comprehend the perfection behind the visible reality, one would find it difficult to do anything but the good. There was no relativism in Plato's ethical system. The moral principle or ethic learned from reflection could then be applied to every situation in every age. Indeed, over the centuries, certain philosophers have pushed this principle to its extreme. René Descartes, as an example, suggested that knowledge of reality is utterly dependent on internal reflection in his classic phrasing of the issue, "I think, therefore I am." Ecofeminist Carolyn Merchant notes the indebtedness of the later rationalists to the Platonic quest for the ideal:

> Other philosophers and scientists such as René Descartes and Isaac Newton conceptualized nature as dead, inert atoms moved by external forces. They removed the soul from the world and the *spiritus mundi* from the heavens. They left the earth as dead matter, devoid of any resemblance to the human being. Nature was described by mechanical laws, God was a mathematician and engineer, human bodies and animals were miniature machines, and the mind resembled a calculating machine that added up perceptions of the outside world in a logical sequence. The "death of nature" metaphorically gave humans power to control and manipulate it for their own benefit.[1]

Ethical thought for Plato (and for his intellectual successors), then, was totally dependent on rational self-sufficiency. Goodness was equated with the compelling power of reason, and the imperfect world in which men and women live out their existence was viewed as of only limited value in developing norms for the perfect society.

A half-century later, Aristotle (384–322 B.C.) developed an ethic that placed more emphasis on the natural world as the instructor of human conduct and action. With Plato, Aristotle affirmed that one must search for the perfection existing behind the visible imperfections of our common life. The intellectual task of comprehending that which might be absolute was important. But to Aristotle, the natural world itself raised most of the basic ethical questions for human beings, and in turn suggested some of the answers. No more formally egalitarian or democratic than Plato, Aristotle nonetheless believed that one should not abstract (as does Platonism) the living self and the conditions to which existence subjects the human being

from the search for truth. Rejecting the Platonic tradition that regards all objective appearances to be deceptive and popular opinion
to be false and ignorant, Aristotle sought for truth at least partially
within human experience. As he notes in the *Nicomachean Ethics,*
"Theory must remain committed to the ways human beings live, act,
and see."

For Aristotle, the search for the good life was to a very large degree
the search for a happy life. But happiness was never to him a matter
of simply doing whatever one wished to do in the hope of finding
immediate sensual or intellectual satisfaction. Rather, it involved
living a virtuous life, and understanding that the most satisfying
human activities always arise from accomplishing worthwhile tasks.
Implicit in this Aristotelian ethic was his doctrine of the golden mean,
which suggested that at all times humans must act in moderation if
they are to be happy. More tolerant than Plato of the physical nature
of people and the ambiguities residing in the change and flux of
nature, Aristotle believed that good resides at least partially in the
realization of our specific nature as human beings. To a certain
degree, we simply are what we are. Such a world perspective suggests
different limits and different possibilities from those intimated by
Plato. Not all of that which is visible and natural is imperfect, as Plato
had suggested. A moderate relativist, Aristotle believed that different
ways of living could be appropriate for different people. We are not
all the same. Rejecting the formal absolutism of Plato, Aristotle
understood that human experience—existence itself—ultimately
plays a substantial role in determining what the good life should be
for individuals and for societies.

Although the subsequent schools of classical philosophy (Epicu-
rean, Stoic, and Gnostic) differed widely in their formulations of
ethics, they tended to agree with Aristotle about the necessary boundaries of human conduct. Epicurus (341–270 B.C.) could say that life is
always the search for pleasure; but that pleasurable activity should
only be moderate since immoderate activity will always lead to pain
and displeasure. Stoicism (c. 300–200 B.C.), although counseling
general noninvolvement in the external conflicts of life, nonetheless
directs people to use the good things of life without guilt but always
with care. One is to live in ways consistent with nature itself. Knowledge must be primarily based on sense perceptions. Gnosticism, the
religious and philosophical movement of the late Greek and early
Christian eras, promised salvation only to those whose special knowledge enabled them to understand that the material dimension of life

by itself could not enable a person to live in proper relationship to the eternal. In all of these systems, the practical ethic is affirmed: Never become so entrapped by self-aggrandizement and the quest for pleasurable activity that your good things would leave you with nothing if they disappeared altogether. Be in touch with the world as it really is.

Christian ethics later incorporated much of the dualistic Greek world view into its system. Matter and spirit were generally seen as disparate and mutually hostile entities. With Plato, the Christian world view emphasized the priority of idea over existence, placing the system of belief (faith) before the system of action in the world (works). Christianity subsequently built an ethical system based on a combination of *rule* and *act* ethics. Rule ethics assumes that ethical precepts should be based largely on adherence to some external absolute. Act ethics takes into some account the consequences of the particular acts in which the human being is engaged. The arguments over the relative importance of faith and of works that emerged in Pauline theology have continued within Christianity to this day.

Indeed, traditional Western theism has always had trouble taking the natural world seriously. It has given priority to creedal formulation rather than worldly action. In this view (best seen in Christianity, although also reflected to a lesser degree in Judaism), God is essentially independent and separate from the natural world and much more concerned about the moral conduct of human beings than about that larger creation over which, scripturally, people were to exercise dominion. This problem was precisely posed in a recent study of the relationship between Christianity and ecology: "Christians have traditionally seen the rest of the world merely as the background for the human drama of salvation."[2]

With Plato, Christian orthodoxy has tended to view nature in its essence as permanent, unchangeable, and essentially separate from the more sectarian and primary considerations of human perfectibility. Nature was supposed to provide resources for those special beings who were created only, as the Old Testament writer notes in Psalm 8, "a little lower than the angels." In such a tradition of instrumentalist ethics, where Earth's bounties rarely have more than a use value and where nature is only a means to other and greater ends, the realm of the really real is human history. And the only portion of that history with any real consequence for believers is its salvation history. This has contributed to a generalized (although by no means universal) religious indifference in the West to nature and to environmental health.

Attempting to deal with this opposition of humankind and the rest of creation and, in the process, developing a natural-law ethic (with much indebtedness to Aristotle) was the great Catholic scholastic philosopher Thomas Aquinas (1225–74). Aquinas proposed that a human action is morally appropriate insofar as that action is in accord with both human nature and our end purpose as human beings. Both motive and consequence are thus important in the moral calculus.

According to Aquinas, every natural creature seeks its own kind of well-being, related to what it is as a species. The order of God's creation forms a "great chain of being" within which each creature is called on to perform that exact role given it by God. Human beings can know at least something of their end goal because they are all at least "dimly aware" of the purpose of human life. Within this ordering of nature are hierarchies both of dependency and obligation. For our species, Aquinas distinguishes several categories of "natural human inclination" that characterize all people and that thus can provide the basis for a code of moral ethics. These natural human inclinations include the preservation of our own existence, procreation, the nurturing of our own kind, the attempt by reasonable people to know the truth, and the need for a just and well-ordered society, freedom, and security. Perhaps overly prescriptive in defining a normative ethic for human beings, Aquinas at least speaks directly about actions connected with securing or reinforcing natural needs or concerns, and helps us to understand them as morally justifiable under normal circumstances. Efforts to maintain some measure of relative autonomy and to secure self-determination are always appropriate goals. Never an absolutist in his theory of means and ends, Aquinas suggests that it is incumbent on the rational person to use appropriate means for the given end sought. This principle is particularly well explicated in his theory of just war, which will be dealt with in Chapter 13.

In the midst of all this, we can always appeal to general principles. The first Thomistic principle is that in all things we seek to do good and avoid evil. Questioning rhetorically how we can determine what is good, Thomas Aquinas responded that we know in practicality what is good by understanding both the purpose (i.e., the motive) and the end (i.e., the consequences) of the considered action.

One of the endearing things about Thomistic ethics is its common sense. Aquinas maintained that, since most of us do recognize to some degree our end goals as individual human beings, we can be reasonably clear about the conduct appropriate for our own lives. Given some guidance, we should be able to steer our way through the many conflicts of everyday existence. Aquinas is also quite cautious (except in certain distinctly religious areas) about suggesting any kind of formal, conceptual moral absolutes that will resolve all problems for all people at all times. The most correct inferences about proper conduct emerge from the everyday struggles of life. Two aphorisms—one from Thomas Aquinas, and the other from his philosophical father Aristotle—make the point:

> The decision always rests with perception.

> For the things we have to learn, before we can do them, we learn by doing them.

Modern Theories of Justice

Surely the most important of the post-Enlightenment ethicists was Immanuel Kant (1724–1804), who posed the basic question, How does one distinguish a moral from a nonmoral act? As a deontologist (i.e., concerned for the nature of duty), Kant affirmed that the paramount factor in the ethical act is the motive behind it. Although one will certainly hope for positive consequences from any act that involves good intention, the consequences of the act are finally irrelevant in the calculus of whether it was in fact good or bad. Do what is right, implies Kant, though the world be damned. As we will see, Kant's approach to moral problems is very different from that of the utilitarians with their concern for the end results of particular actions. What Kant valued is the individual; whereas in most consequence theories, the more abstract general social values are paramount.

With Plato, Kant believed that the moral law can be known by reason, and also affirmed the direct relationship between knowing what is right and doing it. Good motives lead to right and proper actions. That is, right conduct is always predicated on an obligation to be dutiful and obedient to that moral law which one comes intuitively to understand and/or which is a priori imprinted within the consciousness. The act that happens casually and simply from inclination—even though it may appear the same as the act done from a sense of duty or obedience—cannot be characterized as a good act. And even when the consequences of two acts are the same, the only action that can be considered moral is that done in the context of proper motivation.

Abstract as this may seem at first glance, certain Kantian assumptions are eminently practical for the living of everyday life. For example, Kant presumes the absolute value and importance of every human life. One must never act in a manner that would be resented were such action directed toward oneself by someone else. Actions, Kant said, must be based on some form of general principle if they are not to degrade into meaningless relativism. One of the Kantian maxims is that there are universal conditions obtaining in any free and responsible human effort. Thus, rational individuals will normally all act the same way in a given situation, observing certain rules. If we have the right kind of understanding, then we are not simply the objects of an arbitrary external force, but may in fact be able to "will" an event. To will an event is, in Kantian analysis, to command intuitively or direct the self to make a desired goal become reality.

From all of this comes the key ethical construct in Kantian ethics: the categorical imperative. Simply stated, Kant says to "act only on that maxim whereby thou canst at the same time will that it become a universal law."[3] In its traditional reformulation, the categorical imperative insists that human beings never regard other persons as only the means to an end, but always as an end in themselves. Acts based on maxims requiring or using deception or coercion, and that therefore do not involve the consent of the other person, are wrong. Concerned that the demands of justice be met as much as possible, Kant regarded a proper means to be the best assurance that any particular action is a moral act, even though its consequences prove evil. On the other hand, it is utterly impossible for Kant to conceive of a situation wherein an evil means would result in a good or happy consequence.

As with every ethical system, there are problems with the Kantian analysis. This may be particularly true for modern people. At least three dilemmas immediately present themselves. First, it is doubtful that the rational will—for Kant, the basis of every good and moral act—is ever truly as autonomous as he considered it to be. We are not so insulated from other influences and stresses as to be always rational in the way Kant presumed. If the conceptual apparatus of the human mind is as pliable as most modern theories of psychology suggest, then one can hardly trust pure motive based on rationality to be the emergent force of all ethical good. Second, the ultimate theoretical irrelevance, according to Kant, of the consequences of particular actions virtually assures a typical idealist social and political quietism on the part of those who rigidly apply the Kantian assumptions in everyday life. As we have learned again and again, such apolitical idealism is always made use of by those who control power to increase rather than diminish social inequities. An ethic that has less regard for the consequences of individual or social acts than for their good intentions tends toward self-righteousness and social indifference. Third, this kind of ethic reflects the same old arrogant anthropocentrism that may tolerate, but in fact never really cares for, concerns affecting creatures other than Homo sapiens.

Nonetheless, Kantian motivism does correctly presume a going beyond the self in moral decision-making to some form of universal principle as the basis for thought and conduct. That principle may be no more than some simple utilitarian formula suggesting that we should always consider the greater good of the majority, or it may be a construct as firm as the categorical imperative. But some kind of at least minimal ethical beginning must be the baseline for all moral thinking.

At the opposite end of the theoretical spectrum is the utilitarian ethic first formally proposed in the nineteenth century by Jeremy Bentham and John Stuart Mill. Their leading principle was that it is indeed possible to lay down objective standards for determining right and wrong. In this sense, along with Immanuel Kant, they were absolutist in their ethic. We all know, suggest the utilitarians, that in real life some actions are right and some actions are wrong and that human beings are obligated in some way to do the right and, to the best of their ability, to avoid the wrong. Since it is not always immediately apparent as to what constitutes a good action, some system is required to assist us in our evaluations. Utilitarianism is one approach to the problem, and it holds that the positive benefits or negative effects accruing from any particular action or class of actions are solely determinative of whether the action should be considered good or bad.

The overarching standard by which rightness or wrongness in decision-making can be gauged is the principle of maximum utility, which was first systematically described by Jeremy Bentham. What it means simply is that the determining factor in the ethical determination of justice is the provision of the greatest good for the greatest number of people. To the utilitarians, the motive behind an act is relatively unimportant; only the consequences will prove its relative rightness or wrongness. No act is either intrinsically good or intrinsically bad. All depends on the outcome. An act that is painful, for example, may well prove to be positive if it leads to an outcome wherein the good resulting from the pain is greater than the pain itself.

As an operative ethic, utilitarianism suggests at least the following steps for decision-making. First of all, the individual should carefully assess all the different courses of action available in a particular situation and then make the best possible evaluation of the probable consequences of each act. That course of action which maximizes the good and minimizes the evil for the greatest number of people is generally what should be done. Since in the routines of life it is rarely possible to make such an elaborate calculation of consequences, one may reasonably act on the basis of past experience so long as one's earlier decisions reflected such a utilitarian analysis.[4]

Utilitarianism is forthright about the strong probability that, in many different situations, acts will have to be performed that either are unpleasant in themselves, or treat people as means rather than as ends in themselves, or lead in the shorter run to certain kinds of evil. Such acts, however, are good and ethical if the pain they occasion is less than the good that they ultimately produce. The application of the utilitarian ethic has been particularly helpful, for example, in medical research. In many cases, some people are called upon to suffer (e.g., in the evaluation of experimental drugs) in order that larger numbers of patients may be healed. Many experimental protocols in medical research are based on such utilitarian principles.

As noted earlier, philosophers sometimes distinguish between act and rule uilitarianism. The act utilitarian is a flexible philosopher who believes that one must always act in every particular situation so as to produce the greatest balance of good over evil, even though the act may not in itself be completely good. Rule utilitarians, recognizing the cumbersomeness of the act-utilitarian calculus, think one should act simply in accordance with general rules that, based on past experience, can be expected to produce the greatest balance of good over evil. Rule utilitarianism seems, in fact, to be the only practicable form of the theory since it moves the intent of the action from an individual assessment of what is right to a more collective one. An act is morally right, say the rule utilitarians, if one can imagine there to be a moral code embodying and endorsing it. Right actions then are those in accord with those rules or codes that tend to optimize the general good of the society. Indeed, most legislation involving redistributive fiscal mechanisms to assist those who are less well off in the society operate essentially under a rule-utilitarian formula. Progressive income taxes, welfare programs, and food assistance to needy people and/or countries all reflect such an understanding. Implicit in utilitarianism is a constant assessment of the relative costs and benefits of any individual action or social program.

A variety of criticisms can be leveled against the utilitarian method of practical ethics. The most important, and the one that demolishes any absolutist utilitarianism, is that no one can ever know the overall consequences of particular decisions. Try as we may, it is impossible to foretell the future. As we will see in Chapter 13, nations have many times entered into what they considered to be "just wars" on utilitarian grounds, believing that the good to be occasioned by the war would far outweigh the suffering. As history shows time and time again, however, such wars often prove to be anything but just, causing suffering of a kind that could not have been anticipated at the beginning of the action. In many other situations as well, the difficulty of foretelling the consequences of an action before the fact make formal utilitarianism a problematic ethical method.

A second major criticism of this philosophy is that a system in which we must only be concerned for the greater good of the majority will tend to overlook the rights of minorities, whose needs under the principle of utility will have to be subsumed to the will of the majority. In contemporary society, it is all too possible to develop programs that seem to serve the majority of the people but that in the process overlook the poor, racial minorities, or other quantitatively smaller classes or groupings of people. Although utilitarianism can be immensely important in formulating preliminary decisions, it is always limited in application.

Having forsaken the principle of ideological purity, then, it appears that some practical combination of motivist and consequence ethics will be the most helpful approach in making bioethical/ecoethical decisions. Few would argue seriously with the central tenets of either position: The intention of an act, along with the readiness to view other people as ends in themselves, is just as important as trying to accomplish the greatest good for the largest number of people. A working synthesis of the two seems to be an ethical prerequisite. Such flexibility is the norm for many a practical ethicist concerned both for individual rights and for the greater social good.

Four contemporary ethicists deserve attention here as being absolutely clear exponents of the traditional philosophies introduced above. The perspectives of other important ethicists (in particular Peter Singer and Tom Regan) will be considered in later chapters. But here we shall look briefly at the views of utilitarian bioethicist Joseph Fletcher, neoconsequentialist Paul Ramsey, theory-of-justice philosopher John Rawls and environmental ethicist J. Baird Callicott before we move on to the more specific consideration of how any of these approaches can assist us in making decisions on the important issues addressed in the remainder of the book.

Joseph Fletcher, professor of medical ethics at Duke and Harvard universities and probably the most well known of the first generation of U.S. bioethicists, comes down squarely on the side of utilitarianism. For Fletcher, "the only possible moral test of ethical actions lies in their consequences." Any human activity is a good activity if it leads to positive consequences. It is not good if it leads to negative consequences. The moral actor must decide what will offer the most good in any particular situation. From this, Fletcher develops a new conceptual formulation of "proportionate" good—an application of ethical cost/benefit analysis wherein the relative proportion of good over bad in a sequence of events is the determining factor. Accordingly, for Fletcher, there are occasions when good ends can justify less than good means, if the end result of the action totals out to be for the greater benefit of humans or the social order. Fletcher therefore rejects the a prioris of Kant wherein even a very good end can never justify an evil means.

Anything that may promote the general social welfare is—in Fletcher's calculus—to be encouraged, even though it may impinge on the freedom of choice of the individual. A strong advocate of most genetic engineering practices, Fletcher feels, for example, that society should play a larger role in determining population norms and in controlling what he calls "reproduction by lottery." Individual freedoms, he suggests, do not always lead to greater social good, and the maximization of utility in a society may require short-range coercive means. One can easily see why biomedical utilitarians like Fletcher are often characterized as social engineers—applying utilitarian principles in order to modify the conduct of the larger community.

Paul Ramsey, past professor of ethics at Princeton University, builds quite a different framework for ethical decision-making. Ramsey believes there are a great many ethical problems that can never be resolved, and it is unrealistic to imagine that even the general consequences of human actions can ever be accurately assessed. Criticizing the utilitarians, Ramsey maintains that, because of our inability to have any real understanding of final results, we must be extremely careful before discounting the pain or suffering of an individual for some supposed greater good. Similarly, we should be careful about social do-good programs wherein an informed minority presumes to know what is good for the rest of society. What some consider to be Ramsey's "prohibitionist" position relative to biomedical and certain other kinds of scientific research is based on his belief that there are many things that *can* be done in science that *should not* be done, even as there are many things that can be known that should not be known. Only with extreme caution should we propose either scientific or moral trade-offs of the moderate present good for the promise of future better. Of particular concern to Ramsey are the issues of genetic engineering and the manipulation—whether therapeutic or experimental—of the fetus. Allowing that some experimental research on children may on occasion be warranted, Ramsey considers any research on the human fetus to be inappropriate. The ultimate costs of fetal and genetic research, both in terms of the assault on the dignity of the person and the unknown potential consequences of the work, are far greater than the benefit, Ramsey believes. Most biomedical technologies will ultimately create enormous problems for us to solve, rather than providing any real help to the species. Since Ramsey was writing before many of the current biotechnological therapies had been discovered, it is not clear whether he would feel precisely the same today or would take into account the differing approaches and contexts of fetal research. However, Ramsey's entire approach is a basically Kantian and deontological perspective, which suggests he might still feel very much the same. A human life is sacred. The moral dignity of the person must be guarded at all costs. Believing this, Ramsey is necessarily cautious about approving any kind of biological or behavioral intervention that would use even one human being as a supposed means to a greater good.

Paul Ramsey may well have anticipated one of our most trying current dilemmas in scientific and biomedical research. Existentially trusting only ourselves, in practice we have nevertheless tended to transfer responsibility for our physical, emotional, and social well-being to the experts—the scientists and technologists—who seem to promise so much. Paul Ramsey cautions us lest we allow this confusion of values—individualism coupled with a vague and uneasy reliance on the generalized expertise of the technologists—to interfere with our respect for the worth of our own selves and other persons.[5]

John Rawls is a contemporary ethicist who in his important book *A Theory of Justice* attempts to combine the strengths of both Kantianism and utilitarianism by focusing on the problem of justice in modern society. Rawls begins by enunciating two essential principles. First, each person is to have an absolutely equal right with every other person to the basic human liberties affirmed by a particular society—economic, political, social, or medical. Second, recognizing that such liberties are in fact never equally distributed in any society, Rawls then states that social and economic inequalities must be arranged so as to provide the greatest benefit from increases in the overall well-being of a society to those who are least advantaged. The greatest good should be granted not to the greatest number but to those who need the most. Rawls is neo-Kantian in his affirmation of the importance of the individual. But he also believes that justice and fairness in human relationships must be accorded to all. Indeed, the primary subject of justice is social equity. Within this Rawlsian scheme, an absolute ethical requirement emerges that demands the ordering and structuring of institutions to provide for the greatest possible equal treatment for all.

To this end, Rawls believes that modern societies require formal social contracts between the primary groupings in the society in order to protect individual rights and the larger social good. Affirming our elusive quest for both the greatest good and respect for the individual, Rawls finesses the errors of traditional Kantianism and utilitarianism by suggesting *both* as norms and guidelines for an ethical system. Although often criticized by both ends of the ethical spectrum (for being either too much concerned for the individual or too idealist), this perspective enunciated by Rawls will exhibit its immense value as we later consider issues of distributive justice and individual rights within the unjust society.

Environmental ethicist J. Baird Callicott brings the matter of "theories" of environmental justice up to date by categorizing three secular contemporary approaches to environmental ethics: traditional humanism, extensionism, and ecocentrism. Most environmental ethicists follow a traditional humanistic approach (as noted earlier) by focusing strictly on the human component of ecosystems. It is good for us and for future generations (protracted humanism) to treat nature with care and reverence. This leads, suggests Callicott, to a management ethic wherein we do our best to conserve resources but assume that our only real and direct responsibility is to our species.

The second approach attempts to ground the moral issues in environmentalism by extending value to the nonhuman world—which has been popularized by the new concern for animal rights. Ethicists Peter Singer and Tom Regan have spearheaded the animal rights movement, and this extensionist ethic is now everywhere recognized as having value in helping to define nonanthropomorphic value theory. The practical impact of the movement in reducing the number of animals used in scientific experimentation, for example, has been felt around the world. Unhappily, some more radical environmentalists have improperly used extensionism to develop an antihumanist platform, declaring that only by a reduction in human population (e.g., through the spread of AIDS) can the environment be saved.[6] The entire issue of extensionism and the nonhumanist value theory will be reviewed carefully in Chapter 14.

Callicott himself is perhaps the most articulate exponent of the third contemporary approach to an environmental ethic: the ecocentrism described in Chapter 1. Callicott says that, because of Aldo Leopold's dual emphasis on the importance of human beings as the primary moral actors within ecosystems as well as on the necessary limitation of human freedom if we would relate in a healthy and nonexploitative fashion to nature,"—Leopold's land ethic remains the only holistic or ecosystemic game in town."[7] Most ecoethicists, however, will continue to draw insights from each approach: the importance of human beings as dependent entities within the ecosystem; the obligation we have to extend at least certain rights and moral standing to nonhuman segments of the creation; and the need to move from ego- and homocentrism to a more ecocentric model for the future.

From humankind's first reflective moments, men and women have sought to find practical answers to the ethical problems of everyday life. They have been concerned for their own feelings and for discovering those universal truths that go beyond the interest and desire of the individual. Generally, they have given a high priority to the formulation of ideas and to finding out how ideas relate to existence itself. They have debated the questions of means and ends and what it actually means to be at once both faithful to the primary agendas of the self and socially responsible.

Today, the practical ethicist understands that the realm of moral action involves far more than either perfecting ideas or acting responsibly to our fellow human beings. As we are interconnected with the natural world, so are we responsible to and for it. A Wintu Indian woman in California in 1860 reminded us of a heritage that desperately needs correction today:

The Spirit of the Land hates the white man. The Indians never hurt anything but the white people destroy everything. They blast rocks and scatter them on the ground. The rock says "Don't! You are hurting me!" But the white people pay no attention. How can the Spirit of the earth like the white man? Everywhere the white man has touched the earth it is sore.[8]

As noted in succeeding chapters, the motive for our despoliation of the land in earlier centuries was surely more a matter of assumed economic requirement than a total indifference to the health of nature. But it is clear that, today, new moral requirements confront the species. And it is to these imperatives—of ecology, ecoethics, and economics—that we now turn.

Notes

1. Carolyn Merchant, "Can Science and Nature Be Partners? Meeting the Environmental Challenge of the 1990's," keynote address to the Vassar Class of 1993, Poughkeepsie, N.Y., August 25, 1989.

2. Loren Wilkinson, *Earth Keeping: Christian Stewardship of Natural Resources* (Grand Rapids, Mich.: Eerdman's Publishing, 1980), p. 3.

3. Immanuel Kant, *Fundamental Principles of the Metaphysics of Morals* (New York and London: Longman, Green, 1785), sec. 2:1.

4. Many years ago in Chicago my philosophy professor described to the class his switch from neo-Kantian to utilitarian ethics: Living in Holland during World War II, he had passively accepted the occupation of his country by the Nazis, and spent his time writing a philosophy book. However, when the Nazi SS troops began rounding up Jews in his neighborhood and throughout the city for deportation to concentration camps, he determined that the greater good called for his murdering as many SS storm troopers as possible before they in turn could kill many times their number in Jews. Thus, my professor moved from being a principled neo-Kantian idealist concerned primarily for the purity of his ideological pacifism to being a pragmatic consequentialist.

5. See the Supplementary Reading List at the back of the book (re: Chapters 2, 7 and 8, and 13) for some of the major works of Joseph Fletcher and Paul Ramsey.

6. Although not representative of the Earth First! movement as a whole, the suggestion by some organizational editors that AIDS may be good for the Earth since it may massively reduce the human population was extensively covered in the four 1988 issues of the *UTNE Reader,* November/December 1987, January/February 1988, March/April 1988, and especially May/June 1988.

7. J. Baird Callicott, "The Search for an Environmental Ethic," in Tom Regan, *Matters of Life and Death: New Introductory Essays in Moral Philosophy* (New York: Random House, 1986), p. 404.

8. D. Lee, *Freedom and Culture* (New York: Prentice-Hall, 1959), p. 163.

3

World Order Imperatives

Tens of thousands of temporary settlers with gold fever came to California in the first few years of the Gold Rush era between 1848 and 1852. This same kind of migration—fueled by the hope for quick riches and a new way of life—was starting to happen in many other places around the world at that time. California's forty-niners had no intention of staying long in the gold country. They wanted to find the treasure, rip it from the earth, and return home with fat wallets as quickly as possible. Although in fact many of them ended up as permanent residents (surviving, ironically, more by agriculture and trade than by prospecting), their early intent had been clear: maximum exploitation of the mineral wealth of the area in as short a period of time as possible.

World Order and the Environment

All around the world—in Europe, Asia, Africa, and Latin America—the story in the past century and a half has been much the same as in the California Gold Rush, although with different long-range consequences. Poor people, believing the promises of promoters and seeking a better life and more secure future, have tended to pick up and move in droves, one way or another, to the resource-rich fringes of society or the empire to gain wealth or simply to survive. These ordinary people harbored no special desire to destroy nature. In fact, many (like the European immigrants to America who for the first time had access to the woods and fields and streams denied them by the aristocracy in their own lands) came to develop a sense of kinship with nature. Everywhere, however, these migrations were met by an official governmental indifference both to the plight of the poor and working people who were forced into patterns of resource exploitation, and to the rapacious conduct of the industrial entrepreneurs who saw the natural orders only as a means to the accumulation of wealth. Simple necessity often directed that ordinary people exploit nature in whatever ways were required to ensure personal and family survival.

Today, the political assault on the environment has intensified. Nation-states, transnational corporations (TNCs), and international banking and financial institutions establish formal policies to rationalize their assault on planetary resources—on rainforests and minerals and fisheries and land and animals and people. On a scale of assault unimaginable just a few decades ago, there is now a new and equally disturbing dimension to the older and traditional patterns of resource exploitation. Any global survey of nation-states in 1990 will indicate there are few political leadership coalitions anyplace in the world today that do not treat their citizens as well as their natural resources as enemies. Political prevarication within the election campaigns in the Western nations, the popular uprisings in China and throughout Eastern Europe, and the increasing pressure for democratization within oppressive societies everywhere all attest to the pent-up frustrations of people who are seeking honesty, equity, and justice in their everyday dealings with those under whose rule they must live.

The continuing wars of the period—in the Middle East, Central America, Indochina, South Asia, and Southern Africa—have perhaps had the most direct effect on the well-being of both people and nature. We all know by now of both the millions of deaths and the oil and chemical pollution of the Persian Gulf by the Iraqi and Iranian governments so utterly indifferent to the welfare of either citizens or ecosystems. We have heard of the hundreds of thousands of people whose lives were destroyed by preventable chemical poisoning from the Union Carbide plant in Bhopal, India. We witness the exhaustion to both land and people from the tens of millions of refugees in Asia and Africa forced to move from place to place in order to escape war and poverty. We have seen the burning and destruction of rainforests by U.S.-sponsored contra forces in Nicaragua, the decimation of croplands and jungles in Cambodia by political friend and foe alike, the holocaust against both people and nature by South African forces in wars against their own and neighboring native peoples, the frightful assaults on the land and people of Afghanistan by the Soviet Union, and the massive environmental horrors occasioned by both revolutionary and counterrevolutionary armies in Ethiopia, Eritrea,

Somalia, the Sudan, Chad, Angola, Mozambique, and so many other places on that tragic continent of Africa.

A concern for "world order and the environment," then, refers to efforts to explore the linkages between political/economic/military decision-making and ecological health, and to determine what might be the contours of a just, decent, and ecologically healthy society in the midst of a desperately imperfect existing world order. What are the basic privileges that every person in any country should have a right to expect? What are the connections between the positive norms of human justice and environmental health? Some current facts and figures are in order here.

During the UN's International Year of Peace in 1986, global military expenditures reached $900 billion. Between 1960 and 1985, money expended for defense around the world totaled $14 trillion, an amount equal to 23 years of total income for all of the people and all of the nations in the poorest 70 percent of the world. The social deficits for ordinary people caused by this kind of central government military expropriation of a nation's wealth are obscene. Even though 80 percent of global military expenditure occurs in the developed world, the military outlay in the Third World countries alone totals far more than the overall outlay for health, education, and social services in those countries. These trends continue to escalate.

Unhappily, the long-anticipated expectations of people in the developing world for more humane governance in their own post–World War II, post–colonial era nation-states have been almost universally shattered. The dreams passed all too quickly. Most of the newly independent Third World nations were in fact creations of the older colonial empires, which arbitrarily determined both national boundaries and the allocation of resource-rich territorial divisions. Thus, many "independent" countries were formally designed to serve continuing imperial concerns. In other instances, the colonial powers (Britain, France, Belgium) had fostered a native bourgeoisie that became indifferent to anything but the maintenance of its own class privilege. Linkages between the bureaucracies and the military— often the ultimate guarantor of political continuation—were commonplace. After independence, this same basic power structure remained in place (at least until the first coup). While in many instances the indigenous power base was formalized and strengthened in the process, only rarely was there any corresponding effort to improve the welfare of the masses of ordinary people. When efforts at genuine democratization were made in Africa, for example, they were almost uniformly discouraged by the older colonial powers. Superimposing a capitalist economy (with all of the requisite market-system assumptions regarding labor, capital, production, economic priorities, sector investments, and modes of economic development) on an often decentralized social infrastructure created enormous cultural problems. The state apparatus, too often patterned on Western models, tended to grow more rapidly than the tax and support base. Higher and higher percentages of the national wealth were passed to the indigenous oligarchy. The new centralization of power isolated leaders from the survival concerns of the people and opened the floodgates to the inducements of foreign capital.

Environmentally, then, these joint forces—ex-colonial powers and untested new leaders, both concerned essentially for the continuation or the consolidation of power—inevitably affected the well-being of the land. World order concerns—justice for people and nature—did not often have priority on the respective agendas. Enormous human problems stemming directly from the unhappy alliance of old and new leaderships have become increasingly visible throughout the world. The United Nations International Children's Emergency Fund (UNICEF) currently estimates the unnecessary (i.e. easily preventable) deaths of infants and children in the developing world to be at least 15 million annually or 40,000 per day. Of all infants born in the Third World, 20 percent now die before their fifth birthday.

> 4 million children die each year from six diseases which could be prevented by immunization, 2 million from acute respiratory infections complicated by malnutrition, and 5 million from diarrheal dehydration. . . . Then there are the hundreds of millions who survive but are permanently disabled physically or mentally; 10 million babies who are born malnourished; 500,000 who go blind annually for lack of vitamin A.[1]

The trend toward militarized political power in the developing world, often facilitated either by the earlier colonial regimes or the great power armaments dealers (primarily the United States and the Soviet Union), continues. Whereas in 1960 only 28 percent of Third World governments were controlled by the military, by 1985 more than half were militarized. And among the 57 governments currently controlled by the military, institutionalized terror is commonplace. Ninety-five percent of all militarized governments have placed restraints on voting and the expression of political opinion. A large percentage of such countries are cited annually by Amnesty International for their continued assaults on their own people.[2]

Even in the democratic West, most of us have become totally disenchanted with what established power calls the "democratic process." We understand that ordinary citizens have virtually no voice, neither in choosing political candidates nor in helping to establish policy. The arrogance of rulers seems to increase with every new election. A Washington *Post*/ABC News poll taken just after the June 1989 resignations of U.S. House of Representatives Speaker James Wright and Majority Leader Tony Coelho because of ethics and misconduct charges indicated that three out of every four Americans believe U.S. congresspersons routinely "lie, cheat and steal" and that they are responsive only to the concerns of "special interests."

The Poverty—Ecology Connection

The connection between environmental disorder and poverty is revealed more clearly every day. Almost 1 billion people in the developing world do not have the requisite income to purchase food and fuel. The corresponding impact on their immediate environment is extreme. In Asia and Africa, 80–90 percent of the poor live in rural areas; and 60 percent of the poor in Latin America are concentrated in environmentally fragile areas. Overreliance on subsistence farming and the increasing use of land for annual food crops, which cannot be sustained indefinitely, rather than the traditional and ecologically stable perennial crops (grasses, trees) inevitably cause environmental disruption.

With 70 percent of global population, the Third World generates only 7 percent of industrial production worldwide and just 5 percent of global research and development. More than 40 developing nations still export essentially only one or two crops and are thus highly vulnerable to price fluctuations. Parity between the prices received from exported products as compared with the prices paid for imports declined by more than a third in the 1955–75 period, with an even more rapid decrease in the past decade. Because of this parity gap, increasingly destructive extractive processes are employed in the mines, forests, and fields as local producers increase production to compensate for low prices or else switch to cash crops for export. As a symbol of the asymmetry in the relations of rich and poor countries—of unequal and uneven development—foreign debt for Third World nations rose from $139 billion in 1976 to $1.3 trillion in 1990.[3]

Although we normally associate the concept of apartheid with South Africa, the essential structure of apartheid—where a racial minority dominates the majority in the economic, social, political, and cultural framework of a society—is in fact now the global norm. Gernot Kohler has calculated the extent of its economic dimensions manifest in the world today. In South Africa, the white/nonwhite ratio is 1:4.7, while throughout the world it is 1:2. The poorest 40 percent of the people in South Africa receive 6.2 percent of the national income, while the richest 20 percent take 58 percent of the total. Often overlooked, however, are the even more frightening global-apartheid statistics. Worldwide, the poorest 40 percent of the people receive only 5.2 percent of total income, while the wealthiest 20 percent take an amazing 71.3 percent. The global inequities in income are thus far worse than those obtaining in South Africa.[4]

And while global population increase is still seen by many as the major problem in effecting sustainable resource development programs, the fact remains that the 1 billion people in the world who belong at least marginally to the middle class (with minimum per-capita incomes of $2,000 per year) consume resources at rates 5–10 times higher than the more than 4 billion people in the poor and developing world. The environmental impact of this small middle-class segment is thus several times as much as that of the 4 billion have-nots in the world. Population policies based on simply limiting the increase in numbers of the poor, while ignoring the growth of this high-consumption segment of the world's more privileged classes, are shortsighted at best and racist at worst.[5]

Given the apparent inability of the nation-state—developed or developing—to create the proper conditions for world order and basic human and ecological rights, many people are now transferring their hopes to the transnational corporations, whose executives—they trust—may prove more adept than political leaders in dealing with the globally emergent human and ecological crises. Unlike industries in the past, which tended to concentrate first of all on the home market and sought primarily the economic well-being of the company and its nation-state of origin, the new corporation operates internationally and is primarily concerned for global production, capital formation, and profit. Since nowadays what's good for General Motors may not in fact be good for the country (and vice versa), may we not indeed expect more enlightenment from corporate executives of the TNCs who—more so than politicians—are called on to make long-range plans and to cast their eyes beyond the borders of any particular country?

Peace researcher Johan Galtung argues to the contrary, however, that things have not in fact changed so much under the new global economic order. He says that the TNCs, quite as much as their nation-state industrial precursors, are the carriers of economic imperialism. This newer manifestation of the great international corporation still requires "large scale economic cycles in which capital, labor, raw materials, manufactured goods are moved and shuffled around. The administrator of that process, including all stages of financing, extraction, processing, marketing, consumption, and reinvestment . . . is [still] a corporation."[6]

Galtung then suggests a number of factors that should dissuade the innocent from placing too much hope in the redemptive power of the new TNC. These corporations continue to maintain and reinforce the vertical, hierarchical division of labor that makes economic self-sufficiency and independence in developing nations almost impossible. TNCs are quite as much interested today as they ever were in transferring capital and profits from the smaller, peripheral nations to the coffers of the economic centers. The TNC perpetuates the traditional capitalist emphasis on capital/energy/research-subsidized modes of production—practices inimical to the welfare of most developing nations, which continue to be called on essentially to provide cheap labor and inexpensive raw material. Finally, very many of the products produced by the TNC, even within the developing country, are not needed by or affordable to the mass of people in that country. Minimally, then, one can reasonably expect the TNC to evidence little more enlightenment regarding human and natural resources than its predecessors in the world of commerce and industry.

Rights and Just Expectations

In recent years, as the injustice perpetrated by political leaders (whether imposed from without or from within the nation) have become more and more visible, there has been increasing attention given to theories of justice, and to defining the basic rights and legitimate expectations of people, on the part of groups that are seeking to actualize world order priorities (e.g., the World Order Models Project of the Institute for World Order). Happily, theory has also begun to move into practice as the issues of people's rights are being redefined and restructured throughout Eastern Europe and the Soviet Union and in some of the newer independent nations. What are the conditions required not merely to enable us to avoid destruction, but also to live in reasonable peace and security? How can we sustain the elementary goals of social life? As mentioned in Chapter 2, John Rawls has suggested an outline for determining human rights that provides a kind of plumb line for measuring political and social intention within a nation.

1. Each person is to be guaranteed equal rights with access to all basic human liberties within the society: economic, social, political, health, educational.
2. Since in actuality liberties are never equally distributed, social and economic inequalities must be offset by providing larger benefits to those who are least advantaged, when society experiences an overall increase in well-being.

Under such a formula, then, the greatest good would not be granted to the greatest number of people (as utilitarians advocate), but to those who need the most because of past deprivation. The primary proof of justice in a society, says Johan Galtung, is social and economic equity. Even the World Bank began to speak the language of basic human rights during the 1980s as it went about its business of underwriting "sound loans" in the developing world. While John Rawls emphasizes liberty more than welfare, the connection between the two is quite clear from his outline. Social justice without freedom is impossible.[7]

In fact, certain basic categories of rights should be self-evident to the political and economic leaders who bear responsibility for world order. Richard Falk discusses four such categories:

1. Basic Human Needs: food, housing, health, education;
2. Basic Decencies: freedom from political torture and arrest, and from inhumane governance;
3. Basic Participatory Rights: right to share in political decision-making and to choose one's place of residence, employment, and cultural activities; and
4. Basic Security Rights: the right to expect future well-being and national and ecological security.

Those of us who are concerned for planetary survival will necessarily make a connection between social and environmental rights and values. There is a direct link between world order issues and peace. Indeed, all forms of war—both external wars (between separate nation-states) and internal wars (civil wars)—are rationalized by appealing to the most precious liberties and the sense of well-being of the people. Similarly, environmental factors—requirements for land, resources, living room, food—are often used as a justification for war. Contemporary peacemaking thus requires environmental awareness.

Many suggestions have been made in regard to the formation or maintenance of a stable world order and a lessening of the poverty–ecology connection. Richard Falk has consolidated these suggestions into three approaches that may help us in thinking about our global future.

1. System Maintenance. The basic premises of the existing world social and economic orders are worthy of preservation and appropriate for all future planning. The nation-state system is the only practicable means of dealing with the arrangements of global power. Problems that exist can be largely resolved by more efficient management.

2. System Reform. While certain structural modifications will be required within the global economy (perhaps even calling for a new international economic order), the basic ordering of social relationships is sound, and solutions proposed to redress inequities should not seriously challenge or question the predominance of the nation-state in the ordering of global power.

3. System Transformation. The very structure of international relations must be changed by minimizing the role of the sovereign nation-state and by working for the minimization of collective violence and the maximization of economic well-being, social and political justice, and ecological health.[8]

While helpful in considering alternative strategies for the future, virtually every proposal for minimizing the nation-state since the end of World War II has been ineffective. Only the United Nations has been able, partially, to overcome some of the national self-interests—and these only occasionally and modestly. Today, more than ever, the nation-state appears to be firmly entrenched all throughout the world. Neither the older established countries nor the newly independent entities have any intention of giving up even an iota of sovereignty. How then can we find some basis for redefining national security and promoting world order in a continuing nation-state dominated world?

The Nature of Security in the Modern World

One thing is certain: Political realists, those who recognize the importance of the world order–ecoethics connection, do need to begin working toward a reformulation of the concept of national security. At a 1989 conference in Wellington, New Zealand, titled "Security in a Nuclear Free and Independent New Zealand," speakers emphasized the degree to which the very concept of security has changed today. Without ever challenging the functional viability of the nation-state system, the theme was enunciated again and again that real independence requires new formulas for survival. Traditional understandings of security—military and political-economic strength—may in fact have little to do, in the future, with genuine national security. The minimization of stress in race relationships and the promotion of ecological health are much better indicators of strength and well-being than external alliances and defensive preparations. Without internal strength, even the most well-meaning projections of traditional force have little staying power.

Clearly, *glasnost* and *perestroika* are current attempts in the Soviet Union to strengthen internal security in that country, and in quite a dramatic fashion. Similarly, the reformation of political power in Eastern Europe in late 1989 indicated for all to see that external power and armed strength mean little when certain basic rights are unavailable to the masses of the people. And in the United States, Congress finally seems to have understood the double jeopardy this nation faces due to its global economic decline and industrial stagnation (caused by the military preemption of most scientific and engineering research) coupled with a still abidingly imperial foreign policy. This new understanding gives some grounds for optimism in rethinking—if not checking—the nation's rapid drift into second-power status. High unemployment, reductions in social programs, inflationary tendencies, and increasing racial and cultural tensions all work together to create the real problems of national security for the United States, and for virtually every other nation in the world today.

Strength does begin at home, and environmental health is the absolute precondition of national security. It is important that we begin planning now for economic conversion from defense- to more peace-related economic and industrial activities. The recently agreed upon reductions in both nuclear and conventional military forces of NATO and the Warsaw Pact make this issue of economic conversion more compelling than was the case during the period of the Cold War.

The Peace Equation: Economic Conversion Equals Job Insurance

Economic conversion from a system based to a large degree on war production to one more directly geared to serving the peaceful needs of people is a concept that is shown more and more serious consideration in the United States today. Although the political leadership of the nation seems for the moment indissolubly wedded to the profitable deathdance of the war economy, things are changing elsewhere. The recent dramatic changes in the Soviet Union and within Eastern and Central Europe may well force even the conservative U.S. political establishment to consider whether its continuing $300 billion–plus annual defense expenditures really are good for the country. In this time of the crumbling Berlin Wall, political thaw, global movements for democratic reform, and international calls for détente and sanity in great-power relationships, the United States must offer some kind of quid pro quo to the efforts for peace and justice now underway in other parts of the world.

In any case, the changes now being acclaimed everywhere will inevitably shrink the U.S. defense budget in spite of certain opposition by the defense establishment and those who otherwise base their expectations—economic and political—on a continuation of militarism. In December 1989, U.S. Defense Secretary Richard Cheney predicted that a cut in U.S. military expenditures of $200 billion was inevitable by 1995. Even this modest 20-percent reduction (with much higher cuts now being called for by more progressive political forces) will require some fundamental restructuring within the U.S. economy. It seems quite clear that the U.S. containment doctrine—the heartbeat of our post–World War II strategic concern for limiting communist expansion throughout the world—no longer has merit, with the crumbling of economic and military power in Eastern Europe. Since 60 percent of the U.S. military budget is now geared toward maintaining forces able to fight a land war in Europe, the predicted reductions in men and matériel in that theater should have a major impact on overall defense allocations. Armed Forces Chief of

Staff General Colin Powell has already proposed a possible military build-down that could cost the army alone six active-duty divisions, or half its current level of forces. And the February 1990 decision by Presidents Gorbachev and Bush to reduce Soviet and U.S. land forces in continental Europe to 195,000 on either side portends even greater reductions in the near future.

That there will be other changes, as well, in U.S. defense production resulting from the realignment of the Warsaw Pact nations seems a sure bet. The defense sector is now discovering that its entire strategic war-fighting doctrine is being increasingly subjected to public reexamination. The rationale for continuing a huge, high-technology defense establishment with tentacles reaching into every corner of the world has been challenged by both conservative and liberal politicians. Already the stock market has shown some anxiety about the performance of defense stocks. Since the largest of the contractors will in the short range continue to receive the allocated billions in their contract pipelines, the smaller industries that supply parts, personnel services, and planning to the military will be hit first by any reductions.

The current changes in political-economic relationships worldwide have given renewed impetus to the concerns of peace groups (which support the more idealistic vision of full conversion from a wartime to a peacetime economy) and organized labor (which increasingly questions just how many jobs are actually created by defense-related allocations). The heart of the issue turns on whether or not military spending is in fact good for the country overall. The extreme apologists for both capitalism and socialism in the United States say that, yes, military spending is necessary for economic health in the United States. Capitalists understand the enormous and virtually unrestricted profits that bless a handful of large defense industries through the grace of massive military spending. And radical socialists like Alexander Cockburn and James O'Connor agree that military spending is necessary for the health of the economy until such time as a new and more humane social system replaces the antiquated priorities of the old order. They criticize

> those people who say, cut a billion here or a billion there out of the military budget, convert this factory or that factory to peaceful production, like Grumman making aluminum canoes instead of F-14's, without realizing that military spending is essential to capitalism and if you are going to think about cutting it, you have to think pretty radically about

what to put in its place. Of course, these jobs-with-peace theories are well-meaning but mostly hare-brained.[9]

As we have learned again and again, however, social theorists who advocate change only insofar as that change is consistent with their understanding of economic and political theory do not really help in the process of humanizing social structures. It really does not need to be pointed out that defense-industry workers will fight to maintain both their jobs and the parent military contracts if their only alternative is unemployment. New statistical information, however, is now forcing both labor and the smaller industrial corporations (if not the Marxist and capitalist theoreticians) to reconsider their traditional "military spending is good for the economy" position. Of the 4 million businesses in the United States, only 1 percent (40,000) receive contracts from the military for war production. One-third of the total spending in the nation, however, goes to that 1 percent of the industrial sector. The self-interest of the rest of the U.S. economy in reprioritizing the military's national budget is being increasingly understood. Even the U.S. Chamber of Commerce has now gone on record as saying that, so long as 75 percent of all federal scientific research and development (R&D) is geared toward the military, there cannot be a healthy U.S. economy. The views of those who claim that economic conversion is impossible are increasingly irrelevant.

Already, for example, top managers at the Lawrence Livermore National Laboratory (one of the United States' two special labs devoted to the development of nuclear weapons and recipient of billions of Pentagon dollars) are mulling over the implications of massive cuts in military procurement that may affect the lab. Lab directors are now seriously considering the expansion of nonmilitary energy research programs to pick up the slack. There is some doubt as to whether or not the lab will be flexible enough to adapt to peacetime production. In any case, it is likely that adjustments will have to be made in the near future, if the lab is to survive intact.

Corporations around the country are being forced to deal with the same issue: What happens once the military goose that has been laying golden eggs for them decade after decade is there no more? On the upside for industry is the fact that, while Pentagon spending will decline in the next few years, NASA's projected budget increases for space exploration are expected to fill some of the gap. But corporate inertia will make it difficult for many of the larger companies to respond quickly and make needed changes in their production priorities. Defense-industry expert Thomas Lloyd-Butler notes that many industries serving the military sector are, in fact, "quasi-governmental bureaucratic institutions. It is hard for them to compete in commercial markets, not only from a pricing and profit standpoint, but also in product development."[10]

Defense Secretary Cheney has now officially predicted employment reductions in the Department of Defense at "several hundred thousand in the next 3–4 years." Some states may be especially affected by the overall cutbacks. Experts now estimate that, although 200,000 jobs in California alone could be lost by 1995, the biggest problem may not be layoffs so much as the monumental task of retraining both management and workers to make the transition into non–war economy production. The problem of job retraining will fall largely on the federal government, which created this industrial dependency on vast military expenditures in the first place and which is now being called on by all sectors to transfer the expected "peace dividend" over to the massive social deficiencies that have developed as a consequence of the military buildup of the past decade.

The West Coast—home to 40 percent of the aerospace industry—will be one of the hardest hit areas as this anticipated economic conversion gains momentum. Southern California especially—for decades dependent on military procurement—is now generally acknowledged as an enormous, bloated, obsolete defense establishment that will have to be pared down. But with no more than 38,000 jobs annually expected to be lost under the phase-down and with the California economy generating 300,000 new jobs per year for its civilian labor force of more than 13 million, the problems of relocation and retraining for displaced workers—with a little help from Uncle Sam—should be manageable in that state. And if the expected transition does in fact take place, the inevitable transfer of some federal R&D funding from the military to the civilian sector will make the United States more economically competitive, with a consequent increase in employment in consumer-oriented production.

The melancholic concerns of those who feel that the peace dividend will prove impossible for U.S. industry to handle is contradicted by many respected economists. Lester Thurow of the Massachusetts Institute of Technology has said,

> It's a mistake to make any important economic problem out of a cut in the defense budget that would be even as big as 50%. The defense budget . . . employs 40% of the engineers and scientists in the country.

We need those people in civilian industry. The economic question is really trivial.

And economist John Kenneth Galbraith of Harvard says,

Defense budget cuts would be uniformly favorable. If there are cuts in defense spending, we would have to maintain the same budget spending. The dollar difference could be used for the urgent needs of our central cities and . . . to ease the transition in Eastern Europe.

The one thing to be kept strongly in mind is that the two most prosperous countries . . . are Japan and Germany which haven't been burdened by the diversion of talent to weapons production.

Economic projections made by Data Resources, Incorporated (DRI) in calculating the effect of a 5 percent annual cut in the defense budget show a remarkably favorable set of economic indicators in the 1990–95 period. The economy grows, interest rates fall, business spending increases, housing starts accelerate, and machine tool production spurts ahead.[11]

Although the Reagan and Bush administrations have constantly criticized Japan and (what was) West Germany for their "industrial targeting" (providing government financial aid to earmarked industries), the United States has an unbroken record of targeting primarily the defense sector for government underwriting. We will note in Chapter 6 in more detail how and why it is that we allocate three-quarters of our federal R&D funds to the military sector. The main point is clear, however. With our primary economic competitors targeting civilian sectors of their economies (even with its military resurgence, Japan puts less than 10 percent of its R&D money into military projects but very large amounts into consumer durables, electronics, and other export goods), it is little wonder that foreign competitors so often produce higher quality consumer goods. Steadily, the United States has been losing its competitive place in the world market for anything other than military hardware.

Labor unions are now taking seriously the reality of the number of jobs produced for every $1 billion of industrial investment:

17,000 jobs from missile production
25,000 jobs from petrochemical production
48,000 jobs from health-sector production
62,000 jobs from educational services
65,000 jobs from retail trade

Although the structural transition from a permanent war economy to a moderate peace economy will be difficult, the process was already modestly under way even before the changes in Europe took place. The Pentagon and defense procurement scandals, which produced criminal indictments against virtually every major U.S. defense contractor, revealed certain truths about who actually profits from the military-scientific-industrial complex. The current reluctant—but real—movement by the economically exhausted great powers to reduce both nuclear and conventional arms presages the inevitability of positive economic change.

In all of this, it is the long-range interests of labor that need to be held foremost. Political changes throughout the world will accelerate the transition. But the forces pushing for the maintenance of military expenditures at current levels still remain formidable. The MX missile program alone involves industrial contracts in more than 400 congressional districts throughout the country. It is politically risky for incumbent politicians to oppose the continuance of such contracts. In San Diego County, California, one of every four jobs is currently tied to military spending. One of every six jobs throughout California has a military or defense-industry connection. Defense expenditures in the San Francisco Bay Area in 1989 averaged $10,000 for every San Franciscan. In London County, Connecticut, per-capita defense industry spending now totals more than $8,000. With fiscal year 1991–92 defense-sector expenditures now projected at $325 billion, a key factor that tends to prolong the arms race and the maintenance of a permanent war economy in the United States is the structural connection between industry, the Pentagon, the scientific community, and the millions of workers dependent for employment on these economic sectors.

Thus, the problems are very real. It is easy to talk about economic conversion, but difficult to effect the social reconstruction required to make it happen. Still, new programs are being mounted to begin the task. Major labor unions regularly schedule conferences and seminars on jobs, the environment, and military spending. Congressman Ted Weiss (D-New York) recently sponsored the Defense Economic Adjustment Bill (originally House Resolution 229), which stipulates that the federal government may not enter into any contract for military equipment unless the contractor agrees to pay into a special fund the amount of 1.25 percent of the total value of the contract to underwrite future job retraining and worker assistance in the event of contract cancellation. Other economic conversion legislation on both the federal and state levels is being developed. One project that has already been successfully actualized is the recent conversion of the Fort Baker military depot and wharf area in San Francisco into a permanent center for some 40 environmental, peace, and cultural organizations. How pleasantly ironic to find Greenpeace and the Nuclear Freeze headquarters occupying military property! Although major federal legislation may still be a dream, at least in the short run, the current combination of political change in Europe, serious arms-reduction negotiations, and an increasing awareness of the overall negative impact on the economy of a continuation of current-level defense expenditures may make conversion a genuine possibility in the not too distant future. Happily, more of us are discovering that there is in fact a direct connection between jobs, military spending, and world order.[12]

New Politics and Paradigms for the Solar Age

In spite of the continued dominance of nation-states in the world political order, new connections are being constantly forged for a more unified, global economic and political system. International trade is exploding; transnational corporations now have more concern for their global sales than for the welfare of their home countries; transborder telecommunications systems now girdle the Earth. It is becoming virtually impossible today for any one country to maintain the kind of formal independence once considered to be the norm for the nation-state. We are at least approaching the place where we can envision the integration of relatively isolated and independent economic structures into a more unified world economic system. This is not all necessarily a positive development. The dangers suggested earlier of overoptimism about the future role of the TNC are worth remembering. But it is clear that major developments are under way globally toward more creative integration of systems. As Hazel Henderson notes,

> The old economic theories of Adam Smith, John M. Keynes, and their Marxist variants are now about as useless as monkeys for space exploration. Most of today's global crises—the arms race, pollution, drug addiction and social breakdown—are symptomatic of our deeper crisis of

human perception. Many futurists . . . agree that the deeper crisis is no less than a shifting of the entire belief system that burdened the industrial revolution.[13]

Henderson says that one of the pressures for a new global system of mutual sustainable development and a new understanding of common security is the economic exhaustion—fiscal and resource related—of the United States and the Soviet Union. Properly recognizing that the Cold War is or is about to be over and that a "multipolar" world order may now be taking the place of the old superpowers, Henderson (and others) foretells new long-term trends in cultural and social development: "Few countries will follow the now error-prone, per capita averaged, money-dominated, Gross National Product indicators still favored by Eurocentric, Western models, which have often preempted more creative approaches."[14]

In remarkably similar vein, physicist-philosopher Fritjof Capra suggests that we are indeed in the very midst of a "rising culture" (which we may not be able to see clearly since we are so directly immersed in the old one). For Capra, the old dominant world perspective that has provided all of the operative models for Western society since the Enlightenment is now bankrupt.

> At the beginning of the last two decades of our century, we find ourselves in a state of profound, world-wide crisis. It is a complex, multi-dimensional crisis whose facets touch every aspect of our lives—our health and livelihood, the quality of our environment, and our social relationships, our economy, technology and politics. It is a crisis of intellectual, moral, and spiritual dimensions; a crisis of a scale and urgency unprecedented in recorded human history. For the first time we have to face the very real threat of extinction of the human race and of all life on this planet.[15]

Pointing out the failure of mechanistic, reductionist views of science and technology, Capra indicates that new paradigms must include ecologically oriented ethics. An environmental ethic must be developed for exploration of radically new moral and metaphysical principles. The recognition of value inherent in nature stems from the deep awareness that nature and the self are in fact one. "In most traditional ethics, self-interest needs no justification. But if nature and I are one, acting in the best interests of nature becomes enlightened self-interest."[16]

Remarkably, the dilemmas of world order we have discussed do not commonly create the kind of generalized outrage from people in the developing world that we might expect. The consequences of poverty, militarization, ecological disaster, and injustice are today of such a scale that it is hard to imagine right-minded people acquiescing in the brutalities of the era. As Richard Falk has put it, "Despite these dangers and trends, the citizenry in most countries is not aroused. . . . The dynamics of oppression associated with the workings of world order remain largely latent and invisible. As long as social problems remain invisible—not seen as problems to be solved or solvable—it seems almost futile to propose positive responses."[17]

Reflecting on this "politics of invisibility," Falk notes that, for centuries, the social arrangements of power in the poor countries have led people there to believe the oppression is simply in the natural order of things. Is it not written in the Bible that the poor will always be with us? So often there seems no alternative but to accept this apparent fact. The realities of oppression are so extensive that, even among those who know what in fact is going on, there is a tendency to move from a feeling of powerlessness and helplessness into actually denying the truth. The Brazilian educator-philosopher Paulo Freire has remarked that a primary element in the struggle for a just and decent ordering of society is the quest to make the various oppressions visible. Richard Falk agrees: "The emerging enterprise of global reform is commited to shifting oppressive structures of world order into the domain of visibility for millions of people. The world order perspective is designed to make a massive assault on the overall politics of invisibility."[18]

Paulo Freire reminds us, further, that oppressed people commonly fear freedom, and this seems almost universally true. We are so used to being treated as objects, as things whose only value is in serving and being of use to those who rule, that we become resigned to the status quo. Oppression has always been a primary domesticating tool of those who practice inhumane governance.

> To surmount the situation of oppression, men must first critically recognize its causes, so that through transforming action they can create a new situation, one which makes possible the pursuit of a fuller humanity.
>
> Functionally, oppression is domesticating. To no longer be prey to its force, one must emerge from it and turn upon it. This can only be done by means of the *praxis*: reflection and action upon the world in order to transform it.[19]

The earthshaking changes now under way in Central and Eastern Europe show that, when people are somehow enabled to understand and confront the forces of brutality about them, transformation does become possible. During the 1968 Democratic party convention in Chicago, police forces (under the joint control of then Mayor Richard Daley, Sr., and the Democratic party establishment) undertook massive and violent assaults against U.S. citizens protesting Democratic party compliance with the Vietnam War policies of President Lyndon Johnson. As these people—mainly young antiwar activists—were daily brutalized under the watchful eyes of the television cameras, they took up the cry, "The whole world is watching." Praxis had become for these people the practical task of reflecting, analyzing, and then actually taking action on the truth they discovered about the origins and reasons for continuance of the war. The forces of oppression manifested in Chicago could no longer count on a politics of invisibility, neither in their exercise of power at home nor in their conduct of the war in Vietnam. Public disenchantment with U.S. foreign policy developed rapidly and positively as a consequence of this revealing behavior on the part of the political leadership. In an even more dramatic and important symbol of change, the recent democratic revolution in Europe offers new hope for all the peoples of the world. Once awakened, the forces for justice and equity are hard to contain.

New possibilities for positive change are always on the horizon. My old mentor, community organizer Saul Alinsky, used to say about organizing for social change—and about life in general—that "every negative has a positive." There is, ironically, a positive element that can emerge from the escalating assault on the Earth and its people by the organized forces of government and industry. The problems are now so great that it is difficult to keep them invisible. Popular awareness of their severity thus increases day by day. The chickens of past political and economic indifference to ecological health are now coming home to roost. The whole world is watching. And, as we will repeat again especially in Chapter 15, ordinary people must persist in organizing on the basis of world order imperatives if they are to take full advantage of that fact.

Notes

1. Ruth Sivard, *World Military and Social Expenditures,* 11th ed. (Stockholm: World Priorities, 1986), p. 22.

2. Ibid. p. 25.

3. Richard Falk, Samuel S. Kim, and Saul Mendlovitz, "Economic Well Being," in *Toward a Just World Order*, vol. 1 (Boulder, Co.: Westview Press, 1982), p. 290.

4. Gernot Kohler, "Global Apartheid," *Alternatives: A Journal of World Policy* 4, no. 2 (1978).

5. For a helpful perspective on this issue, see Nathan Keyfitz, "World Resources and the World Middle Class," *Scientific American* 235, no. 1 (July 1976), pp. 28–35.

6. Johan Galtung, "The Nonterritorial System: Nonterritorial Actors," in *True Worlds: A Transnational Perspective* (New York: Free Press, 1980), p. 105.

7. John Rawls, *A Theory of Justice* (Cambridge, Mass.: Belknap Press, 1971).

8. Richard Falk, "Contending Approaches to World Order," *Journal of International Affairs* 31 (Fall/Winter 1977).

9. Alexander Cockburn, "Socialist Ecology: What It Means and Why No Other Kind Will Do," *Zeta Magazine* (February 1989), p. 20.

10. Don Clark, "Defense Cuts Probable," San Francisco *Chronicle*, March 2, 1990.

11. The Thurow and Galbraith quotations and the DRI data are from Charlotte Lucas, "The Peace Dividend," San Francisco *Examiner*, March 11, 1990.

12. Further information, materials, and films on economic conversion and the status of pending legislation can be obtained from the following organizations: Center for Economic Conversion, 222C View Street, Mountain View, CA 94041; and The International Economic Conversion Information Exchange, 2161 Massachusetts Avenue, Cambridge, MA 02140.

13. Hazel Henderson, "The Imperative Alternative," *Inquiry Magazine* (June 1986), p. 43.

14. Hazel Henderson, "The Emerging Worldgame of Mutual Development: Toward New Criteria and Indicators," address to the Conference on the Global Economy, George Washington University, Washington, D.C., December 8–9, 1988. Also see Hazel Henderson, *The New Politics of the Solar Age: Alternatives to Economics* (Garden City, N.Y.: Doubleday, 1988).

15. Fritjof Capra, *The Turning Point: Science, Society, and the Rising Culture* (New York: Simon and Schuster, 1982), p. 21.

16. From a personal conversation with Fritjof Capra at the Elmwood Institute, Berkeley, California, July 1988.

17. Richard Falk, "On Invisible Oppression and World Order," in Falk, Kim, and Mendlovitz, *Just World Order*, p. 44.

18. Ibid. p. 46.

19. Paulo Freire, *The Pedagogy of the Oppressed* (New York: Seabury Press, 1971), pp. 31–32.

4

The Moral Demand for the Biological Steady State

As the preceding chapters have hopefully suggested, the time has arrived for a new ethic based on ecological self-restraint and a new morality that can respond to the biological, ecological, and economic necessities of the age. Unless the decision is voluntarily made within the ordered structures of society to move toward a steady-state society incorporating self-sustaining energy and resource utilization systems, the decision will be forced on the people of the world either by the forces of nature or by strong, centralized governmental authorities created to enforce compliance with the new demands of scarcity and survival.

More than a decade ago, Robert Heilbroner emphasized the urgency of the matter. In *An Inquiry into the Human Prospect*, Heilbroner reminded us that, unless measures were soon taken on a popular level to restrain our exploitation of natural resources, our expansion of military technologies, and our general hostilities toward one another, almost inevitably totalitarian regimes would rise to deal with the tensions of scarcity and the imperatives of planning. Because of the inertia in our social systems, however, and in light of the magnitude of the problems, Heilbroner saw little "hope for mankind."[1] Indeed, the environmental literature of the period from 1970 to the present has focused on the general ecocrisis: economic and industrial maldevelopment, the fragility of the closed ecological systems of Spaceship Earth, and the terrifying need for a limitation of growth.

The Club of Rome studies dealing with the limits to growth (*The Limits to Growth, Mankind at the Turning Point*, and *RIO: Reshaping the International Order*) pointed at unrestrained industrial growth and development as the primary culprit in the environmental crisis.[2] In fact, some people were very surprised when these studies uniformly concluded that more important in the survival equation than population growth, resource and food scarcity, or pollution is the tendency in both the capitalist and the socialist worlds to increase industrial development as rapidly as possible. Efforts have subsequently been made by many groups—both governmental and nongovernmental organizations (NGOs)—to outline newer and more rational, organic growth theories capable of replacing the clearly obsolescent patterns of undifferentiated economic growth that have characterized the historical development of the industrial nations.

As we have all now admitted to our dismay, economies based on constant industrial growth and development bring inevitably negative consequences in their wake: scarcity of resources, increased patterns of consumption, planned waste and obsolescence, increased pollution, global competition for supplies of needed raw materials, and competitive social orderings. We have not yet been able, however, to come up with a new social mechanism to deal with these problems. Nevertheless, the steady-state or equilibrium society, wherein material input equals no more than the outflow of waste in a sustainable ordering and utilization of resources, has now become a moral imperative of the highest order. Whereas, in the past, saints and martyrs could call for sacrifice as the highest rule of the personal life, it has now become a social requirement for generalized survival.

Any functional steady-state economic system will require a number of significant changes within society: a reduction to the lowest possible levels in the throughputs of energy and materials so that production will approximate depreciation; the holding of population and resources to survivable ratios; the re-creation of materials and machines to as close as possible a replacement level; the reduction of industrial pollutants to levels compatible with general public health; and a caring for the global have-not population in order to minimize gross demands for land and energy. Reflecting on the emergent moral imperative that less is more, economist Herman E. Daly has said, "Only two things are held constant—the stock of human bodies, and the total stock or inventory of artifacts. Technology, information, wisdom, goodness, genetic characteristics, distribution of wealth and income, product mix, etc., are not held constant."[3]

While such alternative modeling may raise the spectre of an overly minimal and unduly frugal ordering of society, it may not add up to all that in tomorrow's world. Too often our wants have been transformed into covetously anticipated needs that do not necessarily contribute to either personal or social well-being. As resource economist William Ophuls has commented, "It follows from what most writers state (and by similar words uttered by people of every age and tradition) that nothing of real value would be lost if [industrial] development were to cease. Rather the likelihood of men and women leading reasonably happy, sane, fulfilled and harmonious personal lives would be enhanced."[4]

Actually, certain implications of a simple and modest model of the more livable society should be welcome—not ominous—to ordinary people. Ophuls (among many others) has suggested a number of policy reformulations for the development of a hierarchy of values among those who would be involved in creating a new and sustainable society. Community decision-making, rather than our frontierlike "do your own thing" mentality, would come to dominate the social orders. Political sensibilities would involve matters other than market-related concerns and would effect actual needs more than imagined ones. There would be a new and generally enforced stewardship of resources of all kinds. National goals—both personal and those affecting state policy—would have to become more modest. A new morality affirming our links both to other peoples and to the natural order would come to be the commonplace ethic.

The Pros and Cons of the Sustainability Debate

As noted in the Introduction to this book, the worldwide sustainable-development movement has gained new converts in the past few years. The 1987 publication of *Our Common Future* gave the movement direction and credibility. It is worth repeating the central premise of this UN World Commission on Environment and Development (WCED) report: *Sustainable development* is development that meets the needs of the present without compromising the ability of future generations to meet their own needs. The definition contains two key concepts:

> [1.] the concept of "needs," in particular the essential needs of the world's poor, to which overriding priority should be given, and
> [2.] the idea of limitations imposed by the state of technology and social organization on the environment's ability to meet present and future needs. . . . The goals of economic and social development must be defined in terms of sustainability in all countries—developed or developing, market oriented or centrally planned.[5]

The WCED study then sums up the concept of sustainability by suggesting that economic development must always have one primary objective: the satisfaction of human needs and aspirations. (Parenthetically it must be noted that nonanthropocentric value theorists have decried the extent to which editor Gro Harlem Brundtland continues the old "man in the environment" motif with its consequent slighting of and apparent indifference to the nonhuman portion of the creation. In all fairness, however, Brundtland's team was charged by the United Nations solely with responsibility for assessing the environmental future of the human inhabitants of the globe.) The study notes the obvious but terrifying reality that the essential needs of the majority of the world's population for food, shelter, jobs, clothing, education, and health care are being everywhere ignored. A world in which poverty is the dominant reality will be an ecologically unhealthy world. Sustainable development, as defined, holds out policy options that may enable global planners to begin formulating responses to both major problems: unmet human needs, and ecological health.

Although well intentioned, the Brundtland report has been able to do little more than call further attention to these existing dilemmas. Like the earlier limits-to-growth studies, the report criticizes the role that the two dominant economic systems have played in contributing to the problems but it falls short of suggesting viable alternatives to current practice. As one critic has noted, "Sustainable development has emerged in the last few years as the latest development catchphrase." Energy and resources expert Sharad Lele points out the possibility that, in the important debate on sustainability, the concept itself can be trivialized if the serious problems of policy facing its development are not squarely faced.

> Development is a process of directed change; definitions of development thus embody both the objectives of this process and the means of achieving these objectives. While the latter depend upon one's perception of physical and social reality, the former depend upon one's ethical beliefs and concerns. Thus, a paradigm of development must include a statement of objectives, of the perceptions of reality that modify the objectives . . . as well as the means to achieve these objectives.[6]

The sustainability bandwagon can indeed present problems to uncritical advocates. The term "sustainability" is sometimes used to describe a romanticized kind of conservation process to be effected essentially by the goodwill of resource planners. But if we have learned anything in the past 25 years, it is that global resources cannot be subject to sustainable development policies without massive change in the political and economic structures of the world. Resources are limited. Both energy supplies and the biosphere's ability to absorb the waste products of industrial societies have absolute limits. Ecoethical generalizations on sustainability themes cannot substitute for the frank acknowledgment of the limiting nature of biophysical restraints and the need for structural economic realignment.

The WCED focus on the need for permanent economic change must be looked at under the harsh light of present-day international economic policies. The current priorities of the World Bank and the International Monetary Fund (IMF) with regard to developing-country debt repayment virtually mandate a reduction in the living standards of the citizenry in order to meet the demands of debt servicing. Such policies cannot facilitate positive economic growth since they reinforce poverty—and poverty inevitably has a negative environmental impact overall. Most of the entrenched mainstream economic programs forced on debtor nations continue the trend toward impoverishment of the poor and enrichment of the local oligarchies and international bankers.

As Sharad Lele notes, economic growth by itself will never be a vehicle to enhance sustainable development. Even the World Bank has come to realize (in principle if not yet in practice) that large-scale economic development programs based on developed-world models— hydroelectric plants, agricultural projects employing "green revolution" technologies, mineral extraction programs, huge profit-making industrial schemes—are more often than not harmful to the majority when basic human needs (food, shelter, health care, education, sanitation) have not first been met.

As was mentioned in Chapter 1 with regard to the destruction of tropical rainforests, poor people are frequently scapegoated for the visible environmental decay in their countries—as if environmental degradation were somehow a consequence of the "unenlightened" practices of the majority. In almost every case, however, the misuse of land, the destruction of local forests for fuel wood, and the inability to develop and implement appropriate and sustainable technologies are not the fault of inadequate people, but of inappropriate economic systems not suited to the needs of developing nations. As Berkeley development scholar Miguel Altieri has noted,

> Sustainability implies balancing agricultural development and environmental preservation in a culturally and socially acceptable manner and

should not be used to rationalize high-input agriculture and interventionist policies. . . . Technological concentration has had tremendous ecological and social costs, including genetic erosion, long-term hunger and poverty, [and] increased economic stratification among farmers.[7]

Furthermore, the emphasis in most of the sustainability models on the need for free trade overlooks the basic power relationships between the wealthy and the impoverished nations, which inevitably tilt the advantage in arbitration to the richer trading partner. Without clearly defined parity standards (with prices for exports and imports indexed to some accepted standard of equitability), so-called free trade will always benefit the relatively powerful nation.

There is also a need in any sustainability model for what Lele calls "social sustainability"—an institutional tendency to reduce internal conflict and to provide organizational and cultural flexibility—as a necessary condition for both effecting and enforcing sustainable development programs. "Sustainable development is being packaged as the inevitable outcome of objective scientific analysis . . . that does not contradict the deep-rooted normative notion of development as economic growth. In other words, sustainable development is an attempt to eat one's cake and have it too."[8]

Those of us who are involved in the struggle to make sustainable development practices meaningful to our short-range, goal-oriented politicians and economists must be careful not to become so caught up in the rhetoric of sustainability that we forget the inequity in our existing social and economic relationships—imbalances that will ultimately be the biggest single obstacle to effecting new and more appropriate development policies.

The Two Faces of Scarcity

Like the Roman god Janus, whose two bearded faces pointed in opposite directions so that he could see both ways at once, the concept of scarcity in the modern age has two distinct dimensions: real scarcity, and ideological scarcity. The first seems to be the clearest, but also the most controversial: a scarcity of certain resources necessary for survival that does exist in different places in the world today. This global fact of life has an enormous implication for the survival of millions of our fellow human beings. Already, millions of people starve to death throughout the world each year, with hundreds of millions more existing on the very edge of disaster. It does no good for these people to be told by political economists (true though the statement may be) that in reality the problem has to do with the production and distribution mechanisms of society and that, when the economic machinery is properly oiled, there will be plenty for everyone. Starving people understand only that there is not plenty for everyone today and that they are starving. Scarcity in some places is terribly real.

On the other side of the coin, there has always been an ideological aspect to the discussion of scarcity. The assumptions made here often determine the context in which the actual scarcity is to be seen. In the early nineteenth century, the English parson and economist Thomas Malthus was convinced, for example, that the only way for industrial societies to maintain some equilibrium was for at least a fair number of the poor to die in order to balance population with food supplies. Reflecting on the relative expendability of the less fortunate, Malthus stated,

> To act consistently . . . we should facilitate the operation of nature in producing mortality; . . . we should seduously encourage other forms of destruction. . . . Instead of recommending cleanliness to the poor, we should encourage contrary habits. In our towns we should make the streets narrower, crowd more people into the houses and court the return of the plague. In the country, we should build our villages near stagnant pools, and particularly encourage settlements in all marshy and unwholesome situations. But above all, we should reprobate specific remedies for ravaging diseases . . . that annual mortality may be increased.[9]

Happily for his theory—if not for the poor—Malthus's enunciation of the supposedly "iron law" of population and resources came to justify his retrospectively quaint and morally repugnant stance. Yet his iron law was but a myth constructed to justify certain social assumptions of the British ruling class. Such intentional misapplications of the concept of scarcity have long been used by neo-Malthusians as the formal justification for limiting those segments of the population that seem most to threaten established values and understandings. It is, therefore, important to look very carefully at our two faces of the scarcity problem.

Few would argue with the fact that at least relative scarcity is common in many parts of the world today. The pressures of population growth in some of the poorer countries, where annual rates of increase are approximately 2.5 percent and sometimes appreciably more (implying a population doubling time of 20 years or less), have placed enormous pressures on the supplies of food and fiber required to sustain such burgeoning populations. There is no question that the local inadequacies of political and economic systems, supported by the harsh supply-and-demand requirements of the global market, have exacerbated these problems. When Haitian peasants—among the poorest and hungriest in the world—stop growing beans and rice in order to make pastureland for the fattening of cattle for fast-food outlets in the United States, it is clear that some scarcities in food supplies are not absolute, but relative. They are nonetheless real in terms of the needs of the people and the unwillingness of political and economic leaders to act in the best interest of the people of their own country.

Throughout history, there have almost always been relative scarcities of certain materials created either through inadequacies in the production or in the distribution systems. In the few centuries since the emergence of the scientific-industrial revolution, however, many of these scarcities have been temporarily overcome in certain societies by new ways of structuring the economic and social orders. New technologies, the opening of new areas of the world for the production of food and raw materials, and the marshaling of economic forces to process these materials have made many of us forget the earlier periods of scarcity in Western history. It is a basic element in our understanding of life in the industrialized world that there seems to be plenty to go around for most people here.

Today, the global scarcity problem has been complicated by spin-offs from technological society itself. The new threat to human life and survival through poisoning by pollution and biospheric contamination has become commonplace, adding a new dimension to the routine problems occasioned by regional resource scarcity. Everywhere today, hungry people are being poisoned by the chemical contaminants of the industrial system. This is now such a common part of the life of virtually every poor person on Earth that it tends increasingly to be ignored by those affected.

Economic and political leaders, most particularly, have been able to fool themselves about the realities of abundance. Both capitalist and socialist economic orders have structured their ideologies around the myth of abundance and ecological plenty. But such an era of dreaming innocence is now gone. We know that the demands of advanced industrial societies have in certain ways brought us back to where we once were—with newer and more serious scarcities in energy supplies, food, and resources and with distributional inequities now generalized throughout the world. We may ethically covet the extension of our own standard of living to less privileged people in the developing world, but the very fact that the 5 percent of the Earth's population now living in North America consumes almost one-third of total world resources demonstrates the limitations in such a fantasy of global consumption. If only 15 percent of the total world population consumed food, fiber, energy, and raw materials at the rate that the U.S. Americans and Canadians do (followed by Japan and Western Europe), virtually nothing would be left for the remaining 85 percent of the world's people. Furthermore, a number of studies have shown conclusively that capital stocks and mineral resources could never supply the developing world with the same materials infrastructure needed for its rapid development to advanced industrialization. There is simply not enough steel, lumber, mineral resources, and energy available to enable developing nations to replicate the Western systems, even under the best of circumstances.

Given these realities, it is understandable that there has been in the past two decades a flood of warnings from the cosmic doomsayers to the effect that, even if we do reorder our global systems (which now seem to be able to do no more than ensure the continuance of inequity), there are only a few decades left. According to their assessments, we have reached the point of no return in all of our systems: moral, economic, political, and social. Other commentators feel the one hope remaining is for the emergence of "iron" leadership within both the nation-states and the international community that will impose new frugal and steady-state policies, since it seems so clear that we will never take such actions voluntarily.

It is most certainly clear that some new balancing between population needs and environmental requirements must be developed. New economic and political models are quite desperately needed to deal with the emergent reality and realization of scarcity in the world. Constraints of one form or another, whether communally or bureaucratically enforced, do seem to be in order. The limits-to-growth studies, assessing the global future through analysis of the five big survival elements—industrial outputs, food per capita, population growth, pollution, and resources utilization—calculate a last-ditch transition time of at most 100 years. Even those who disagree with the macabre sensibilities of neo-Malthusians such as biologist Garrett

Hardin, who believes in essence that the rich should keep what they have and the poor be left to starve, now agree with the likes of Hardin that, sooner than we would like, we may have to develop some forms of "mutual coercion, mutually agreed upon" if we are to stave off biospheric collapse. Technological fixes will not solve this global problem since the most they can do is simply rearrange existing supplies through the pricing mechanisms of the market. Such methods can provide short-range amelioration, but no long-range answers to the materials/food/population perplexity. Market manipulations cannot create permanent new supplies. It is probably true that, at least to a degree, the era of benign politics has ended wherein existing environmental dilemmas can be continually pushed aside. Scarcity—whether absolute or of the more common socially mandated type—has brought a new sense of urgency into the world.

There is a second and equally important way of viewing the scarcity issue, however, by first looking at the assumptions that define the problem itself. Assumptions always color how we see and understand a problem. Food, for example, is not considered scarce in Japan, which nonetheless imports up to 80 percent of its food and virtually all of its energy, nor in Holland, which imports more milk solids to feed its veal than all of the developing world combined. But food is scarce in many of the nations that provide exports to those two countries. The irony is that, while protein is scarce in the developing world, it exports more protein to the richer nations than it imports. And while overall there is no shortfall in calories produced by the world agricultural systems (a global average of at least 3,000 calories produced per day per person), somehow or other we manage to assume that there is not enough to go around, worldwide. It is a function of the global market system that scarcity will be overcome in one area because of its ability to purchase needed foodstuffs but exacerbated in another by that same move.

Assumptions color reality in other ways, as well. Europe overall uses only half as much energy per capita as the United States, but it does not follow that energy is therefore scarce in Europe. People starve in large numbers in many areas of South Asia, even though their governments maintain extensive grain storage facilities and grain supplies. Unfortunately, scarcity is here again a function of the ability to pay for food, rather than its availability. It is normal for the means to sustain life to be scarce among those who cannot afford to purchase or grow the needed materials.

Many so-called scarcities, therefore, are not absolute. They are created and managed by social forces, rather than rising somehow automatically from nature itself. Social and cultural factors are as important in the definition of scarcity as are actual supply factors. Those who generally agree with a neo-Malthusian approach to scarcity—that population pressure invariably constitutes the primary dynamic in food and material shortages—have fallen prey to an overly simple analysis.

Although, as noted, there do seem to be emerging pressures on food and materials that may lead to more absolute scarcities, those we most often encounter—and think we understand—are the creation of inadequate political, social, and economic institutions. It is terribly dangerous to allow the concept of scarcity to become the new determinative norm of social do-gooding without some serious and reflective analysis on what the origins of scarcity actually are. The fact is, whenever scholars talk about how absolute scarcity has come to exist in the world, they wind up setting an outside limit on total planetary population. Operating from these findings as a cultural assumption, it is then easy for people in the advanced industrial world—whose impact on world resources is many times per capita that of people in the developing world—to call for severe limitations on the population elsewhere. Ever since Malthus, the overpopulation theory has been used to justify various kinds of racial and class oppression. Although it is clear that Earth does have a limited carrying capacity for life of any kind, it is also clear that, if the developed world were to limit its consumption, support the production of appropriate foods in normally dependent economies, and redistribute its own surplus to the have-not peoples, there would be little need to talk about either absolute scarcity or zero population growth.

The political biologist, considering the great dilemmas of ethics and human survival today, needs to acknowledge the reality that scarcities in both food and materials—whether real or ideologically contrived—may soon present an insurmountable barrier to the maintenance of existing populations. It is the task of the ecoethicist, however, to understand that such scarcities are almost always the result of inadequacies in the production and distribution systems of human society, rather than absolute extensions of the teeth of nature. The problem of scarcity must be dealt with by those who seek the moral imperative of the steady state, but not on the terms of those elitist forces who either created the problem in the first place or have exacerbated it. Advocates of sustainable development must take such realities into account.

Biological Ethics and Thermodynamics

The history of the ethical development of human society is essentially the story of the determination of social and cultural values. Ethics has thus been an instrument used by the species to develop suitable social orderings related to the routine, day-to-day needs of human beings. In the future, however, ethical malfeasance will be more a matter of the violation of the biological and physical parameters of life, than of issues of individual moral conduct in society. During the recent era of imagined abundance, humankind could overlook the extent to which nature places constraints on its activities. Today, however, it is not possible to ignore those essential limiting laws of the universe, which remind us of our place in the biosphere and of our absolute connection with the natural world. One way to view the current ecoethical dilemma is to see it in the context of the inexorable laws of nature to which we are all subject.

The first law of thermodynamics states that energy is never lost although it may be changed from one form to another. The corollary is that neither can energy be created. There will never be more nor less than there is today. As we transform energy from one form to another (chemical energy to thermal energy, or coal to sulfur dioxide and heat), we simply replace the more usable energy forms with others that may be of less value to us.

The second law of thermodynamics says that the energy available to us constantly decreases. Each energy conversion, whether as the result of natural or human causation, creates a loss in the total energy available. A certain amount of the energy in the biosphere is thus no longer capable of being converted into work. For all practical human purposes, when it is gone, it is gone! Here the vital concept of entropy comes into play. Entropy refers to the disordered physical state that results from the decrease of available energy and the consequent environmental degradation. It is not possible for nature to perform energy-related work at constant rates, since the total energy available is constantly diminishing (not in total supply, but in availability). To the extent that we ignore this reality and continue to use energy at constant and nonsustainable rates, to that same degree do we contribute to an increase in the high-entropy gradient in the biosphere. High entropy indicates randomness or uselessness, while a low-entropy situation refers to structure, concentration, and order.

Ethically, there are powerful consequences to these two basic physical laws that affirm constancy in the energy content of the biosphere but also the constantly diminishing usefulness of that energy. It is the low-entropy stored resources of nature that we are using up when we burn fossil fuels, primarily in the production of heat. Thus, order tends inevitably to end up as chaos. The cosmos tends constantly toward disorganization and randomness, rather than structure and orderliness. The process of aging, the condition of a teenager's room, the inability of decayed organic matter to reconstruct itself in its original form, the heat-producing decay in every natural process are all eloquent testimony to this reality. Nature does exact a penalty in some fashion for those heat-producing activities that make our lives more comfortable today.

It is certainly possible (as we humans know so well) to push entropy backward for short periods of time—but only (as we are coming to admit) at the cost of a greater increase in total energy use and an increase in the entropy of the surrounding environment. An air conditioner can make life more comfortable in the short run, although its heat-producing activities will cause greater entropy just outside its margins. Evolution has produced relatively greater order for some species, but in the process has exacted certain penalties on the environment itself. This has been most notable in the case of Homo sapiens. The major developments of human society (science, technology, the manipulations of the natural order) have for the first time placed one species—our own—in disharmony with the rest of the biosphere.

As Jeremy Rifkin has pointed out in assessing the energy–entropy connection, our industrial age—the age of managed consumption fueled by some form of fire wherein stored fossil-fuel reserves have been rapidly consumed in order to provide for the wants as well as the needs of human societies—has generated pollution and enormously increased the level of carbon dioxide in the atmosphere, which may in turn cause a massive raising of the global temperature in the very near future (see Chapter 1).[10] As Barry Commoner has reminded us, in nature there is no such thing as a free lunch. There are always consequences to any intrusion into the natural order.[11]

All economic systems that are based on continued growth and development (with their concomitant increase in energy use) directly flout the first and second laws of thermodynamics. Thermal pollution via the heat-producing activities of energy transformation provides a basic limiting factor in human control over biospheric systems. Whether we can develop the social mechanisms needed to control and limit such activities at this time in history is doubtful. We have basically altered the ecological pathways in our indiscriminate utilization of low-entropy raw materials with their subsequent transformation into high-entropy pollutants. Since there is no reversing of entropy (when heat is released into the biosphere it cannot be retrieved or contained), a new moral imperative has been injected into human affairs. The ethicist of the future will find that the primary determinants of morality are our personal and collective efforts to live more in harmony with nature. Energy cannot forever play the role in the production of materials currently assigned it. As entropy economist Nicolas Georgescu-Roegen has said,

> The maximum of life quantity requires the minimum rate of natural resources depletion. By using these resources too quickly, man throws away that part of solar energy that will still be reaching the earth for a long time after he has departed. And everything that man has done in the last two hundred years or so puts him in the position of a fantastic spendthrift. There can be no doubt about it: any use of natural resources for the satisfaction of non-vital needs means a smaller quantity of life in the future. If we understand well the problem, the best use of our iron resources is to produce plows or harrows as they are needed, not Rolls-Royces, not even agricultural tractors.[12]

Realistic moralists should clearly recognize the need for a new ethics based on the reconsideration of what are appropriate means and ends for modern people. Our end goals must be at least related to the survival of our own and other species. Accordingly, more sensible means than we have traditionally used to support these life systems are now requirements rather than options. Progress made on the "soft" energy pathways wherein increasing reliance is placed on the utilization of renewable energy resources (wind, solar, biomass conversion), rather than continuing down the "hard" paths (nuclear and nonrenewable fossil fuels), would be one way of developing a more reasonable approach to our survival goals. The means we use must be appropriate to the end of biological and biospheric survival.

What all of this adds up to is that biospheric survival now requires a global movement toward some form of a steady-state system utilizing only the most appropriate kinds of science and technology and wherein the throughputs of materials and energy can be structured on a permanently sustainable base. The moral imperative for such a system is apparent and, as always in ethics, clearly related to practical need. Unless we move to systems that encompass equity in resource use and distribution and that are structured to be self-sustaining, Homo sapiens will more than likely join the ever-growing list of endangered or extinct species.

Notes

1. Robert L. Heilbroner, *An Inquiry into the Human Prospect* (New York: W. W. Norton, 1974).

2. Although now dated, the Club of Rome studies on the limits to growth significantly altered global thinking in regard to resource utilization and the ability of the biosphere to absorb the garbage of the industrial era. The three major studies were Donella H. Meadows, Dennis L. Meadows, Jorgen Randers, and William N. Behrens, *The Limits to Growth* (New York: Universe Books, 1972); Mihaljo Mesarovic and Eduard Pestel, *Mankind at the Turning Point* (New York: E. P. Dutton, 1974); and Jan Tingbergen, *RIO: Reshaping the International Order* (New York: E. P. Dutton, 1976).

3. Herman E. Daly, "Entropy, Growth, and the Political Economy of Scarcity," in *Steady State Economics: The Economics of Biophysical Equilibrium and Moral Growth* (San Francisco: W. H. Freeman, 1977), pp. 16–17.

4. William Ophuls, *Ecology and the Politics of Scarcity* (San Francisco: W. H. Freeman, 1977), pp. 239–40.

5. Gro Harlem Brundtland, ed., *Our Common Future* (Oxford, U.K.: Oxford University Press, 1987), pp. 43–44.

6. Sharad M. Lele, *Sustainable Development: A Critical Review*, Energy and Resource Group, University of California, Berkeley, December 1988.

7. Miguel Altieri, "Sustainable Agriculture," *Environment* 31, no. 3 (April 1989), p. 2.

8. Lele, "Sustainable Development."

9. Thomas Malthus, *An Essay on Population*, vol. 2 (London: J. M. Dent and Sons, 1958), pp. 179–80.

10. Jeremy Rifkin, *Entropy* (New York: Viking Press, 1980).

11. Barry Commoner, *The Closing Circle* (New York: A. A. Knopf, 1971), p. 45.

12. Nicolas Georgescu-Roegen, *Analytical Economics* (Cambridge, Mass.: Harvard University Press, 1966), as quoted in Daly, *Steady State Economics*, p. 312.

5

Economics as if Nature Mattered

When E. F. Schumacher recommended in 1973 that we should think about developing an economics "as if people mattered," he was surely on the right track. In the intervening decade and a half, however, we have come to broaden that category and be even more inclusive in our notion of what might constitute a relevant economics for a world certainly facing imminent environmental crisis. Particularly, we now understand the imperative for nonanthropocentric economics—for an understanding of economics that extends beyond the requirements of our species—as an integral part of the Gaian value system. Such an understanding was actually both explicit and implicit in Schumacher's thought. But ever since Adam Smith first systematized classical economic theory in the middle of the eighteenth century, economists have tended to give themselves too much credit for figuring out what is actually happening in the world. Their attempts to analyze social trends and then prophesy what might happen in the future have generally had dismal results. Two decades ago, economist Joan Robinson—always a realist—sought to demythologize economic systems and deflate any overly optimistic expectations about their ability to solve the great problems of human society. Robinson had this to say: "It is impossible to understand the economic system in which we are living if we try to understand it as a rational scheme. It has to be understood as an awkward phase in a continuing process of historical development."[1]

Although many theorists insist that we now finally have our economic act together (a particularly arrogant belief of scholastic economists), it is a fact (as Robinson notes) that in every society—socialist, market, or mixed—this children's ditty of the nineteenth century still holds unhappily true:

> The rich man in his castle,
> The poor man at his gate,

God made them high and lowly
And ordered their estate.

Most recently, and yet typically, those economists who specialize in the arcane numerical and social calculations of "econometrics"—the attempt to express economic theory strictly as a set of mathematical and statistical relationships—have demonstrated themselves to be indifferent to the social dislocations occasioned by continuing class antagonisms in the real world. It is always interesting that economists—who, after all, are social scientists—can believe in the ability of their own formulas to redeem the world, all the while ignoring the real problems of real people all about them. John Maynard Keynes, benchmark liberal capitalist economist of the twentieth century, long ago sought to define the enduring ethical problem facing the economist in the Western world:

> Europe was so organized socially and economically as to secure the maximum accumulation of capital. While there was some continuous improvement in the daily conditions of life of the mass of the population, society was so framed as to throw a great part of the increased income into the control of the class least likely to consume it.
>
> In fact, it was precisely the inequality of distribution of wealth which made possible those vast accumulations of fixed wealth and of capital improvements which distinguished that age from all others.
>
> Thus, this remarkable system depended for its growth on a double bluff or deception. On the one hand the laboring classes accepted from ignorance or powerlessness . . . or were compelled . . . into accepting a situation in which they could call their own very little of the cake. . . . And on the other hand the capitalist classes were allowed to call the best part of the cake theirs . . . on the tacit assumption that they consumed very little of it in practice.
>
> And so the cake increased; but to what end was not clearly contemplated.[2]

Keynes's response to the situation was to rationalize capitalism so that, through his formulation of a series of economic checks, balances, and redistributive mechanisms, the worst faults of capital accumulation under the market system could be avoided or minimized. Not surprisingly, the high point of socialist theorizing under Marx and Engels took place in the same era that Keynes so picturesquely described, when vast concentrations of capital and resources were accumulating in fewer and fewer hands. Denouncing both traditional and liberal economic theory, socialist economists (pre- and post-Marx) sought to construct an entirely new social and economic structure—one in which the value of labor would be affirmed and the distributive injustices of capitalism eradicated. Although neither economic alternative succeeded (as we shall soon be pointing out), each sought constructively—but awkwardly, to use Joan Robinson's word—to turn the corner.

Table 5.1 delineates three different approaches to the task of evaluating past economic theory and developing a more appropriate modern theory of economics:

1. *Traditional* or neoclassical capitalist—the ideal of those favoring supply-side systems (e.g., Reaganomics in the recent era);

2. *Liberal* or neo-Keynesian—still practiced by most of the advanced industrial nations of the West; and

3. *Socialist* or neo-Marxist—favored generally by the Soviet Union, post-1948 China, Vietnam, Cuba, and the Eastern European bloc of nations between 1946 and 1990.

Table 5.1 compares these three alternatives on some of the key aspects of economic development: ownership, economic surplus, the priority of supply or demand, planning, attitudes toward labor (and nature), and the overall motive force deemed appropriate by the protagonists of each system. Three trends emerge from the comparison:

Table 5.1   Economics and the Environment: Three Historical Approaches

Issue	*Traditional*	*Liberal*	*Socialist*
Ownership of means of production	private	private plus regulation	public
Surplus	private	private plus redistribution	public
Supply/Demand	supply	demand	need
Planning	private	private plus regulation	state sector
Motive force	profit	profit plus need	need
Labor/Nature	commodity	commodity	intrinsic value

1. *Traditional* market-oriented economic values affirm the sole right of the private sector in ownership of the means of production (capital, tools, resources); are trusting of the apparatus of production to regulate the market through controlling supplies of goods and materials; believe that labor is simply another neutral commodity in the production process; and affirm that, while value does arise from the productive role of labor (as Adam Smith said), the sole and indeed redemptive motive force for the entire economic process is laissez-faire self-interest and the bottom line of profitability. Nature is transformed into "resources" or "commodities"—economic concepts denoting something of worth that can demand exchange value in the marketplace.

2. *Liberal* economic theorists unabashedly affirm the right of the private sector to control the variables within and the profits from production, but believe that certain redistributive mechanisms are required (income taxes, welfare programs, regulatory bodies) to overcome the tendency within the market to concentrate wealth and surplus within the hands of those who control production; hope to orient the entire system toward demand stimulation, rather than production control (compare here the pump-priming efforts of the New Deal to stimulate consumption through increasing demand with other earlier and more primitive attempts to control production—destroying livestock and agricultural produce in order to limit supply and thus force prices upward); and view labor—with the traditionalists—as essentially only another means toward the end of maximizing production and consumption, but agree with the socialists that public need on occasion can outweigh private profit on the scales of both justice and economic efficiency. Nature is again viewed as essentially a commodity, but with the understanding that resources need to be carefully managed if they are to last.

3. *Socialist* economists believe that the state—or, rather, the representatives of the public within the nation—must control planning, production, and economic surplus; that social need as the only legitimate motive force of economics must determine both production norms and goals; that labor has intrinsic value that goes beyond simple commodity valuation; and that efforts should be made to keep the entire production process from alienating the workers and that the wages of labor should reflect the actual value of the production rather than simply the number of hours worked. While lip service is occasionally given to the intrinsic value of nature, socialist resource economics is in fact much like that of the capitalists. Nature is

understood as the horn of plenty from which all good things will continue to be made available to those who have the ingenuity to harvest them.

Thus, while market forces may push toward maximizing economic efficiency, the theoretical side of socialism appears to give better protection at least to the human environment, since labor is seen as more than simply the means to economic ends. And it is certainly difficult to value nature if human beings are not first regarded as having an intrinsic worth that is reflected in their social and economic contributions. In practice, however, we know that the tendency to turn both labor and nature into commodities has been quite as forceful in socialism as in capitalism. It must also be noted here that, whereas both traditional and nontraditional economic theorists emphasize the overwhelming importance of "ownership" of the means of production, the actual control over economic activity within a nation-state, an industry, or a transnational corporation may be even more important nowadays. Rigidly bureaucratic party control over economic planning under socialism can be quite as detrimental to the public welfare as capitalist control of resources within the market. And while Lee Ioccoca is surely only a minority stockholder in the Chrysler Corporation, his control over corporate activities makes it quite clear that he wields far greater power than all the majority owners lumped together.

Capitalism and Socialism

We must forgive the current economic and political leaders of the West for their understandable tendency to gloat ever so modestly about the disarray in world socialism, especially in the Soviet Union, Poland, Hungary, (what was) East Germany, and Czechoslovakia. Given the 1990 merger of the two Germanys and the now imminent move of their socialist neighbors from bureaucratic socialism to a mixed market structure, those who remember Nikita Khruschev's famous boast at the United Nations in 1954 that Soviet-style socialism would "bury" world capitalism can be permitted a bit of a smirk.

It is clear that the market system has in fact proven itself to be more dynamic and resilient than socialism. Although paid for at a high price (as we will note later in our critique of the human and environmental costs of allowing the market to go its own way), personal freedoms (of speech, travel, security) are both better guaranteed and more diverse under the market system, at least in the advanced liberal societies. Contrary to basic socialist theory, social freedoms (job opportunities, health and educational guarantees) have at best been no better than those provided by market economies and often very much worse. Whereas the recent upheavals in Eastern and Central Europe have been occasioned in part by shortages of material goods, the essential motivating factor for throwing off the old governments (as attested by every new political leader in these countries) has been the lack of political freedom and the poor quality of the social infrastructure: of educational opportunity, health and medical service, housing, and work opportunities. Of great but probably lesser importance, goods and services are provided in better quality and more abundance in the market societies than in any socialist state. Shockingly, even the internal distribution of wealth is not so equal as socialism's uncritical advocates would have us believe. Though socialism is certainly better than the market system in this regard, the special arrangements—salaries and privileges—of socialism's elite have exacerbated a similar discord within their own societies. The fact that there was only a slight difference in the income distribution within socialist East Germany and liberal West Germany in 1980 shows how the egalitarian dream has eroded within the socialist world in recent years. Table 5.2 suggests that the distribution of justice is problematic in any existing society.

But while this so-called victory of the capitalist alternative in portions of the socialist world in late 1989 indicates that a market-oriented economy may have advantages for many of the people who live in those societies, and while such a system may have been good for the American, Japanese, and other Western upper and middle classes, it has been a dismal failure for the environment and for its impact on most people living elsewhere in the world. American Indian Movement (AIM) leader Russell Means has accurately stated,

> You cannot judge the real nature of a European revolutionary doctrine on the basis of the changes it proposes to make within the European power structure and society. You can judge it only by the effects it will have on non-European peoples. This is because every revolution in European history has served to reinforce Europe's tendencies and abilities to export destruction to other peoples, other cultures and the environment itself.[3]

Table 5.2 Income Distribution for Selected Countries, c. 1980

Country	Lowest 20%	Highest 20%	Highest 10%
Africa			
Ivory Coast	2.4	61.4	43.7
Egypt	5.8	48.0	33.2
Kenya	2.6	60.4	45.8
Americas			
Brazil	2.3	63.7	48.3
Canada	4.6	41.6	25.0
Guatemala	5.3	56.4	42.1
Mexico	3.5	53.8	36.3
Panama	2.0	61.8	44.2
U.S. (1985)	4.6	43.5	25.8
Asia			
Bangladesh	6.6	45.3	29.5
China	11.8	31.7	n.a.
Hong Kong	4.3	47.0	31.3
India	5.0	50.4	34.9
Philippines	5.2	56.5	40.9
Europe			
Denmark	5.4	38.6	22.3
France	4.0	49.9	34.5
Germany (E.)	12.2	29.8	17.5
Germany (W.)	7.2	38.1	22.8
Poland	10.1	34.7	20.6
Switzerland	6.6	38.0	23.7
United Kingdom	5.8	39.7	23.4

We do tend to forget that First World/Third World, North/South, center/periphery economies do have a kind of interdependence that essentially assures the existence of the gap between rich and poor, and keeps it growing. The one side cannot live without the markets for raw materials to which it has historically been tied; the other cannot survive without the resources to fuel its factories. The rapid industrial growth in the West—of the "overdeveloped" capitalist and segments of the socialist worlds—may have given the majority of citizens of those countries economic blessings and advantages unprecedented in other eras. But the consequences elsewhere of such advantages for the few—increased resource and energy use, escalating chemical pollution of the air and water, climate-changing impacts of industrialization, assaults on the public health—illustrate the truth in the observation of Russell Means. Economic theory cannot be judged simply by the visible impacts of that theory on the welfare of the few.

A detailed accounting of the indifference to nature of both capitalism and socialism will continue to be documented throughout this book. My intention here is simply to review certain political-economic realities as they relate to the ordering of human life in a healthy environment. This will be done via a short critique of the two dominant economic systems in light of their impacts on nature, and a brief exploration of certain economic relationships between North and South (the have and have-not sections of the world economy), with some final comments regarding alternatives for the development of a more humane Gaian economics. Later in the book, we will deal extensively with the need for an economics that is more democratic, more "green," and more appropriate to the needs of the majority of the world's population.

Dilemmas of Political Economy

From the very beginning of the human social orders, individuals and groups have been impacting the natural systems—the environment—in which they found themselves. Human society has always required the means to effect the production and distribution of various forms of goods and services. Thus, from the beginning, the question of resource management (although rarely explicit) has been implicit within the social order. What do we need to survive? How much is there? How do we go about getting it? A popular economist once noted that even Robinson Crusoe faced the urgent task of accumulating sufficient surplus to guarantee his own survival; he first found himself a slave (Friday) and then accumulated a bit of unearned income through his own and Friday's work.

In fact, while typically identified with capitalism, surplus accumulation is the requisite first task of any society. Historically, it has taken several different forms, as Figure 5.1 indicates. Human *labor* has been everywhere recognized as a primary means of social enrichment. The work of people has value beyond any other kind of economic achievement. Economic surplus, as Marx notes, has also been "*primitively accumulated*" throughout the ages of civilization. Powerful individuals and nations have regularly imposed their will on others—on groups and on nations—to forcibly extract wealth for the sole benefit of the

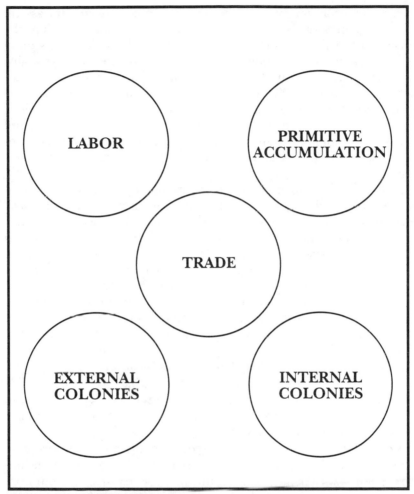

Figure 5.1   History of Capital/Surplus Accumulation

dominant nation. Colonial powers established *external colonies* in order to acquire both inexpensive raw materials and cheap labor so as to sustain their increasingly resource-dependent societies and to provide new markets for finished goods. *Internal colonies*—national groupings, slaves, a permanent underclass—within countries have been established in order to maximize the well-being of the few against the many. And since the beginning of the mercantilist era, *trade* has been a dominant force in the acquisition of economic wealth and power.

However, economic power by itself cannot long withstand the assault of alien values or alternative schemes of development. Thus the concept of political economy, wherein the values of the reigning economic and political tendencies are continually reproduced socially, is a requirement for understanding many of the antisocial intolerances of advanced economies. Determining the processes for the production and distribution of the goods and services of the society, positing the rules regulating the consumption of material goods, and deciding on dominance and subservience in the class relationships of the society have in fact all been a historic part of the basic economic task.

So it is that economics has the responsibility for developing systems that will lend order both to the productive apparatus and to the social services required to sustain life within particular societies. Usually failing in the traditional task of meeting human needs (although relatively more successful in the politically more important task of the social reproduction of values), economics has failed even more frequently in providing even minimal care for the resources it is called on to develop. Yet it is a simple economic truth that the way in which natural resources are finally transformed into products clearly affects the well-being of human society. Economics is a vulgar, imperfect, awkward, but inevitably necessary science. Both the capitalist and the socialist dream of a perfectly balanced social order kept in equilibrium on the one hand by economic checks and balances (the "invisible hand" of Adam Smith), or on the other by a social order infused with humanist ethics, distributive justice, and a belief in the ultimate equality of all people (Karl Marx).

More specifically, each of us is acted on by the economic system in which we are placed. Our lives—our personalities, our relationships with family and friends, our attitudes toward nature, and our consciousness—are constantly undergoing change as we engage in economic activity and find ourselves subject to the powerful formative influence of the ideological descendent of the economic system: its science and technology. As Michael Albert and his coauthors of the book *Liberating Theory* have noted,

> Changing a person's role in the economy—from capitalist to worker, for example—will change many of the social pressures (and benefits) that mold his/her life. Change the nature of the economic system as a whole—from feudal to capitalist, for instance—and you will change the pattern of roles and economic circumstances facing everyone. Economic

activity therefore affects the qualitative human dimensions as well as the quantitative material dimensions of life. It affects social relations and people as well as things. A first priority in a complementary holist approach to economics has to be to include personality, skill, knowledge, consciousness, and different kinds of qualitative social relationships as central economic concepts.[4]

Comparing the competing systems, certain economic failures within Marxist practice stand out:

1. Traditional rigid Marxist class analysis—which posits the overall understanding that the industrial working class alone has both the social cohesion and the economic power to change the nature of the productive forces in the society—totally overlooks the emergence of powerful new classes within the modern industrial world that have quite as much potential power as the old working class: managers, service-sector employees, and white-collar workers who control data and much of the flow of information within societies. The vast array of technical and organizational knowledge that is either conceptualized or serviced by the new working classes is perhaps more important today than the old blue-collar working class—particularly in an era of the co-optation or weakening of the industrial union by management and government.

2. The tendency toward one-dimensional political thought (never the sole inheritance of capitalism, no matter what Herbert Marcuse said)[5] has had a stultifying effect on creative individualism within much of the socialist world. While Marxist theory has always held that the economic freedoms (job guarantees, the social safety net) usually guaranteed by socialism far outweigh the personal freedoms (expression, political activity, freedom to travel) usually guaranteed by market societies, today's socialist workers know that even these economic freedoms have in fact never been fully realized in practice. The appeal of capitalist culture and capitalist goods to those who have never had access to them is now apparent almost everywhere in the world. Although time will tarnish the allure of material goods as people come to resent the conditions that accompany market production (high structural unemployment, pollution, workplace hazards, competition, economic stress), the magnetism of consumer productivity is inescapable to those who have in the past been able to satisfy neither wants nor needs.

3. The economist tendency latent within socialism—ignoring or

downplaying all noneconomic forms of domination (racial, cultural, sexual) as being absolutely secondary to economic domination—has made it impossible for Marxist economic theory to stay abreast of cultural change and the real life situations of millions of people.

> But more than this, marxist economic theory fails to provide conceptual categories that help us discover how different kinds of economic activity have different effects on the development of human characteristics and needs. This omission not only devastates our ability to *evaluate* different economic institutions, it debilitates our ability to *analyze* some of the most important dynamics that influence social stability and change. In its fixation on the material, quantitative aspects of economic activity, marxism has largely ignored the human, qualitative aspects. Or, put differently, marxist economics has never become a theory of economic "praxis"—in fact, we do not live by or for bread alone.[6]

A critique in kind may be directed at the market system. Indeed, many of the concerns expressed here as criticisms of the one are in fact characteristic of both systems. Experience has illuminated the following patterns within capitalism, for example:

1. Work tends to be regarded as a privilege, not a right—even as workers are viewed essentially not as individuals so much as if they were commodities to be used as the production schedule requires. Any revised market approach to labor should in the future include a redistribution of work loads so as to lower the average workweek— thus providing employment to some of the currently unemployed— and guarantee minimum wages and the right of workers to know about the not so obvious conditions and hazards of their workplaces. The rapid development in the United States of a new permanent underclass comprised of the uneducated or undereducated poor (White as well as Black and Hispanic), coupled with the historic readiness of economic and political leaders to take advantage of the inexpensive availability of such people, portend major problems for both democracy and equality in this country.

2. The need to key all market strategies to social objectives must be constantly affirmed. As we will point out again in the chapters on biotechnology (especially Chapter 7), research and development on products that may harm the general public health (e.g., breeding resistance into plants so that more herbicides can be used in agriculture) must be subject to human and environmental cost/benefit analysis. As noted earlier, the social imperatives for developing sustainable resource systems must enter into every market maneuver.

3. The dominance within the economic system of components of the permanent war establishment in the United States suggests an increasing inability to compete within the world economy except in the military realm. The fact that the military now siphons off fifty-six percent of the national budget and represents a far higher share of the gross domestic product (GDP) in the United States than in any other major industrial nation shows the lopsidedness of the U.S. economy. The direct correlation between military expenditures and trade and budget deficits (budget deficits increase in almost direct proportion to increases in military expenditure), and the impact on productivity from the dedication of almost half of our capital resources to military uses (compared with West Germany's 14 percent and Japan's 3.7 percent), reveal a major structural deficiency within the U.S. political economy.

As will be noted again and again throughout this book, the disparity in the relative well-being of the rich and poor, North and South, center and dependent economies of the world indicates an ominous future for all but a handful of wealthier nation-states. Third World countries—uniformly demanding the establishment of a "new international economic order"—regularly cite the facts of life as they pertain to the relationships among nation-states today. The rich/poor gap is growing constantly. All current growth and development schemes worldwide basically favor the rich over the poor. Within 30 years there will be another world on top of the one we now know—equal perhaps in numbers, demands, and expectations. When economist Robert Heilbroner spoke of future global "wars of redistribution" unless more peaceful means of overcoming the rich/poor imbalance were developed in the nick of time, he was perhaps acting more the prophet than he then understood.[7] If nations absolutely cannot survive under current standards of equity and justice, should we be surprised when they choose other avenues of redressing the historic wrongs done to them?

Minimally, then, those who favor new Gaian economic orders include on their agendas these facilitating elements:

• A plan in every society to begin moving toward sustainable use and development of natural resources;
• International agency control of key natural resource systems (mineral, marine, and other renewable and nonrenewable resources

should not continue to be controlled simply by those who have dominant economic and military power);

• A taxation program for those who pollute the international commons of the air and water (those who contribute most to environmental degradation should pay the economic and social costs of cleanup and restoration);

• The stabilization of commodity prices (the vagaries of supply and demand on the international market—controlled largely by the Western nations—create roller-coaster changes in the prices of raw materials, which must be stabilized by international agreement);

• Parity indexing of raw materials and manufactured goods (if manufactured goods increase in price, then the raw materials used in the production of such goods must be similarly priced);

• Restructuring of the international debt (the $1.3 trillion now owed by Third World countries to the center economies must be constructively refinanced, either by reducing interest rates and terms of repayment or by reducing the outstanding principal); and

• Equality of voting in international monetary agencies (the current voting on the basis of financial contribution leaves the developing world with no voice in affecting policy of the World Bank and its related agencies).

In succeeding chapters, much more will be said about the interactions of ecology, ethics, and economics. There is, in fact, no room for gloating on the part of either market or socialist political economists about any of their self-proclaimed successes past or present. Both have significantly failed to meet the needs of all of their subject people and to contribute to an ecologically healthy and sustainable system of global development. A new democratically based Gaian economics must incorporate both the intrinsic-value and economic-security affirmations of the best socialist theory and the economic efficiencies and personal freedoms of those who live within the market structure. Nothing less can resolve the dilemmas and meet the hopes of the billions of people in the world who have been ill served by the existing global arrangements of economic power.

Notes

1. Joan Robinson, *Economics: An Awkward Corner* (New York: Pantheon Books, 1967), p. 3.

2. John M. Keynes, *Economic Consequences of the Peace* (Cambridge, U.K.: Cambridge University Press, 1914), pp. 16–17.

3. Russell Means, "The Death of Europe," *Mother Jones* (December 1980), pp. 27–28.

4. Michael Albert, Leslie Cagan, Noam Chomsky, Robin Hahnel, Mel King, Lydia Sargent, and Holly Sklar, *Liberating Theory* (Boston: South End Press, 1986), p. 47.

5. There is always a tendency within the U.S. left to identify cultural one-dimensionality with societies incorporating a market-oriented philosophy; see Herbert Marcuse, *One Dimensional Man* (Boston: Beacon Press, 1964).

6. Albert, *Liberating Theory*, p. 52; emphasis in original.

7. Robert L. Heilbroner, *An Inquiry into the Human Prospect* (New York: W. W. Norton, 1974), pp. 43–46, 79.

6

Bioethical Limits to Scientific Inquiry

The new discipline of bioethics—the narrower focusing of environmental ethics that attempts to bridge the widening gap between science and human values—has emerged in large part because of the political nature of the physical and biological sciences. Ethical dilemmas unprecedented in human history have arisen from the almost absolute control over science and technology now exercised by a relative handful of immensely powerful private and governmental organizations.

That science has always been to some degree under the political control and direction of nonscientists has been a fact of life for hundreds of years. There has always been a politics of science. Contrary to both popular opinion and the cherished myths of the science professions, scientific options do not simply flow unimpeded from some neutral pursuit of truth, unobstructed by the attempts of outsiders to control the direction of inquiry. Nor is technology—the creation of tools and methods to apply science—as benign as many would like to think. Careful observation of the work of any major scientific or technological enterprise today reveals that the questions posed to the scientific community for response and decision inevitably have a political and economic cast. The socially neutral problem is almost never brought to the attention of those who do the nation's funded research.

As I mentioned in an earlier book, Galileo provides a spectacularly good example of the perpetual predicament of the scientist. After popularizing the telescope in 1525, Galileo was only able to capitalize on his work by utilizing the instrument's military potential. In his memoirs, there is an account of what he told the Venetian authorities he had in mind for his future research:

> The writing of some books about military matters such as the practice of fortification, ordnance, assaults, sieges, estimation of distances, artillery matters, and the uses of various instruments and so on.[1]

Unfortunately, for Galileo as for the modern scientist, the funds required for research and problem-solving have always been determined in large part by the dominant political or economic power of the day. Defending this first of his great compromises, Galileo illustrates the point.

> Great and remarkable things are mine, but I can only serve princes; for it is they alone who carry on wars, build and defend fortresses and in their royal diversions make those great expenditures which neither I nor other private persons may.[2]

Even more so today than for Galileo, the modern scientist must reckon with the question of who will pay the bill for his or her work. Although some universities and research institutions pride themselves that they are involved in doing "pure" science, such is rarely the case. At a 1987 seminar for nuclear technologists held at the University of California at Berkeley, I queried the director of one of the nation's more important energy labs as to whether he ever had second thoughts about carrying on a line of sponsored research because of ethical concerns over how the research would be used. At first almost disbelieving the question, he finally answered by saying, "Ethics is not our business in government funded research. We do what we get paid to do."

In the best of all possible worlds, pure science—that is to say, the kind of scientific inquiry that has no immediately intended application and that seeks simply to unlock a few more of the secrets of the universe—would be free from either public or private funding. Since this is impossible in our world, it is perhaps true that opportunities for doing pure nonintentional science no longer exist. To the extent that outside funds are provided, to that same extent will special self-interested concerns and questions be posed to science. The hope and expectation of the funding agency has always been that the final result of an assigned scientific task will transform the world in ways consistent with the interests of the donor. To industry and government, problem-solving is far more important than simple discovery.

This dilemma becomes particularly disturbing when science continues its quest for knowledge into matters regarding the nature and destiny of humankind. As in other contexts discussed throughout this book, the value assumptions science makes about those factors that constitute "humanhood" are normally determinative of the research task undertaken. For example, the researcher who believes that Homo sapiens can be reduced to a set of biochemical equations will necessarily tilt toward a mechanistic view of human nature, and in the process will tend to ignore the spiritual, cultural, and other nongenetically determined aspects of the species.

The Militarization of Science

When Winston Churchill declared the advent of the Cold War in a speech at Fulton College, Missouri, in 1946, the rationale for new government spending on military research and development was established. Over the next 40 years, the military segment of the R&D budget increased regularly, most rapidly under the Reagan administration. By 1980, according to the National Science Foundation (NSF), the military portion of the total U.S. research budget had reached $37.8 billion or fully 50 percent of the total R&D effort. In 1986, after six years of Reagan-era military buildup, the annual expenditure for research and development was $54 billion. The military portion of this was 72.7 percent. When George Bush became president in 1989, the military R&D percentage was estimated at 75 percent of the total.[3]

The overall economic implications of this disproportionate allocation of the research dollar are clear. Almost no money is available today from government sources to fund consumer-related commercial or industrial product development. Our primary competitors on the world market—West Germany and Japan—invest less than 10 percent of their research budget in military development, and thus have ample funds to underwrite research in electronics, automobiles, and other consumer durables. Many experts now agree that, so long as the United States continues to target only the military sector for its primary research effort, U.S. consumers will continue to buy better researched and higher quality foreign products.

Perhaps the most significant social impact of the militarization of research and development, however, is the human factor. Young engineers and physics majors often wind up in the military-industrial complex, it being the employer of last resort. Young scientists with doctorates in these fields find there are virtually no jobs in nondefense-related sectors. Research grants for instructors in these fields are largely from the defense establishment. Many professors at major universities are now reluctantly engaged in Strategic Defense Initiative (SDI), or Star Wars, research because the money is readily available for this kind of work; it has largely dried up elsewhere.[4] Berkeley Professor John Holdren, current chair of the National Fusion Energy Program, states that

> The unseemly haste with which long-term energy projects have been closed down to free up money for booming military R&D was well illustrated in February [1986] at the Lawrence Livermore National Laboratory. There, one of the centerpieces of the national program of research in magnetic fusion energy—the huge new Mirror Fusion Test Facility just completed at a cost of some $360 million—was mothballed the same day it was formally dedicated by Department of Energy officials. The Reagan administration proposes to let the new facility sit idle in order to save the few tens of millions of dollars it would cost to operate it.
>   Meanwhile, scientists . . . are understandably although probably reluctantly seeking jobs in the burgeoning SDI (Star Wars) programs where the money has gone. At the Livermore Lab, displaced fusion researchers need only walk across the street to the building where research on particle beam weapons is growing by leaps and bounds.[5]

A shortsighted and Procrustean approach to their work is often adopted by those caught up in the contradictions of contemporary science. In Greek legend, the giant Procrustes sought to produce uniform results on his visiting acquaintances by utilizing a somewhat arbitrary methodology. Insisting that they conform to his own predetermined norm for proper positioning on a bed, Procrustes either stretched or mutilated his "subjects" to make sure the fit was perfect. In these manipulations, Procrustes was anticipating a familiar practice within modern science and technology, where the overwhelming concern is no longer to discover new insights into the workings of nature, but to provide acceptable answers to those funding the research. Yet in today's increasingly stressed and fragile web of life, the scientific and technological communities can ill afford to be so naive or indifferent as historically they have been to the social and political impact of new discoveries. The implications for our future from much of the new hierarchically directed and highly intentional research are awesome. Scientists and engineers have an obligation these days to themselves and to the public both to better understand and then also to declare their political and value assumptions.

Professor Edward Teller (known popularly as the father of the hydrogen bomb) once became extremely irritated with me over the way I introduced him for a guest lecture in one of my Berkeley courses. I had told the audience that, because of his key role in the development of thermonuclear weapons, Teller was a major architect in the formation of a new post–World War II imperial U.S. foreign policy and a determinative shaper of U.S. Cold War values. Teller informed the students that he was not really such a big factor in these developments. And anyway, scientists simply "do good science and stay away from policy." Although Teller's defensive "Aw shucks, I'm no more important than anyone else" response was probably intended to mystify the students (since Teller most certainly understands the science–policy connection), the vast majority of scientists are in fact unaware of or indifferent to the kind of cultural and social determinism that can be implicit in much of their work.

Whenever scientific opinion enters the public forum (in spite of its traditional pretensions of objectivity and neutrality), it loses its claim to special standing. The social rearrangements that have occurred, for example, in the biological, health, and medical sciences in the past 25 years are the inevitable consequences of a change in technology— change that carries its own momentum, precludes certain alternative options, impels a certain kind of high-tech social transformation, and directly affects the lives of countless millions of people. It must, therefore, be as subject to public scrutiny as any health, educational, or cultural policy.

Closely related to the value concerns of bioethics are the more generic questions related to the nature of scientific inquiry. Does science, for example, have the right (as it now universally proclaims) to do whatever is possible for it to do? As the methodologies of science and technology become ever more sophisticated, can some kind of substantive control be exercised over their real-life application by any other than the establishment's in-house practitioners? I once asked a well-known nuclear scientist whether he ever felt any obligation to seek more general public or ethical input into the formulation of his nuclear research programs. He said, "Of course not. Only scientists and those providing funds should be involved in setting science policy." It is to this issue—the isolation and invisibility of science and science policy from public review and input—that we will now turn our attention.

The Limits of Science

Traveling through the United States in the early nineteenth century, the French writer-politician Alexis de Tocqueville discovered some truths about the U.S. political economy and its accompanying social psyche that give clues to the nature of U.S. science today. De Tocqueville found that Americans—unlike most of their brethren in the other industrial societies of the West—had somehow formulated certain unique and socially determinative attitudes about the nature of progress. Americans have traditionally believed, for example, that all change and growth is positive, that the resources of our respective frontiers have been given us for whatever type of exploitation we feel to be appropriate, and that the costs of growth should be reckoned only after needed changes have been effected. In spite of economic and political ups and downs, we have historically affirmed that there is no real problem facing human beings in their confrontations with nature that cannot be ultimately resolved.

Americans have never been very critical when it comes to exploitation of natural resources. During the industrial age (what social critic Jeremy Rifkin calls the "age of fire"), we have overutilized fossil fuels in order to maintain our well-being, and (at least until quite recently) been utterly acquiescent in accepting the consequences of this action. Although we know that these nonrenewable energy sources cannot last much longer at current rates of consumption, it is still hard even to consider putting the brakes on their use. Constantly we suck nourishment from the natural environment surrounding us in orders of magnitude unprecedented in Earth's history—taking, but never returning. We seem incapable of understanding that, in the process of all this exploitation, we may be dooming ourselves. The political biologist, however, will understand the psychological need of Homo sapiens to rail against any suggestion that there may be limits or boundaries to human existence, but will not be content with such moral myopia. De Tocqueville's critique of individualism in America is remarkably applicable to the current situation.

Limits suggest that we are not omnipotent; furthermore, they presage decay and death. Although we know better, we wish to keep ourselves insulated in whatever way possible from the truth that ours is only one of more than a million existing species, and not all that different in fact from many others. The U.S. presidential candidates in 1988, each of whom must certainly have had at least some minimal understanding that traditional patterns of capitalist economic growth cannot be sustained forever if the biosphere is to survive, found it absolutely impossible even to recommend a more modest use of Earth's resources to the American people. George Bush did manage to declare himself a "lifelong environmentalist," though—in spite of his longtime service to Ronald Reagan as chairman of the Committee on Government Reorganization (known to environmentalists as "the environmental wrecking crew"). In politics, first things must come first—and only rarely are environmental concerns ranked near the top of the list.

Politicians elsewhere are little different. Even though they may perhaps know better, they recognize that the call to develop more modest and sustainable economic development programs is hard to sell politically. And when the awareness of actual human limitation— and the intimations of mortality perhaps engendered by such an awareness—occasionally do intrude, our leaders in science policy seek to mystify the people and preserve the status quo once again by developing new and ever more exotic technologies—genetic engineering, nuclear technology, "smarter" weapons—few of which will ever contribute to the well-being of the general public. Jeremy Rifkin has said, "Today we spend far less time planning the future than eking out what is left of the past. The industrial epoch marks the final stage of the age of fire. After ten thousand years of torching fire to ore, the age of pyrotechnology is slowly burning out."[6]

Although second thoughts are cropping up more and more these days in the plans of policymakers, we still receive official assurances from them that the Earth will remain a bountiful cornucopia of inexhaustibly rich and wonderful things. Even when the rare politician does proclaim this to be a "new era of limits," policymakers (or is it the people themselves?) still seem to believe that those who can access the goods needed to fuel the economic machine must seize them, regardless of any of the outside costs of production—the impairment of health, threats to the general welfare, or the increasing terrors of pollution. And although these operative myths of progress are coming under ever-increasing scrutiny as we are forced to pay some of the human and ecological costs of undifferentiated economic growth, little attempt has thus far been made in the developed world of either East or West to formulate more rational paradigms for the operation of science and technology.

We all know that our value systems inform our world views on almost everything. They support and shape our beliefs and opinions on the proper role of science in the modern world. But it is increasingly difficult in the midst of a contrary propaganda barrage fostered by government and industry to grasp the importance of imposing new limits—of even occasionally saying no to the masters of science and technology. Historian of science Arnold Pacey states,

The political issue concerns the totalitarian nature of many of the institutions that control modern technology; it is associated with the difficulty encountered at almost every level, of opening any real dialogue between experts and users, technocrats and parliamentarians, planners and people. On the government level, the growth of bureaucracy has tended to shunt parliament away from the center of political life. The executive apparatus functions increasingly without adequate political control. That has led to a widespread sense of political impotence, and some loss of faith in elected government, and so to the growth of protest movements concerned with the environment, the arms race and nuclear energy.[7]

A remarkable lack of reflection and self-criticism infects much of the technological community today. Like a virus, the belief in human progress that initiated the era of the Enlightenment has spread to every corner of the West. We fully believe, in spite of all the evidence, that there is an absolute and relevant connection between technology and human well-being (perhaps because we do not know how the money is actually being spent). German philosopher Bertolt Brecht provides insight into one of the dilemmas of science when (in a play) he depicts Galileo saying,

I take it that the intent of science is to ease human existence [but] your progress may become a progress away from the bulk of humanity. Your cheering at some new achievement could be echoed by a universal howl of horror.[8]

Technology expert Langdon Winner believes that, as part of overall human activity, technologies are powerful forces in the reshaping of societies. Winner suggests that we are all called on to reproduce social roles and frameworks "with the rise of the sun each day."

From this point of view, the important question about technology becomes, "what kind of world are we making?" Are we going to design and build . . . to enlarge and enhance possibilities for growth and freedom . . . or are we heading in an altogether different direction?

We usually do not stop to inquire whether a given device might have been built in such a way that it produces consequences logically . . . and prior to any of its professed uses.[9]

As noted, the knowledge industries of business and government have long tended to exploit science for their own particular ends. As perceptive critics have pointed out, government funding of research has tended to be concentrated in two spheres: military development, and subsidies of various types to private industrial enterprise in order to increase the profit potential of U.S. industry. Government funding of corporate activity is thus the key to scientific and technological development in the United States and (to a lesser degree) in most other Western societies. Industrial research is geared to satisfy the demands of either state policy or the production of goods for profit. Rarely in the United States does public need interfere with the satisfaction of these often antisocial end goals of government and industry.

One problem facing the average person, in even our most well-intentioned attempts to assess the impacts of social change, is a growing inability to distinguish between the powerful institutions of government and industry and the roles we picture these institutions as playing. To have a school, for example, presumes that the institution is in fact "doing education," when in fact it may be doing nothing of the sort. The point applies fully as well to the institutions of science. Structure tends to equate with function, and individuals become psychically dependent on the continuance of such institutions to solve their problems.

The institutionalized forms of politics and economics thus become the functional parents of the scientific enterprise, ministered to by a bureaucratic managerial class often unwilling to ask the value-related questions that might interfere with technocratic progress. For example, this writer is acquainted with some of the technocrats who manage the design and development of the nation's nuclear weapons in the radiation labs at the University of California's Lawrence Livermore National Laboratory. So many of these good people, protesting that they are only doing their job, and ignoring the fact that there are always value determinations implicit in such a definition of duty, well illustrate the truth that evil is often quite banal. The issue at hand—in the biological, medical, and physical sciences—is never simply a struggle between science and antiscience, nor is the critical questioning of the function of modern science in any way an anti-intellectual retreat. Quite to the contrary, contemporary anti-intellectualism is most often found in those who are unwilling or unable to question the management of science when such questioning might interfere with either personal security and professional advancement or corporate-industrial-government end goals.

On the functioning of the contemporary scientific establishment and its penchant for publicizing potentially profitable (and occasion-

ally fraudulent) research, *Science* magazine editor Nicholas Wade has
this to say,

> Science may in one sense be a community, but in another way, equally
> important, it is a celebrity system. The social organization of science is
> designed to foster the production of an elite in which prestige comes
> not just on the merits of work but also because of position in the scientific
> hierarchy. Members of the scientific elite control the reward system of
> science and . . . have a voice in the allocation of resources. . . . The
> system favors the search for personal glory over the search for truth . . .
> and [provides] immunity from scrutiny to the work of the elite. . . . They
> are the product and beneficiaries of a social organization that fosters
> careerism and creates the temptations and opportunities for fraud.[10]

Science and technology (of whatever kind) always carry and display
certain visible marks that are imprinted on them by the nature of the
operative economic and production systems. Characterizing our own
Western, state-capitalist system of production are tendencies toward
capital-intensive, centralized, large-scale, hierarchically organized,
and energy-dependent forms of production. These same development norms apply fully to the production of science. Although we
prefer to think of science as being somehow isolated from the rough-
and-tumble of the marketplace, in fact it is not. The macro world of
the Western political economy is fully revealed in the micro world of
science and technology.

One end result of this form of science and technology is a deepening of the social constraints that operate within a given society.
Inevitably, the worker ends up as little more than an appendage of
ever more sophisticated machines, thus losing all sense of any direct
role in the process of production. The massive shift currently under-
way in the technology of mass production in the United States has
accelerated this tendency and, with the movement from specialized
human labor to electronic and robotized controls, has dramatically
increased the number of industrially displaced workers. In human
terms alone, the development of industrial systems that rely on labor-
intensive, decentralized, small-scale, and democratically organized
production units is a goal worthy of pursuit. Small-scale operations
also carry plenty of potential for alleviating some of the technical and
creative problems of greatness (or largeness) experienced within the
current organization of the scientific endeavor.

Science, Systems, and Nature

Table 6.1 lays out some of the major assumptions that have under-girded science, with their correlative views as to its purpose. Although some may protest that there was no functional science before Ptolemy, it appears in fact that science has always been around—to a large degree an intrinsic product of the social system of the era, reflecting both its priorities and allegiances.[11]

The schematic representation in Table 6.1 suggests that science and technology as we know it today have been essentially Western or

Table 6.1 Scientific Paradigms as They Have Developed throughout History

Type	*Actors*	*Assumptions*	*Function/Purpose*
Prescientific, Hebrew, Greek, etc., cosmologies	priests	all events are acts of God	to protect people from capricious acts of God
Ptolemaic, 2nd–16th centuries	astrologers/ alchemists	motionless Earth at center of the universe	to "divine" the hand of God and predict the future; the cosmos has a soul; organic view of nature
Copernican, 16th–17th centuries	the scientist as an observer of nature	heliocentric solar system	much the same as Ptolemaic
Newtonian, 17th–20th centuries	scientists working within "disciplines"; whole equals sum of parts	universe is a great machine that can only be understood through laws of mathematics	to discover those universal laws that can enable us to bring the cosmos under human control
Einsteinian, 20th century	scientists also working in interdisciplinary modes; whole greater than the sum of parts	everything is connected; all is in flux; no absolute laws; all is relative	to synthesize all info/knowledge to better understand the functioning of the universe

Source: Adapted from personal communication with Professor John Ratcliff, School of Public Health at the University of California, Berkeley.

occidental developments. The West has historically been better than the East at applying science to solve particular problems. This may have been due in part to the needs of the emergent political-economic systems in Europe. The mercantile capitalists of the period between 1500 and 1800, caught up in the requirement to develop new products and to enlarge foreign trade, desperately needed both the insights and applications of science. State policy was used to create a vast new skilled class of industrial workers—all dependent to some degree on the scientific and technological innovation of their respective eras.

During the sixteenth and seventeenth centuries, the possibility of actual human control over nature was enhanced. The Earth would then take on new economic meaning since it provides "resources" (an economic term) that, properly managed, can lead to the accumulation of wealth. Progress thus came to be measured by two relatively recent norms: material accumulation, and scientific and technological innovation. The Earth was increasingly seen as a machine. Science, as Darwin later noted, became the task of "grinding out the universal laws of nature."

More recently, in a hopeful development, some philosophers of science have suggested that the new physics—quantum mechanics, relativity theory, new cosmological understandings—have the potential for integrating science and religious/philosophical perspectives. As Table 6.1 notes, the newer science is interdisciplinary and process oriented. It sees the cosmos not as a machine, but as an ongoing interactive structure of creation and re-creation. All is in flux; nothing is absolute; truth is finally relative at best. Believing that the time is now ripe for a merging of the best in modern physics and Eastern philosophy, physicist-philosopher Fritjof Capra notes,

> Modern physics has confirmed most dramatically one of the basic ideas of Eastern mysticism; that all the concepts we use to describe nature are limited, that they are not features of reality, as we tend to believe, but creations of the mind; parts of the map, not of the territory. Whenever we expand the realm of our experience, the limitations of our rational mind become apparent and we have to modify, or even abandon, some of our concepts.[12]

Although little noticed in our cultural optimism regarding science and technology, the fact is that modern science has brought with it a new set of rather severe constraints on human behavior and action, rather than an opening of unlimited vistas of progress. Since the discovery that the Earth is not the center of the universe, and the corresponding psychic readjustment by human beings required to understand the more limited grandeur of our planet and our species, science has told us more of what we cannot do—of what our basic limits are—than anything else. Those laws of thermodynamics that relate to thermal pollution remind us of the outer and absolute limits of the Earth's capacity to absorb heat and still maintain life. They similarly remind us (as we daily rediscover) that, if we continue to use energy at the current rates, we will soon raise the temperature of the globe to such a degree that Planet Earth will become uninhabitable.

Quantum mechanics, in spite of the new horizons opened by its profound insights into the physical universe, affirms all of the uncertainties that exist relative to our ability to measure subatomic particles. Wondrous as our knowledge may be, it is always imperfect. Relativity shows us new dimensions of understanding with regard to space and time, but it also tells us of the outer limits of velocity within the universe. Although some of us may not like it, we are essentially earthbound, and our feet will always (perhaps in a spiritual as well as a physical sense) be essentially rooted within our own biosphere.

The lessons for biology and its related ethical systems are clear: to treat the Earth and its inhabitants carefully and with humility, treading gently indeed wherever cautious human beings should fear to go. The time has come to acknowledge first of all the depths of our lack of knowledge and understanding, rather than the peaks of our certainties. The inevitable interactions of scientific, technological, and cultural perspectives provide new subject matter for those attempting to solve our immediate biological dilemmas. Unhappily, the effort to know more and more about less and less seems to be the norm in contemporary scientific inquiry. If technology can in fact lead both to social change and at times to correlative restrictions on individual liberties (because of the difficulty in effecting popular control over highly complex and technical systems), then bioethics and ecoethics must raise many uncomfortable questions about both the means and the end goals of individual and group conduct and political action.

To an ever-increasing degree, then, society at large is organized by the imperatives of those scientific methods that emerged in past historical epochs and that continue to govern advanced science and technology today. Economic and cultural development—in transportation, educational systems, health-care maintenance, science and technology, energy use, and industrial production—is now, to a larger extent than we would probably think appropriate if asked for our opinion, determined by changes in the organization of science. And clearly, it will be impossible even to begin to challenge and reformulate science without at the same time attempting to alter the form of production and the social relationships obtaining within the society. Technology does indeed mimic the rest of the industrial system.

Although logical positivism (the view that science always provides an objective, true, and accurate basis for knowledge about reality) is in theory a somewhat outmoded philosophy of science, it is still very much in the driver's seat in the practical realm of science. The radical empiricist will normally look only to the descriptive sciences for verification of our assumed knowledge about how Earth functions. According to most traditional science, nature alone provides the verification of hypotheses. From this perspective, there can be neither an ethical nor a moral dimension to scientific inquiry since science is, after all, simply the task of description. Science and technology are thus value free. This is rather consoling to the nuclear physicist and the genetic engineer since they can then assume there is nothing wrong that a scientist can possibly do.

A better perspective would be that science is never more than the transitional articulation of what "appears" to be the way nature functions, reflecting no more than the consensus of the majority of the scientific community and the accepted norms of the larger society at any given moment. As Thomas Kuhn explained in his description of the historic paradigms of scientific development, pure science is essentially a theory-testing method wherein science studies the myriad puzzles of nature, models out hypotheses about these puzzles, and—when the accepted answers no longer fit—formulates more reasonable contemporary paradigms that reflect a bit more accurately the present state of knowledge.[13]

Such a perspective affirms that, in most instances, knowledge is relative and that what is considered scientific truth varies in both perspective and affirmation at different historical moments. Above all, science is a reflection of our current understandings of social reality. Whereas such a temperate approach is no guarantee that ethical and value questions will be raised, it does provide for a kind of ongoing scientific self-criticism that considers the propriety of the intellectual quest as well as its procedure.

The realization that the scientific quest is determined to a very large degree by decisions in the political and economic realms impels us to a consideration of the ethical and moral aspects of contemporary science and technology. We have already reviewed some of the traditional theories of ethics and justice. In the next four chapters we will move to a case-study consideration of some of the primary bioethical dilemmas of the modern age. Before we move on, however, the reader is reminded of the central assumption of the bioethicist, as pointed out in this chapter. Biology (and all of science) has a political and economic bias structured into its very core. It can never, therefore, be truly neutral or objective. One need not lament this fact so much as understand it. As we consider in later chapters the functioning of science in the biotechnological, medical, biological, and behavioral realms, questions regarding the proper goal of the scientific task will be raised over and over again.

Notes

1. Stillman Drake, ed., *Discoveries and Opinions of Galileo* (New York: Doubleday Anchor Press, 1957), p. 63.
2. Ibid., p. 64.
3. National Science Report 85-322 (1986); and *Bulletin of the Atomic Scientists* (March 1986).
4. For a description of science priorities at the Lawrence Livermore National Laboratory, see William Broad, *The Star Warriors* (New York: Simon and Schuster, 1985). Also see below in the text.
5. John Holdren, *The Militarization of Scientific Research and Development,* Energy and Resources Group, University of California, Berkeley, September 1986, p. 11.
6. Jeremy Rifkin, *Algeny: A New Word—A New World* (New York: Penguin Books, 1984), pp. 5–6.
7. Arnold Pacey, *The Culture of Technology* (Cambridge, Mass.: MIT Press, 1983), p. 160.
8. Bertolt Brecht, "Galileo," in Eric Bentley, ed. *From the Modern Repertoire* (Bloomington: Indiana University Press, 1978).
9. Langdon Winner, *The Whale and the Reactor: A Search for Limits in an Age of High Technology* (Chicago: University of Chicago Press, 1985), pp. 14, 25.
10. William Broad and Nicholas Wade, *Betrayers of the Truth: Fraud and Deceit in the Halls of Science* (New York: Simon and Schuster, 1982), p. 214–15.
11. I am indebted to Professor John Ratcliffe of the School of Public Health at the University of California, Berkeley, for insights into the paradigms of "science, systems, and nature."
12. Fritjof Capra, *The Tao of Physics,* 2nd ed. (New York: Shambhala Publications and Bantam Press, 1984), p. 147.
13. Thomas Kuhn, *The Structure of Scientific Revolution* (Chicago: University of Chicago Press, 1962).

7

Genetic Engineering

Ever since the double helix of the DNA molecule was discovered in 1953—raising for the first time in human history the possibility of intentional alterations being made in the genetic material of our and other species—the question of whether or not humankind is moving into forbidden territory has occupied the attention of both the scientific and the lay communities. Many ordinary people and experts alike have been concerned about what has been called the "Frankenstein factor." Our new ability to create entirely unique forms of living beings by recombining the cells of higher and lower organisms or the genetic material of plants and animals has awakened both enormous possibilities and grave problems.

The real issue, however, is not between Frankenstein and Einstein—between evil science and good science—but between those who hope to use the new science and technology in an appropriate fashion (to help those in the world who are most needful of good people-oriented science) and those who will focus on providing high-cost services to the already overprivileged portion of the world's population in order to maximize market returns. When huge amounts of investment capital are combined with the very best in biological science and technology, quite remarkable things can happen very quickly. If within a decade or two the mechanics of the life process become the private property of big business—as happens now when new organisms are patented—the ordinary people of the world will inevitably end up the losers.

Whether we—as individuals, groups, or nation-states—are prepared to handle the economic and social consequences of such a trend is doubtful. Our apparatus for developing sound and protective public policy has never been very effective, and biological innovations from the new biotech companies seem to be sprouting up much more quickly than our cultural understanding of the implications of the

technologies. Although many dimensions of biotechnology are socially benign—some kinds of new medical machinery; research on
diseases like AIDS, cancer, and cystic fibrosis; strengthening plant
resistance to certain diseases—the focus in this chapter will be on
genetic engineering and whether or not this new technological science
is subject to control by any other agent of society than the experts in
the think tanks of government and industry who issue the production
orders to the scientific community.

Already today, cells from different species have been fused together
in quite amazing fashion. New recombinations carry the characteristics of rabbits and mice, humans and plants, the blood cells of
chickens and yeast, cancer and carrots, and a variety of other mixes.
Once the natural barriers guarding against the transfer of genetic
material between lower life forms such as bacteria and across higher
plant and animal types had been breached, a new and qualitatively
different factor entered into the evolutionary process. As Lewis
Thomas, one of the most respected medical philosophers in the
United States, has said,

> The recombinant line of research is already upsetting, not because of
> the dangers now being argued about but because it is disturbing in a
> fundamental way, to face the fact that genetic machinery in control of
> the planet's life can be fooled around with so easily. We do not like the
> idea that anything so fixed and stable as species line can be changed.
> The notion that genes can be taken out of one genome and inserted in
> another is unnerving.[1]

In the same vein, religious leaders have warned that

> We are rapidly moving into a new era of fundamental danger triggered
> by the rapid growth of genetic engineering. Albeit, there may be oppor-
> tunity for doing good, the very term suggests the danger.[2]

The social dilemmas posed by genetic engineering and its related
technologies are quite as great as the physical potentialities. We live in
a world characterized by growing disparity between rich and poor,
haves and have-nots, overdeveloped and developing nations, North
and South. A long view of the history of science suggests that new
technologies always tend to favor the powerful in their relationships
with the less powerful. New elitist sciences—like those that led to the
development of the recombinant technologies—do little if anything

to address the survival needs of ordinary people whose biggest daily concerns are inequality and injustice. As noted by one speaker at a conference in Bogeve, France, that dealt with the socioeconomic aspects of biotechnology in the Third World,

> For the poor, struggling to keep their young alive and reduce the fertility of those who feel they have enough children, biotechnology is helping the rich keep the old alive and make the infertile fertile. A world which needs clean water and tropical vaccines is being offered new cosmetics and organ transplants. While the poor search for solutions to malaria and diarrhea, biobusiness plumbs the yuppie market for genetic screening and human growth hormones so that every girl can be a Barbie doll and every boy can look like Ken.[3]

Nevertheless, in spite of the dilemmas, molecular biology is (to this writer, at least) the single most exciting frontier of modern science. Sending out spaceships and probing ever deeper into subatomic structures also have their enchantments. But penetrating the nucleus of the living cell and rearranging and transplanting the genetic material of heretofore separate and distinct life forms is a kind of science conceptually removed in many orders of magnitude from the traditional frontiers of human thought and technology. Creating new medicines like insulin and interferon through genetic cloning procedures, enabling agricultural products like corn and sunflowers to produce their own nitrogen fertilizer, developing bacteria with the ability to eat up oil spills, curing human genetic disorders, and diagnosing fetal abnormalities within the womb are only some of the beginning possibilities within the field.

Simple genetic manipulation is not new. For millennia, humans have been deliberately structuring genetic change in plants and animals by methods ranging all the way from simple selective breeding policies to hybridization and other naturally induced means of influencing hereditary change. The primary concern today is not really so much the inducement of genetic change, but the creation of new life forms. And it is the history and development of this new science and the ethical dilemmas arising from it that will constitute the substance of this chapter.

During the past decade, changes in the field of research in molecular genetics have been so rapid—often with major developments occurring over periods of months and even weeks—that most cautious observers have felt the need for more formal controls over the application and utilization of such research. Few within the industry, however, have evidenced much concern for the kind of problems raised at the Bogeve conference. In order better to understand the history of recombinant technology, an overview of the basic structure of molecular biology is a necessary beginning point. We need to be able to assess the direction of the new science, the kinds of controls that should perhaps be invoked on further research endeavors in recombinant biology, and the nature of the ethical questions raised.

The History and the Science of Recombinant DNA

Exploratory work on the part of Gregor Mendel in the early 1860s led to his discovery of the discrete factors of inheritance that we commonly refer to as genes. It was not until the early part of this century, however, that proper attention was given to Mendel's theories about the genetic basis for transmission of heritable physical characteristics. The brilliant monk's elegantly detailed study of reproductive traits in the simple pea plant—"rediscovered" in 1900 by three independent investigators—gave rise to the more controversial genetics we know today as molecular biology.

Chromosomes, which control the heredity of plants and animals, carry within them the genetic material that determines the specific characteristics of inheritance. Each chromosome includes a long string of DNA (deoxyribonucleic acid), wrapped up in a protein sheath. The DNA is made up of a variety of chemicals called nucleotides, which consist of one sugar molecule, a phosphate group, and one of the four nitrogenous bases that make up the four letters of the genetic alphabet: A, G, T, and C. The letters represent the four nucleotides adenine, guanine, thymine, and cytosine, which are linked end to end in different combinations to make up the two strands of the helical DNA molecule. The particular genetic message encoded in the DNA is structured by the sequence of the nucleotides. The A, G, T, C arrangement determines the sequence of amino acids within the protein molecule. This protein structure within the DNA ultimately determines every physical and chemical characteristic of the organism. Each chromosome is essentially divided into a number of segments (genes), and the particular sequence of DNA in each gene gives a coded set of quite explicit instructions to each cell to perform a certain kind of function. The genetic information is then transferred from the DNA by RNA (ribonucleic acid) in a very particular fashion, the upshot of which is that individual cells are enabled to switch on certain genes and turn off all the rest.

When an error (not at all uncommon) in this process of cell replication (the mechanism of switching the genetic material on and off) occurs due to some event like radiation or chemical poisoning of one kind or another, the sequence of transmission within the DNA molecule is altered. When such changes occur in active genetic material, the cell may be killed or it may function defectively. A cancer tumor, for example, can occur from a mutation that originally may have affected only one cell but then copied or replicated the defect.

Natural gene splicing within species does occur in nature. Many insects, for example, become immune to pesticides by defensively reconstructing segments of their genetic material. Certain people develop immunity to antibiotics after extended use. Bacteria in the body, as a means of self-protection, recombine genetic material in order to immunize themselves against the invading antibacterial agent. What we now know as recombinant DNA (rDNA) became possible in the early 1970s with the discovery of the first of more than 150 restriction enzymes that make it possible to cut the DNA at a quite specific point where a particular A, G, T, C nucleotide sequence occurs. A segment of DNA from another organism, whose nucleotide sequence has been cut by another restriction enzyme in exactly the same fashion, is then attached by its chemically sticky end (so to speak) to those of the original segment. As the fragments grow together, the new matter is incorporated into the old genetic material. All other things being equal, this recombined DNA will then copy itself and be reproduced as the material replicates.

Controlling Recombinant Research in the Laboratory

Much controversy has surrounded this new science from the very beginning. When Herbert Boyer and Stanley Cohen of the University of California in San Francisco first rearranged the DNA molecule in a laboratory in 1973, certain fears were immediately raised. One major problem had to do with the fact that, early on, attempts were in process to combine a tumor virus with a special form of the common *E. coli* bacterium. Although bacteria have never been known to cause cancer in humans, some viruses have produced cancer in animals. The possibility of there being developed for the first time in evolutionary history a cancer germ had seriously to be considered. Other equally serious issues were raised by critics of the new science.

Concerned about the potential for creating a new and virulent bacteria that might do harm to human beings, some members of the molecular biology establishment called for a moratorium on recombinant research until procedures to monitor the research and protect the public interest could be established. Paul Berg of Stanford, later one of molecular biology's fiercest defenders against question-askers from the nonscientific community, chaired a small committee that published the following letter in *Science* on July 26, 1974:

> Recent advances in techniques for the isolation and rejoining of segments of DNA now permit construction of biologically active recombinant DNA molecules *in vitro*. . . . Several groups of scientists are now planning to use this technology to create recombinant DNAs from a variety of other viral, animal and bacterial sources. . . . There is serious concern that some of these artificial recombinant DNA molecules could prove biologically hazardous.
>
> The undersigned members of a committee . . . propose . . . that until the potential hazards of such recombinant DNA molecules have been better evaluated or until adequate methods are developed for preventing their spread, scientists throughout the world join with the members of this committee in voluntarily deferring [certain] types of experiments.

The upshot was the calling of a conference at the Asilomar conference center in California in 1975 to consider the situation. Operating procedures for such research were developed by the gathering, and this led subsequently to the guidelines for rDNA research established by the National Institutes of Health (NIH). Controversial from the start, these guidelines did provide some standards for laboratory safeguards until they were liberalized in 1978, further weakened by removing 85–90 percent of all rDNA research from review or inspection in 1981, and functionally discontinued in April 1982. Many of the major figures in molecular biology were opposed to any kind of effort to moderate the freedom of the scientists to do whatever they wished. James Watson, a Nobel laureate for his work in discovering the structure of DNA, has said,

> Although some fringe groups . . . thought this was a matter to be debated and decided by all and sundry, it was never the intention of those who might be called the molecular biology establishment to take the issue to the general public to decide. . . . We did not want our

experiments to be blocked by overconfident lawyers, much less by self-appointed bioethicists with no inherent knowledge of, or interest in, our work. Their decisions could only be arbitrary. Given that there were no definite facts on which to base danger signals, we might find ourselves at the mercy of Luddites who did not want to take the chance of any form of change.[4]

Although an original signatory of the Berg letter, Watson always opposed any kind of control over rDNA research. He later

characterized the Asilomar conference as "nonsense" and "theater of the absurd," and referred to opponents of unregulated research variously as "hysterics," "kooks," "incompetents," and "shits." He also boasted unabashedly that "I, for one, have never given a moment's thought to whether my passion about the nature of the gene might be misplaced, much less a major danger to mankind itself."[5]

However, as C. K. Boone of the Hastings Center pointed out,

What irked scientists the most . . . was neither scientific nor philosophical disagreements, but the insolence of their colleagues in "going public" with their anxieties. While the non-scientific community viewed these public doubters as responsible professionals, many in the ranks of scientists saw them as apostates to the hallowed tradition of scientific self-determination. Who were they to cast the pearls of scientific inquiry before untutored masses who were incompetent to make judgments about such abstruse matters?[6]

The later decisions essentially removing any kind of control on rDNA laboratory-related research were based on the belief that the earlier warnings were no longer relevant to recombinant research. There was, researchers said, little possibility of new organisms hazardous to human beings establishing themselves outside the laboratories. This optimism may in time prove to have been shortsighted. Subsequent investigation has shown that recombinant microbes ingested by laboratory workers can indeed survive outside the lab, can develop and grow in city sewer systems, and have the potential for doing genuine mischief to the population.[7]

When the National Institutes of Health finally gave up any effort to control recombinant research under its guidelines (which anyway governed only that work funded by the federal government and excluded all privately funded research), it brought to an end the one serious attempt to date to regulate this powerful new industry.

That rDNA technology is now flourishing in a regulatory vacuum, subject to less scrutiny than virtually any other manufacturing process, is a function of the times. . . . It should not diminish the fact that this was the first new technology to stimulate a national discussion on risk prior to its widespread implementation. As it turned out, the go-ahead was won despite the accumulation of problematical data. Those with a concern for the rational use of technology can learn from this episode that only by demanding even greater public discussion of, and scrutiny over, productive processes can the potential for future disaster be averted.[8]

Fully as important as the institution of the original guidelines, however, is the fact that the scientific community had for the first time in history gone public with doubts about the nature and wisdom of its research. Even though most controls have now been removed from such work, researchers in other controversial fields of science may perhaps be a bit more self-critical in the future, given the precedent of the early rDNA debates.

Finally, because "no governmental body was exercising adequate oversight or control, nor addressing the fundamental ethical questions . . . of genetic engineering," a President's Commission for the Study of Ethical Problems in Medicine and Biomedical and Behavioral Research was inaugurated in 1980. Although many different governmental agencies are now involved in one way or another with regulating genetic research and testing, the lines of responsibility are far from clear. As the following section will indicate, it may now be a bit too late to close the barn door; the recombinant horse may have already escaped.

From the Laboratory to the Fields

In the early days of genetic engineering, the major worry of concerned members of the environmental and scientific communities focused on issues of safety within the laboratory. As noted, in the United States, carefully formulated safeguards were established by the National Institutes of Health to ensure that genetically modified organisms (GMOs) would be contained within research facilities. Today, however, the safety focus has shifted: Both public and scientific concerns are centered on the complementary issues of the field testing of GMOs and the production of new products based on such research.

The drive to develop commercial applications of GMOs is under-standable. Enormous investments in genetic biotechnology have al-ready been made, and even greater profits may be just around the corner. Globally, many nations now see new product development via genetic engineering as an absolute key to the maintenance of inter-national economic competitiveness. But too often in the past, early and legitimate warnings have been ignored (one need only note the history of the nuclear and petrochemical fields) in the hunt for immediate results and quick profits. As one observer has put it, "The desire for quick review, quick implementation, and quick reward leads to an exaggeration of benefits and a denial of risks."[9]

In 1988, agricultural researchers at the University of California at Berkeley gained approval for the first field testing of a unique genetically altered organism: the so-called ice-minus bacterium. Since that release, several other field tests of new life forms created by DNA technology have been conducted. Dozens are now waiting approval. A large percentage of the more than 600 genetic engineering com-panies around the country will sooner or later be planning similar experiments.

At Berkeley, Professors Steven Lindow and Nick Panopoulos have removed the ice-nucleating gene from *Pseudomonas syringae*, a com-monly occurring bacteria in nature. *P. syringae* secretes a protein that acts as a nucleus in the formation of ice crystals. By genetically engineering this gene out of the bacterium, culturing it, and spraying it on target vegetation, plants can be enabled to resist temperatures well below freezing. The university has granted a license to the Advanced Genetics Company (AGC) near Berkeley for the production and sale of this new biological product, which will be marketed under the trade name "FrostBan."

Enormous controversy accompanied the research and field testing of this altered bacterium. For some time, lawsuits and bureaucratic maneuvering interfered with the environmental release of the new organism. Many scientists and most environmentalists protested its field test, saying that the "ice-minus" organism poses a threat to public and ecological health. AGC was first criticized and then fined $25,000 by the federal government for conducting certain early tests without federal approval and for failing to inform the public properly about the intended scope and location of the experimental releases. After extended delays, the actual tests took place in April 1988—and aroused remarkably little further public outcry.

The problem of how to regulate both research and testing of the new life forms made possible by molecular biology has now reached a critical phase. There are no less than 18 separate federal regulatory agencies involved with GMOs. In June 1986 the White House Office of Science and Technology instituted the Coordinated Framework for the Regulation of Biotechnology. Its intent is to enable the agencies to "operate in an integrated and coordinated fashion covering the whole range of plants, animals, and micro-organisms derived by the new genetic engineering techniques." Unhappily, certain of the agencies involved (like the U.S. Department of Agriculture) have responsibilities both to regulate and to promote genetically altered plant products. This kind of conflict of interests has been known to cause trouble in the past, such as in monitoring nuclear power developments when the Atomic Energy Commission had a similar dual function.

In any case, critics claim that the bureaucratic Balkanization of the regulatory process means there is in fact no effective regulation. The pressure is mounting to place all responsibility for monitoring both research and testing of genetically engineered products within a single agency—most probably the Toxic Substances Control Office of the Environmental Protection Agency (EPA) or else the Department of Agriculture. But a new study released in early May 1988 by the Office of Technology Assessment (OTA) proposes a quite different direction for DNA product regulation.

New Developments in Biotechnology: Field-testing Engineered Organisms, the official report of an OTA congressional study, appears to minimize any overall risk to the public health in the field testing of new genetically engineered organisms.[10] Stating that "commercial biotechnology is advancing into areas that depend on the introduction of genetically engineered organisms into the environment" and that "the application of such biological approaches may prove more benign to the environment than traditional technologies," the report then qualifies its optimism by stating that "planned introductions of genetically engineered organisms into the environment are . . . not without potential risks." It is the very enormity of this potential risk factor that makes both environmentalists and researchers in the older sciences of agriculture uneasy. The introduction of exotic plant and animal species has often in the past created tremendous problems for agriculture and forestry. Now the spectre of new life forms being released in both small- and large-scale research efforts all around the country—some combining the DNA from plants, animals, and even human beings—frighten most observers not directly attached to the industry.

Further exacerbating the problem is the fact that the EPA is preparing new rules that would take the first few steps toward relaxing even the modest current restrictions on smaller field tests of genetically altered microorganisms. Under the new rules, biotech companies planning outdoor tests on "nonhazardous" altered microbes would be required to submit much less health and safety data than is now required. In many cases, corporations and universities would be authorized to establish their own safety panels for review of their own proposed field tests. Such procedures for "voluntary compliance" with federal environmental regulations—now common throughout U.S. industry under the relaxed environmental standards of the Reagan and Bush administrations—show an increasing reluctance within government to interfere with the profit potential of industrial biotechnology. Indeed, the OTA study goes so far as to state that unspecified "common sense" rules established by industry will normally be adequate to protect people and nature in open-air testing of genetically engineered organisms.

Two primary factors seem to have occasioned what appears to be a strategic backing off by the government in its efforts to regulate rDNA research and testing. One factor has certainly been the massive lobbying effort by the industry to quell public fears about the release of new life forms into the environment. As one industry spokesman stated to this writer, "The issue of public acceptance is now critical. Our industry could die if we don't overcome public fears of environmental releases." The other factor is a recognition on the part of government that it does not really know much about how to regulate new life forms. Accordingly, as one EPA spokesman recently suggested in a background statement, the simplest way for the government to handle the problem is simply to fit the regulation of new research and product development within the scope of existing legislation, thus minimizing any points of potential conflict with industry.

Biotechnology is now an international concern, making any kind of effective regulation difficult at best. Some nations are already targeting the industry of genetic engineering (the United States, Japan, members of the European Community), with their respective governments underwriting both research and product development. Other nations (Brazil, Israel, the Philippines, Mexico, Argentina, Israel) are moving ahead but at a slower pace.

Newer and developing nations will often be very relaxed in their regulatory stance, which may lead the industrial nations to undertake research and field testing in those locations. Thus, the need for international control over biotechnology is particularly compelling. All such regulating must focus on public and environmental health issues, rather than on satisfying the more short-term interests of science and industry.

Social policy critic Mark Sagoff has suggested that the biotech industry sees nature as "one huge LEGO kit" that it can use and manipulate in whatever way seems appropriate in order to maximize profits from what is predicted will soon be a $100 billion industry. No one would argue the point that biotechnology and genetic engineering are here to stay. The questions now being asked by those who want to see the industry monitored have to do with who will control the science and who will profit from the commercial applications of the research efforts. Beneficial products to improve the general health and welfare of the citizenry have already been developed. Many more may be just around the corner. Whether the research and manufacture of such products will in the long run do more harm than good is the big question that requires the further attention of ecoethicists.

Molecules and the Military

The early controversy about laboratory safety in genetic engineering experimentation—while important—may well have obscured other socially related concerns of equal importance. Foremost among these concerns are the military use of the new technologies and the extent to which our social institutions are equipped to deal with policy questions arising from the new technologies.

Early in 1970, for example, the U.S. Army announced that it was planning to build a major research installation adjacent to the Letterman Hospital at the Presidio in San Francisco, which would be known as the Western Military Institute of Research (WMIR). Its announced purpose was to conduct research on tropical diseases. During this period, the author received a letter from a medical researcher at Letterman, containing information that the new WMIR facility was in fact to be a sophisticated chemical/biological warfare (CBW) research facility. My informant stated that it was the military's apparent intention to use the WMIR to replace the old Fort Detrick, Maryland, Research Center for CBW research. Preliminary blueprints of the building were obtained, and they indicated that the new facility could indeed be used to carry out such an assignment. At the time, military journals were for the first time paying attention to the enormous potential of new and promising forms of CBW such as ethnic warfare—biological weaponry that would take advantage of enzyme and other racial and/or genetic idiosyncracies.[11] Whether or not such research was in fact ever conducted at the WMIR was neither confirmed nor denied.

Subsequently, the Bay Area press was full of stories leaked about how the biological warfare division of the U.S. military (through the services of the Naval Biosciences Laboratories) had introduced disease-carrying bacteria and viruses into the transportation systems and atmospheres of New York and San Francisco in order to study the effectiveness of current methods for dispersing chemical and biological agents. At least one person reportedly died as result of these activities.[12]

Unhappily, the U.S. Department of Defense (DOD) has regularly expressed great interest in molecular biology and in rDNA research. DOD is now on record officially with the following concerns:

New threats to the national security may be opened up by various technological and scientific advances. As examples, recombinant DNA technology could make it possible for a potential enemy to implant virulence factors or toxin-producing genetic information into common, easily transmitted bacteria such as *E. coli*. Within this context, the objective of the work is to provide an essential base of scientific information to counteract these possibilities and to provide a better understanding of the disease mechanisms of bacterial and rickettsial organisms that pose a potential biological warfare threat, with or without genetic manipulation.[13]

Earlier, the DOD itself had requested permission from the now defunct NIH Committee on the Oversight of Genetic Engineering to clone toxins in naturally occurring *E. coli* bacteria. Regularly, the military advertises in the science journals for proposals relating to its biological interests. In *Science,* for example, on September 12, 1980 (209:1282), the DOD requested proposals from adventurous scientists on how it might introduce by DNA methods a genetic enzyme (acetylcholinesterase) of the human nervous system into a bacterium. As those familiar with the human health problems of pesticides and herbicides will remember, the cholinesterase enzyme is involved in the transmission of nerve impulses. Literally thousands of argicultural field-workers have been poisoned recently in the United States and other countries by these chemical nerve poisons. The interest of the military in the further development of even more sophisticated "enzyme inhibitors" is historically consistent. One can only assume that, as always, the military will find its takers within the scientific community for further biocidal research in the field.

During this same period of the early 1980s, the NIH oversight committee defeated a resolution by the National Academy of Sciences that recommended a ban on the use of genetic engineering to make biological weapons. And the distinguished British journal of science *Nature* (which first published the Watson–Crick article on the structure of the DNA molecule in 1954) reported on June 24, 1982, that "The U.S. Army is planning a substantial expansion in its biological warfare program, and may be particularly interested in the potential role of recombinant DNA in the development of biological weapons." According to the *Nature* report, the army has requested hundreds of millions of dollars for classified work on biological weaponry. As always, the research would be classified under the protections of national security, with no possibility of the U.S. public ever knowing the nature of the research or how their money was being spent. It is clearly symbolic of the current state of affairs that funding for basic research and development related to biological warfare increased 60 times between 1981 and 1986, under the Reagan–Bush administration.[14]

Patents Pending

On June 16, 1980, in the case of *Diamond v. Chakrabarty*, the U.S. Supreme Court ruled (by a 5–4 decision) that live, laboratory-modified microorganisms were now subject to patent under the federal law. Until that decision, living creatures (excepting for a few plant forms) had been excluded from the provisions of patent law through the common understanding that living things are part of the public domain and belong to the heritage of the entire society. If this legal precedent holds, however, patent requests on genetically modified plant and animal life may become commonplace.

The Court's decision has not been well received by much of the scientific community. Sometimes we forget that plant, animal, and microbial life forms—because of their interrelationships with one another and with the environment—provide the necessary biological foundation for the development of all communities—including human society. Accordingly, they are far too important—if only in terms of human health, prosperity, and survival—to be the property of corporations and modified according to the narrow interests of the profit makers.

Also, like most of science these days, genetic engineering has been developed at the expenditure of billions of taxpayer dollars. The idea of private profits being made through special-interest utilization of public funds brings to mind many great questions of scientific and corporate ethics. As Senator Albert Gore stated in congressional testimony in June 1981, the new research agreements of private enterprise are simply "skimming off the cream produced by decades of taxpayer funded work." And although two-thirds of all basic research in this country is now carried on under federal grants, the public sector continues to be totally excluded from any participation in scientific decision-making. Given the investment of public funds in genetic research, the benefits of the technology developed should by rights be shared equitably and the old distributional gaps of income and power narrowed in the process. Unhappily, the *Chakrabarty* decision guarantees enormous profits to industries able to receive such patents and makes distributive justice in science seem less likely than ever. Corporate control of the biosciences is now only the tip of the iceberg.

> In fact, what is now emerging throughout the corporate sector in the U.S., Europe and Japan is a new, unprecedented institution of economic and political power: the multi-faceted, transnational life sciences conglomerate—a huge company that will use genes to fashion life-necessity products just as earlier corporate powers used land, minerals, or oil.[15]

This new ability of the companies to patent genetic research also virtually guarantees a change in the customary flow of information between researchers. Scientific productivity has usually been enhanced by a free exchange of data. Now, under the rules of proprietary interest, this free exchange will become increasingly difficult. With all of the billions of dollars at stake, the new biotechnology raises enormously complicated questions for the major research institutions in this country. In some ways, molecular biology—traditionally but one dimension of the research task of the university—has become the tail that wags the dog. All throughout the United States, the tendency in academia for the past decade has been to give absolute priority to molecular and recombinant research. The reason is simple.

Much federal and private grant money is now geared in this direction. The word is out on campus that employment in the field of biology is directly related to one's ability to clone! Sheldon Krimsky, environmental policy expert and member of the original NIH rDNA advisory board, states the problem precisely:

> Many biologists . . . are being courted by companies specifically to provide . . . industrial uses for microorganisms. Among those biologists whose areas of expertise are not commercially marketable, envy has become infectious. Meanwhile, the species of molecular biologists who are able to augment their academic salaries but choose to remain devoted to pure science is becoming extinct. A gold rush mentality is permeating academic biology. The psychological dimensions of this mood are not difficult to comprehend. "There's big bucks to be made and if I don't make it, somebody else will." Already rumors abound about: graduate students and postdocs who feel abandoned by entrepreneurial senior scientists; a restricted flow of information and new microbial strains between scientific colleagues; professors with industry ties grooming students for private sector biotechnology as opposed to academic positions; research topics developing around monetary rather than intellectual rewards.[16]

Clearly, the passion for quick profits has prompted genetic engineering companies to try to adapt the environment to the needs of industry, rather than industry to the needs of at least people. European researchers, for example, are attempting to gene-manipulate trees into withstanding what apparently will be ever higher and higher doses of acid rain. Social dislocations can also occur from good science being used in a culturally disruptive fashion. U.S. biotech companies are now producing a natural vanilla flavor that has the potential to eliminate the market for vanilla beans, which currently provide the sole income for 70,000 vanilla growers in Madagascar. A host of other ventures of this type are under way that will produce corporate profits but have a major negative impact on people in developing countries.

Science for People or Science for Profit

As noted especially in Chapter 4, the introduction of new technologies into unjust societies has always tended to exacerbate the gap between rich and poor. This has been true both between nation-states (as when wealthy, center economies bring new technologies into raw material–

Table 7.1   Third World Needs and the New Biotechnologies

Basic Need	Potential Contribution of New Biotechnologies	Dominant Research of Biotech Industry
Conservation and improvement of diverse poor people's crops emphasizing hardiness, nutrition, and yield.	Crop production. Tissue culture technology could support conservation and breeding objectives.	Rather than pest resistance the focus is on gene transfer for pesticide resistance, encapsulated embryos, and yield improvement for major crops only.
Key concerns are durability, nutrition, and cost. Product and production should be culturally and environmentally sensitive, making the best use of local resources.	Food processing. Improvement of traditional fermentation methods and development of new possibilities.	Focus is on reducing or substituting raw materials and the factory production of agricultural products.
Conserve diversity and broaden breeding efforts for foraging animals to develop healthier, more efficient livestock. Develop multipurpose domesticates.	Animal husbandry. Vaccines and diagnostics can support these efforts, and embryo transfer can help preserve diversity.	Attention is on complete control over fertility and reproduction to develop high-yielding, uniform, but highly vulnerable breeds and also on veterinarial packages and on use of livestock as bioreactors for drugs.
Best way to improve health is to eliminate poverty. Following that, preventive health care focusing on improved sanitation, nutrition, and drinking water. Next, new vaccines for tropical diseases and AIDS.	Health care. Biotechnologies could help with monoclonal anti bodies for water testing and gene technology for vaccine research and production.	Emphasis is on diagnostics and clinical assays, help against infertility, production of hormones and drugs related to aging, cancer, AIDS, heart disease, and organ transplants and gene therapy.

Source: Cary Fowler, Eva Lachkovics, Pat Mooney, and Hope Shand, "The Laws of Life: Another Development and the New Biotechnologies," *Development Dialogue* 1/2 (1988), p. 51; slight editorial changes made; reprinted with permission.

Table 7.2   The Green and Gene Revolutions Compared

Green Revolution	Gene Revolution
Summary	
• Based in public sector	• Based in private sector
• Humanitarian intent	• Profit motive
• Centralized R&D	• Centralized R&D
• Focus on yield	• Focus on inputs/processing
• Relatively gradual	• Relatively immediate
• Emphasis on major cereals	• Affects all species
Objective	
– To feed the hungry and cool Third World political tensions by increasing food yields with fertilizers and seeds	– To contribute to profit by increasing input and/or processor efficiencies
For whom	
– The poor	– The shareholder and management
By whom	
– 830 scientists working in 8 institutes reporting to U.S. foundations	– In the U.S. alone, 1,127 scientists working for 30 agbiotech companies
– Industrialized countries	
– Quasi-UN bodies	
How	
– Plant breeding in wheat, maize, rice	– Genetic manipulation of all plants, all animals, microorganisms
Primary targets	
– Semi-dwarf capacity in cereals	– Herbicide tolerance
– Responses to fertilizers	– Natural substitution
	– Factory production
Investment	
– $108 million for agricultural R&D (1988)	– Agbiotech R&D investment of $144 million in U.S. (1988) by 30 companies
General impact	
– Substantial but gradual	– Enormous—sometimes immediate
– 52.9 percent of Third World wheat and rice (123 million hectares)	– $20 billion in medicinal and flavor/fragrance crops at risk
– "500 million would not otherwise be fed"	– Multibillion-dollar beverage, confectionery, sugar, and vegetable-oils trade could be lost

cont'd

Impact on farmers
- Access to seeds and inputs uneven
- Small farmers lose land to larger farmers
- New varieties improve yield but increase risk
- Reduced prices

- Increased production costs
- Loss of some crops to factory farms
- Input/processing efficiencies increase farmer risk
- Overproduction and materials diversification

Impact on farms
- Soil erosion due to heavy use of crop chemicals
- Genetic erosion due to replacement of traditional varieties
- Species loss due to overplanting of traditional crops with maize, wheat, or rice
- Pressure on water resources due to irrigation
- Deforestation

- Continuation and possible acceleration of green revolution effects, plus:
- Release of potentially uncontrollable new organisms into the environment
- Genetic erosion of animals and microorganisms
- Biological warfare on economically important crops

Impact on consumption
- Decline in use of high-value "poor people's foods"
- Export of food out of region

- Emphasis on feeding the rich yuppie market
- Increased use of chemical and biological toxins

Economic implications
- Direct contribution of $10 billion p/a to Third World food production
- Indirect contribution of $50–60 billion
- Gene flow to U.S. alone contributing to farmers' sales of $2 billion p/a for wheat, rice, and maize

- Contribution to seed production of $12.1 billion p/a by year 2000
- Contribution to agriculture of $50 billion p/a by year 2000
- Absorb benefit of gene flow from the Third World

Political implications
- National breeding program curtailed
- Third World agriculture Westernized
- Germ-plasm benefits usurped
- Dependency

- System geared to corporate interests
- Genetic raw materials and technologies controlled by genetics supply industry through patents

Source: Cary Fowler, Eva Lachkovics, Pat Mooney, and Hope Shand, "The Laws of Life: Another Development and the New Biotechnologies," *Development Dialogue* 1/2 (1988), pp. 62–63; slight editorial changes made; reprinted with permission.

producing countries just to produce profits for repatriation) and between classes in developing nations (as in the export of military technologies and nuclear power from industrial nations to the dependent economies). The best example of this is the "green revolution" that followed World War II. Western scientists developed innovative technologies in plant breeding and agricultural machinery that led to substantial increases in cereal grain production in many areas of Asia, Africa, and Latin America. Unhappily, these green revolution technologies led to even further gaps between rich and poor in the developing world, since only the wealthy farmers could afford to pay for the new technological innovations (fertilizers, pesticides, and tractors). Poor farmers were forced to sell their land to the rich farmers, and the spiral of inequality was further accelerated. The intentions of the green revolution were essentially good, but the results were mixed. Far more controversial, however, has been the move from green revolution to "gene revolution."

> The public sector's Green Revolution has been superceded by the private sector's Gene Revolution—with little recollection on anyone's part of the socioeconomic lessons learned during the Green Revolution. Further, the new revolution has created an atmosphere of confusion and uncertainty about the future of agriculture. As the new age of biotechnology unfolds, two forces are competing for control of agriculture—the suppliers of agricultural inputs and the food processors.[17]

When one compares the real needs of Third World peoples with the prospective contributions and research directions of the biotech industries—as shown in Table 7.1—the reality gap is clearly revealed.[18]

Similarly, when one contrasts the green revolution with the gene revolution, the latter makes the former look relatively benign. Whereas green revolution technology was concentrated in the hands of eight semipublic international centers, the gene revolution is concentrated in the leading industrial countries and totally controlled by private industry. Table 7.2 compares the two.[19]

Already rocked by the substitution of petrochemical synthetics for natural fibers, Third World economies are now threatened even more by new kinds of substitutions made possible by the genetic engineers. Some examples of the extent to which biotechnology and genetic engineering are focusing on the welfare of the rich and developed nations illustrate the point.

> Cacao is one of the most important agricultural crops produced in the developing world with Africa now accounting for 57% of total world

production. Companies in the U.S., Europe and Japan, however, are now working on ways to produce cocoa butter in the laboratory using biotechnology. When commercialized, the substitution of biotechnology for human labor will devastate the lives of millions of Africans involved in cacao production.

Biotech companies in the U.S. and Europe are now using genetic engineering to produce thaumatin protein which is normally derived from a West African plant. Thaumatin is thousands of time sweeter than sugar and when produced in the lab for commercial distribution has the potential to destroy the livelihood of 8–10 million people now involved in sugar production in the Third World.

Private companies in Germany, in consort with major universities, are studying 29 bioengineered compounds which have the potential for eliminating food industry dependence on the agricultural crop production of food flavors.

Green *nori* seaweed, traditionally grown in Asia, is now produced on nylon mats in America due to the discovery of a new cloning process. The impact on this traditional $600 million overseas industry will be great.[20]

What now seems to be certain is that the gene revolution will not benefit most sectors of the international agricultural community. As usual, science tends to be more interested in profits than in people.

Policy and Regulation

The history of scientific development in general shows a distinct tendency for those in power to seek to control all information either presently beneficial to them or of possible future use in maintaining and extending their power. As our ability to manipulate genetic material increases, so will the pressure to use the new technologies for reinforcement of the existing class structure of the society. As we learn how to bioengineer new products considered necessary for profitability by corporate hierarchies, or how to increase human intelligence via gene therapy, it will become even more difficult to constrain the powers that be. The well-heeled plans of government, industry, and the scientific community represent a crushing coalition of forces. The issue, then—the only hope of providing any kind of long-range protection for the citizenry—is in the arena of public policy.

What now seems incontrovertible is the need to provide increasingly effective means of public involvement in determining both the priorities for and the control of the research task in the United States. Scientists fall prey to the temptation to "generalize their expertise"— feeling that, since they know what to do in the laboratory, they should also be free to establish all of the policies that would guide and evaluate their work. Historically, this has been actual practice. To the extent that science has been regulated, it has been self-regulated (i.e., by the scientific community itself and by those who control the funding of research).

While the NIH Recombinant-DNA Advisory Committee (RAC) and the 17 other federal agencies involved within the coordinated framework have recently been making an honest effort to regulate biotechnology and recombinant research in the United States, very little effective control has come of it. Technically illegal recombinant research has been performed on university campuses for years now, with impunity. And although it is correct to place the primary emphasis on federal guidelines, local communities must also be involved in the supervision and regulation of both research and product application. Since privately funded industrial research has heretofore never been subject to strict governmental guidelines, local watchdogs may be necessary to ensure that a careful and thorough job of monitoring be done. Certain communities have in fact developed local guidelines for monitoring recombinant research (Cambridge, Massachusetts; and Berkeley, California), and the Massachusetts Public Health Association has developed a model ordinance to assist local communities in drafting appropriate regulatory procedures.

Implicitly, the possibility of unwanted and unexpected evolutionary impacts on human beings hangs over us when we are dealing with the funding and regulation of such research. Species lines, as noted earlier, have always been seen as natural protective barriers that should not be circumvented, even if they could. Futhermore, the growing concern about reduction of the gene variants in a population—an inevitable corollary of molecular genetics as weaker or less desirable strains are weeded out—raises other long-range considerations. Diffused and complex genetic strains, rather than simplified ones, are thought to be evolutionarily preferable (the heterozygote advantage) for species lines. Efforts to simplify and/or standardize the gene pool may well have tragic consequences in the long run.

Given the understanding of science enunciated earlier—that is, that the nature of the scientific endeavor is almost totally dependent on the questions posed and the funds provided by large government or corporate organizations—it will be difficult even with a good regulatory apparatus to control genetic research. The questions raised by such research regarding our human responsibilities and obligations to the larger community will never be answered adequately by the scientific practitioners themselves. The history of science in the twentieth century proves this point again and again.

Accordingly, ordinary people should constantly be raising questions regarding the allocation and distribution of scientific resources. The President's Commission for the Study of Ethical Problems has stated,

> As new technological capabilities raise the standard of normal functioning or adequate health, the scarcity of societal resources may raise anew the very difficult question that theorists of distributive justice have strongly disagreed about: where does justice to future generations end and generosity begin? This question is of vital practical import, for the demands of justice are characteristically thought of as valid claims or entitlements to be enforced by the coercive power of the state, while generosity is usually regarded as a private virtue.[21]

Who pays for such technology and who benefits from it are questions that demand our attention. Without adequate public safeguards, both the cost and direction of molecular genetics may reinforce and even worsen our existing social, cultural, and democratic inequalities. And in fact, a survey conducted by the National Science Foundation discovered that two-thirds of the U.S. people have doubts about further studies in genetic engineering.

Public policy objectives must be formulated that both regulate the industry and also incorporate the lay community into the decision-making process. The following policy guidelines of the Bogeve seminar sum up well the concern for more adequate regulation of genetic engineering:

- Biotechnology shall always be regarded as a tool, not an aim in itself.
- If the potential impact of a biotechnological innovation turns out to be detrimental to society or to the environment, other measures should be sought.
- If the impact assessment of an innovation seems benign, society must still determine if the innovation will divert resources or expertise from more important tasks.

• The release of genetically altered organisms into the environment should be undertaken only after the most careful assessment of environmental impact.

• Genetic manipulations of higher organisms should not be regarded as methods of first choice.

• Genetic manipulations involving human beings should be subject to broad public debate and probably regulation and restriction.

• Reproductive technologies in human beings must also undergo broad public debate, keeping in mind cultural and religious feelings and the necessity of not exploiting women.

• Biotechnological diagnostic and screening techniques should be monitored to avoid abuse, discrimination, and racist application.

• The conservation, utilization, and improvement of genetic resources and genetic diversity must not be hindered or endangered by biotechnological innovation.

• Biotechnological research that results in significant or unnecessary torment of animals should not be allowed.

• Research projects imported from another country shall not be carried out if banned in the country of origin.

• Research projects using public monies must prove that the aim is to benefit the majority of the people, and that the project will harm neither the people nor the environment in the vicinity.

• Researchers must abide by all relevant laboratory and experimentation safety regulations—for example, the recommendations of the Office of Economic Cooperation and Development (OECD) of the United Nations.

• The socioeconomic impact of biotechnology on poor people, small farmers, and small business should be given special consideration.

• Whenever government establishes agencies to regulate any dimension of the genetic engineering process, it must include on such agencies equal numbers of experts and lay representatives to ensure that both the perspectives of science and the public welfare are protected.[22]

The difficulty rests not in defining such principles but in actually formulating the policymaking mechanisms to enforce them. Policymaking and the correlative development of regulatory agencies in the United States has essentially been a matter of asking those institutions that society says need to be regulated to themselves establish the guidelines under which they are to be regulated. The decentralization of much environmental regulation in the United States (wherein the federal government essentially delegates to the states the implementation and enforcement of federal law and policy) will be ineffective in providing for effective management of laboratory or environmental research in the recombinant fields. Altered and genetically modified life forms are simply too different from other kinds of pollution to be so similarly regulated. Unhappily, the federal government has no intention at this time of establishing any separate bureau or superagency to monitor rDNA research and development. Unlike most items subject to governmental regulation, the issue here is control not so much over the products to be developed, but at least equally over the techniques to be employed in production.

The EPA has now asserted jurisdiction over all microorganisms that are not pesticides (which remain under the regulatory supervision of other agencies), under the Toxic Substances Control Act (TSCA). EPA's assumption is that genetically modified organisms fall within the chemical-definition standards of TSCA, and believes it is thus the agency best equipped to monitor and regulate such organisms. Recognizing that genetically modified organisms are at least to some degree unique, the EPA has proposed a new decentralized structure to assess risk/benefit factors in regulating field releases of new organisms, much like the existing local Industrial Biosafety Committees that regulate research. Unfortunately, however, each institution to be regulated—company or university—would form its own Environmental Biosafety Committee (EBC) to regulate itself. The history of all previous efforts at self-regulation in research shows that such groupings become basically rubber stamps for their own institution.

Realistically, it is now certain that the federal government does not intend to create a special agency or agencies to monitor and regulate either the research and development or the environmental releases of new genetically altered organisms. This does not mean, however, that it should be constrained in developing special mechanisms *within existing agencies* to accomplish these tasks. Certainly the lead agency in regulation will be the EPA. But the EPA should not have its hands tied by having to treat biotechnological research and field testing under antiquated and inappropriate toxic-substances regulation. The very minimum that a skeptical public must demand is the formulation of new policy mechanisms—rules and regulations—to guide both research and releases of genetically altered organisms by both private biotechnology companies and universities.

Neither recombinant science itself nor the social implications of the science can be confined within traditional categories of policy or ethics. Recombinant organisms are qualitatively different from products developed in earlier historical periods. Production techniques are absolutely unique and thus require special regulatory oversight and care. For one thing, as genetically engineered changes become more and more commonplace, there may be a tendency among people in power to identify social problems as genetic deficiencies of certain individuals or groups. The only guaranteed ways by which society can control the new science and technology are a continued commitment to individual rights, the further institution of federal and local controls on research and development, and a renewed vigor in alerting the public to both the promises and the perils in genetic engineering. As the President's Commission for the Study of Ethical Problems has forcefully noted,

> Like the tale of the Sorcerer's apprentice, or the myth of the Golem created from lifeless dust, . . . the story of Dr. Frankenstein's monster serves as a reminder of the difficulty of restoring order if a creation intended to be helpful proves harmful instead. Indeed, each of these tales conveys a painful irony: in seeking to extend their control over the world, people may lessen it. The artifices they create to do their bidding may rebound destructively against them—the slave may become the master.[23]

Notes

1. Lewis Thomas, "The Hazards of Medicine," *New England Journal of Medicine* 296 (February 10, 1977), pp. 324–26.

2. *Splicing Life,* report of the President's Commission for the Study of Ethical Problems in Medicine and Biomedical and Behavioral Research, November 1982, p. I-1.

3. Cary Fowler, Eva Lachkovics, Pat Mooney, and Hope Shand, "The Laws of Life: Another Development and the New Biotechnologies," *Development Dialogue* 1/2 (1988), p. 49.

4. J. D. Watson and J. Tooze, *The DNA Story* (San Francisco: W. H. Freeman, 1981).

5. C. Keith Boone, "When Scientists Go Public with Their Doubts," *Hastings Journal* 12, no. 6 (December 1982), p. 13.

6. Ibid.

7. Susan Wright, "Hazards and Controls in rDNA," *Environment* (July 1982); and Stuart A. Newman, "The Scientific Selling of rDNA," *Environment* (July 1982).

8. Ibid., pp. 56–57.

9. Scott D. Deatherage, "Scientific Uncertainty in Regulating Deliberate Release of Genetically Engineered Organisms," *Harvard Environmental Law Review* 11, no. 1 (1987), p. 234.

10. John H. Gibbons, ed., "New Developments in Biotechnology: Field Testing Engineered Organisms: Genetic and Ecological Issues," U.S. Congress, Office of Technology Assessment, document OTA-BA-350 (Washington, D.C.: U.S. Government Printing Office, May 1988).

11. Carl A. Larson, "Ethnic Weapons," *Military Review* 50, no. 11 (April 1970), p. 3.

12. Leonard A. Cole, *Clouds of Secrecy: The Army's Germ Warfare Tests over Populated Areas* (Totowa, N.J.: Rowman and Littlefield, 1988).

13. Charles Piller and Keith R. Yamamoto, *Gene Wars: Military Control over the New Genetic Technologies* (New York: Beech Tree Books, 1988).

14. "Reagan's Biowarfare Research Budget," *Bioscience* 137, no. 6 (June 1987), p. 372.

15. Jack Doyle, editorial in *Catholic Rural Life* (November 1987), p. 11.

16. Sheldon Krimsky, "The University: Marketing Theories, Not Toothpaste," *Environment* (July 1982), p. 46.

17. Fowler et al., "Laws of Life," p. 60.

18. Ibid., p. 51.

19. Ibid., pp. 62–63.

20. Ibid., p. 66.

21. *Splicing Life*, p. III-9.

22. In addition to these summary comments from the Bogeve Conference Declaration in Fowler et al., "Laws of Life, " pp. 226–28, note also the draft model law, "The Biotechnology Safety and Environmental Protection Act," in ibid., pp. 233–36.

23. *Splicing Life*, p. III-19.

8

Genetic Counseling

Genetic engineers are enormously optimistic about their long-range ability to understand and one day to solve many of humankind's oldest ills. As Galileo explored the heavens and Columbus charted Earth's physical parameters, the molecular geneticists are by and large similarly convinced that their explorations of the genes of living creatures are uniformly good and proper, and will be of ultimate benefit to humankind. As this chapter will suggest, that optimism may not be so well founded.

At the beginning of this fourth decade since the discovery of the double helix of DNA, genetic screening is being lauded as one of the most hopeful and practical tools available to the molecular engineer. Its purpose is to identify a variety of genetic diseases and, to the extent diagnostic skills permit, either cure them or at least minimize their impact. Current techniques in genetic screening include programs of different types:

1. to identify carriers of heritable diseases like sickle-cell anemia, Tay-Sachs disease, and phenylketonuria or PKU;
2. to determine whether an unborn child has been affected by negative genetic characteristics carried by the parents through testing procedures like amniocentesis;
3. to provide genetic testing programs and therapies for the newborn;
4. to develop genetic counseling services for prospective parents, informing them as to whether or not they may be carriers of genetic disease and about their options to deal with this reality if it exists; and
5. as R&D efforts within the science progress, to enable actual cell alteration via genetic therapies to erase the possibility of the transference of heritable disorders.

Earlier, we noted the extent to which scientists have learned some of the secrets of the genetic control system in the human being and its ability to turn genes on and off in accord with the chemical signals of the body. Aberrations in the nucleotide sequence in DNA regularly cause mutations with consequences that can lead to lives of pain and deformity, or to death. With thousands of human diseases now recognized as the direct result of a single abnormality in the blueprint pattern of a single gene, medical geneticists are able to identify and diagnose a variety of such problems long before birth. Although little can currently be done to prevent or cure most of these genetic abnormalities, the ability to recognize and understand the causes can at least give prospective parents, as an example, information and options never before available.

One of the primary clues assisting scientists in trying to solve some of the genetic riddles has been the discovery of what have been called "marker" genes. The principles that enabled geneticists first to discover and then to use genetic signposts is relatively simple. As we know, many diseases have components embedded in the structure of the DNA. Once these distinctive marker genes have been identified for a particular disease (through genetic analysis programs like amniocentesis), the way is open to test individuals through routine chromosome scans for the distinguishing genetic characteristics, find out who is susceptible to particular diseases, and then try to do something about them. With time, more and more of DNA's genetic "prophets" (as ethicist Marc Lappe calls them) will be discovered.

As always, however, the benign possibilities of the new genetic technologies make up only one side of the coin. These manipulations performed by scientists also have their darker side. The traditional problems of professional control and dominance over sophisticated new technologies apply in this field as in all others. As Harvard biologist Ruth Hubbard has said,

> The more sophisticated a technology and the more training and skill it requires, the more likely it is to be controlled by elites, to increase inequalities, and to reinforce hierarchies. Those who are able to use it of necessity know more about it, and hence, have more power over its use than the people on whom it is used. When thinking about medical technologies, we must also take into account that . . . most scientists and physicians are part of the social and economic elite. The great majority is male and white. . . . Therefore scientists and physicians are an elite not only in knowledge but also in terms of the other variables that shape the pyramid of power in this society.[1]

Given the reality that most genetic counseling and therapy involves the reproductive systems of women, some of the implications of the manipulation of genes and embryos require special attention. We will explore the pluses and minuses of these developments in the remainder of this chapter.

Genetic Screening: The Identification of Genetic Disease

The first mass screening program in the United States—begun in 1962—was an effort to identify newborns with the genetic disease phenylketonuria (PKU), a rare recessive genetic trait in which the child inherits one defective gene from each parent. PKU leads to irreversible mental retardation and, like many genetic diseases, is linked to particular population groupings. Normally, only children born to parents of Northern European descent are affected. Happily, a simple, inexpensive, and usually accurate test can be administered to newborns as early as the third day after birth to determine whether or not they have the disease. Dietary treatment has been effective in therapy by simply removing certain proteins from the nutritional intake of the child. Not without controversy (since neither the testing nor the treatment has been quite as accurate as was first envisioned), the process has nonetheless been enormously beneficial to thousands of families. PKU screening is now mandated by statute in all but three states. Unhappily, adequate follow-up medical services have not always been provided by public health agencies, nor efforts made to deal with the physical and psychological disruptions to families occasioned by the complicated procedures required to maintain PKU-affected patients.

Another major screening program during the early 1970s—one long demanded by leaders of the Black community in the United States—was for sickle-cell anemia. Based to some degree on the earlier success of the PKU program, the test for sickle-cell could not, however, distinguish between those who actually had the disease and those who simply carried the genetic tendency or trait. This long-awaited and initially much heralded program came back to haunt its early advocates. As screening programs were established, those identified as carriers of the trait were sometimes discriminated against by organizations that had made certain requirements (and assumptions) about "perfect" health for their candidates (e.g., the U.S. military academies) and were simply unaware of the fact that trait carriers do not have the disease itself.

An integral part of any screening program for any genetically based disease must be to help affected persons in considering alternative options for both parenting and treatment. Unhappily, however, little assistance has been available so far. Parents are too often forced to play genetic roulette after a negative diagnosis. Should they choose to have the child and simply hope for the best—that the child will not develop the disease? Should pregnant women who are carriers of the sickle-cell trait, for example, abort their fetuses? Many persons affected by sickle-cell have relatively minor health problems, though for some it is a terribly debilitating disease. Follow-up counseling after the screening-program diagnosis should complete the medical analysis, but seldom does.

Like PKU, sickle-cell screening programs have also ended up in the legislative arena. Not always well informed about basic genetics and the distinction between having such a disease and simply carrying it, legislators in 12 states by the early 1970s had passed laws mandating sickle-cell screening programs. In many of those states, the law required screening before entry to school or in order to obtain a marriage license. That programs with such grave social implications could be so easily and quickly passed by state legislatures raises enormously important concerns. And when the programs are focused on persons or groups who have good historical reason to be suspicious of the intentions of the dominant classes in the society, the problems of state-mandated screening are intensely magnified. The best intentions, without accurate information and analysis, can have bad effects. Although fetal blood tests for sickle-cell are now available, clear-cut choices still elude doctors and parents because of the great difference in severity of this disease among different persons.

Less controversial and of great help to prospective parents has been the Tay-Sachs screening program. A rare disease normally limited to Ashkenazi Jews of Eastern European descent (but also found occasionally in the Mediterranean), Tay-Sachs is a terrible affliction leading to blindness, paralysis, and inevitable death by the age of four. "There is no adequate treatment for the disease, but prenatal diagnosis makes possible identification of an affected fetus early enough for a legal abortion."[2] An autosomal recessive (both parents must be carriers before it is possible for a child to have the disease), with Tay-Sachs there is a one in four chance according to the rigid laws of genetics for any particular double-carrier pregnancy to result in an affected child. Parental decision-making is much less a matter of controversy in such screening programs than with sickle-cell, since Tay-Sachs children will live short and painful lives, while sickle-cell children often lead essentially normal lives. But since only one in four children born to parents carrying the defective gene will in fact have the disease, even here the decision to abort is painful for most parents.

Inevitably, mass screening programs are a cause for concern to both the people involved in the screening and the larger society. Since genetic information from large numbers of persons (both normal and carriers) are obtained, immense problems arise regarding confidentiality of the data, informed consent for procedures undertaken, and possible misuse of the information acquired. The subject of the screening program experiences a number of unanticipated psychological, medical, social, and ethical dilemmas. A research group from the Hastings Center for Bioethics has proposed a set of principles for guiding the operation of genetic screening programs. Their recommendations emphasize the need for well-planned objectives and clear and understandable goals.

> Although there are three distinguishable categories of goals that screening programs may serve, we believe that the most important goals are those that either contribute to improving the health of persons who suffer from genetic disorders, or allow carriers for a given variant gene to make informed choices regarding reproduction, or move toward alleviating the anxieties of families and communities faced with the prospect of serious genetic disease.[3]

Further explicating these goals, the Hastings group lists a number of concerns that must be considered by any genetic screening program.

1. Screening programs must benefit individuals and families by providing information to couples who may be at risk for transmitting a genetic disease.

2. Serious attempts must be made, through the screening process, to acquire knowledge about particular genetic diseases.

3. Caution must be exercised in initiating any program to reduce the incidence of apparently deleterious genes, since the means needed to achieve such an objective must be seen as morally and practically acceptable to the subject group itself. As the Hastings group understands,

Virtually everyone carries a small number of deleterious lethal recessive genes, and to reduce the frequency of a particular recessive gene to near the level maintained by recurrent mutation, most or all persons heterozygous for that gene would have to either refrain from procreation entirely or to monitor all their offspring in utero and abort not only affected homozygote (affected) fetuses but also the larger number of heterozygote carriers for the gene.[4]

The need for standards becomes ever more important as the prospects of a huge demand for genetic screening looms on the horizon. Increasingly today, parents express their fears of having defective children. Some of this concern is due to the ubiquity of environmental chemicals in the atmosphere that are mutagens (mutation causers), terratogens (causing disease in the fetus), or carcinogens (causing cancer). As the Presidential Ethics Committee noted, "Genetic screening and counseling are certain to become major components in both public health and individual medical care." The study then suggested the probability of a new and potentially terrifying reality for the average American.

The time can already be envisioned when all information about a person's abnormal genes and chromosomes will be readily accessible. . . . Mandatory screening is not justified as part of a program to produce a genetically healthy society or other vague and politically abusive social ideals. In the hands of repressive and exploitative political movements, such notions could be used to justify extreme eugenic measures.[5]

Molecular Genetics and Medicine

Given the new research techniques, it is now possible to engineer new capabilities into microorganisms for use as therapeutic or diagnostic agents. Although still in their infancy stage, such procedures are already being utilized. It is the process by which living cells work as protein factories—manufacturing materials that correspond to the genetic code active in the cell—that can be turned to human benefit. As we noted in Chapter 7, bacterial cells can be altered so that they will turn out the product encoded by a foreign gene that has been spliced into the plasmid of a bacterium. Relying on basic bacterial reproduction, great supplies of beneficial medical products can then potentially be harvested. Such methods are already being used to produce insulin and other hormones for treating diabetes and human growth problems. Hopefully, there will come the day when cancer may be similarly controlled. Already, the Genentech Corporation of South San Francisco, the largest commercial genetic-engineering firm in the world, has reproduced a powerful hormone that apparently seeks out dangerous cancer cells and destroys them. Called a lymphotoxin, the product is a natural part of the immune system and is able to distinguish between healthy and malignant cells, breaking down the cell membranes in the cancerous tissue. The Genentech engineers first determined the exact protein structure of the hormone and then constructed an artificial gene that was subsequently inserted into *E. coli* bacteria, which reproduced the lymphotoxin. The substance is yet in the early stages of testing. Breakthroughs in the production of vaccines are also projected for the near future, since genetic engineering can be used to produce pure viral components that are safer to use than the whole viruses currently used to immunize against diseases like polio and hepatitis.

Of longer range interest (and potentially of enormous consequence for the future of our species, as suggested above in the context of screening) is the possibility of treating human genetic disorders. Some 2,000 human disorders result from single-gene mutations. Since human cells can have as many as 100,000 genes, multigene disorders clearly present far greater therapeutic problems and may forever be removed from the possibility of treatment. Many single-gene disorders, however, may well someday be treated by gene therapy. The introduction of a normal gene, for example, into a cell in which its defective counterpart is active, or a kind of genetic surgery replacing an improper genetic sequence with a normal one, may soon lead to heretofore unheard of technologies. One illustration of the controversy surrounding such research, however, is the case of the medical researcher at the University of California in Los Angeles who removed bone marrow cells from patients suffering from betathalassemia (a rare blood and bone disease), mixed these cells with DNA coded for normal bone marrow functioning, and then reintroduced the new mixture into the patients. Although the new experimental procedure apparently neither helped nor hurt the patients, the UCLA institutional review board and the National Institutes of Health have now imposed sanctions on any further work in this field.

Many exciting alternative developments in gene therapy are now under way, however. In July 1990, after years of ethical and scientific debate, the Human Gene Therapy Subcommittee of the NIH Recombinant DNA Advisory Committee (RAC) approved plans by researchers to exploit rDNA technologies in order to implant a foreign gene into the blood cells of certain affected children in the hope that this will enable them to overcome an enzyme deficiency that destroys their immune systems. The same technique can be used to treat skin cancer in adults. Such gene transfers are expected to begin in the fall of 1990.

Mapping the Human Genome

Genetic researchers always envision the day when their new science might be used to treat genetic diseases and abnormalities on a large scale. Recently, the U.S. government decided to invest up to $3 billion ($200 million each year for 15 years) to map the complete human genome. Thus, it looks like the dream of the scientific community may soon be realized. Whether this will be entirely good for the human community remains to be seen.

The idea in the new gene hunt is first to identify and then to apply the secret messages hidden deep within the chemical codes of the gene. The genome (the complete genetic structure in DNA) contains a full set of instructions to create a human being (or any other form of life). These detailed directions can be found in the genetic nucleus of each of the body's 100 trillion cells. Of the 100,000 genes in the human genome, only 4,500 have ever been identified, and only 1,700 of these actually located on the chromosome. If the 15-year federally funded effort is completed, new avenues of research into gene therapy will undoubtedly open up.

Presumably, thousands of inherited diseases and disorders could be identified. Various forms of genetic intervention should then be possible. The new information will also foster the development of exotic pharmaceuticals, enabling treatment of diseases that heretofore were simply considered the uncommon but inevitable chance occurrences of a diverse gene pool. Already, for example, efforts are under way to transplant bacterial genes into cancer patients in order to monitor the progress of the disease and the effectiveness of the therapy.

But our technical skills may have already outpaced our actual ability to use all of the new information available. Just because scientists discover new techniques is no assurance that society really wants them. The diagnosis of a genetic predisposition to cancer or heart disease, for example, raises concerns about future job discrimination.

Most certainly, as such genetic information becomes more readily available, insurance companies will use it to screen applicants.

As we will examine later in more detail, this expected removal of our genetic fig leaf raises a host of new moral dilemmas. Once the gene scientists have determined the "norm" for a human being, will we at some point attempt to reconstitute all persons who do not conform to this standard? With the ubiquity of data storage and retrieval, what will be the consequences for an individual flagged as a carrier of an undesirable genetic trait? How many of us really want to have our genetic histories programmed into computer banks controlled by government and industry? Since today the most basic health care—food, sanitation, disease control—is not available to even half the global population, it is clear that gene therapy (like all other exotic medical procedures) will be available only to the richest of the rich in the world. Those who are enthusiastic about the possibilities of changing the course of human heredity must understand that they will also be changing the course of human destiny. In the past, most efforts to perfect the species have ended up doing more harm than good. Our human arrogance wears many guises.

The already common in-vitro or test-tube-baby fertilization presents in itself remarkable new possibilities for genetic therapy on reproductive cells. Since it has the potential for affecting future generations, it is enormously controversial. By introducing normal genes into the in-vitro fertilized egg of a couple with a heritable disease, the child resulting from such a conception would be made free of the disease. Any such alteration of the gene pool in order to erase negative characteristics is a form of eugenics. A concept popularized by Francis Galton in the late nineteenth century, eugenics is based on the Greek word *eugenēs,* which means essentially to be wellborn. It signifies, in Galton's words, "the improvement of the human race by better breeding." What with all of our twentieth-century experimentation in behavioral eugenics (attempting to influence behavior through better breeding practices—e.g., sterilization of mental defectives and otherwise "unfit" persons) and the controlled breeding practices of the Third Reich to create a super-race, many thoughtful people today are skeptical about any renewed investigation into eugenics, no matter where it takes place. In 1982, the Council of Europe, recalling other efforts in this century to create a new eugenics, requested "explicit recognition in the Human Rights Convention of the human right to a genetic inheritance which has not been interfered with . . . except in accordance with principles which are recognized as being fully compatible with respect for human rights."[6] Recombinant-DNA procedures in reproductive-cell biology clearly open up enormous possibilities for both positive and potentially destructive social change.

Prenatal Screening Programs

Of all the recent developments in molecular biology, one of the most practical is that of prenatal diagnosis. Physicians report a 50-fold increase in the past five years in requests for such services. Although few prenatal diagnoses were undertaken before the 1960s, new techniques for chromosomal and biochemical analysis of amni-otic-fluid cells have been developed since then. (Sonic imaging or ultrasound—while not a genetic therapy—enables the visualization of internal tissue by a sonarlike instrument that maps the fetus on a picture tube. The process is simpler and safer in allowing medical staff to note certain characteristics of the fetus. It is of only limited value in assaying genetic disease.) Prenatal genetic screening tests are now widely utilized. Hundreds of abnormalities can be diagnosed in the womb.[7]

Amniocentesis—a simple procedure wherein approximately two-thirds of an ounce of amniotic fluid is withdrawn from the uterus at some point usually between the fourteenth and the twentieth weeks of pregnancy—can detect dozens of fetal abnormalities. Most of the requests for amniocentesis since it was first clinically introduced in 1966 have been due to parental anxieties about the possibility of the fetus being affected with Down's syndrome (mongolism), certain metabolic diseases, Tay-Sachs, and other brain and spinal-cord mal-formations. Cystic fibrosis and sickle-cell anemia are now also subject to amniotic-fluid analysis. Since amniotic fluid contains significant numbers of living body cells from the fetus, the fluid can be mixed with a nutrient tissue-culture solution and incubated at normal body temperature. Fetal cells will then multiply and, after about four weeks, can be analyzed chromosomally to determine any recognized bio-chemical abnormality.

There is a certain amount of risk involved in the procedure, although miscarriage rates after amniocentesis appear to be only slightly higher than normal rates at this period of pregnancy. Some risk does accrue from the danger of striking the fetus with the needle used to withdraw the amniotic fluid. Even when this occurs, though, the skin of the fetus is usually only slightly scarred as a result.

Concern has also been expressed that there may be long-range effects on the fetus due to lowering the intrauterine pressure in withdrawal of the fluid. The issue has not yet been subjected to hard analysis since data are so limited. In 1986, Laurence Karp came to this tentative conclusion:

> If we add up all the actual and theoretical risks of amniocentesis, we arrive at a total risk figure of approximately 0.5 percent. Admittedly, this is a "soft" figure, since, so far, only a few thousand taps have been performed and then reported in the medical literature. . . . The performance of diagnostic amniocentesis is certainly reasonable when the risk of diagnosable disease is one percent or higher.[8]

During the past decade, a new method of obtaining fetal cells for analysis has been developed. Chorionic villi sampling (CVI) is usually performed between the ninth and eleventh weeks of pregnancy. A simple suction device is inserted through the vagina and cervix. When the edge of the placenta is reached, a few villi (placenta-forming cells) are extracted. Since it is not necessary in CVI to set up tissue cultures, the result of the test is available in a few days, in contrast to a delay of several weeks with amniocentesis. Although initially it seemed that the procedure might entail less risk to the fetus than amniocentesis and that it would soon be the method of choice in prenatal genetic testing, a few cases of spontaneous abortion following CVI in recent years have pushed doctors to more caution in recommending the procedure. Both tests—amniocentesis and CVI—appear to be reasonably safe. Neither of these enormously helpful diagnostic tools should be used for any but the most serious reasons, however, because of the dangers involved for both mother and fetus. Genetic counseling following identification of a major chromosomal or other genetic abnormality inevitably poses the question of abortion. Prenatal diagnosis should be directed toward the end goals of saving fetal lives as well as providing parents with the choice of determining whether or not the risks in bringing a seriously handicapped child to full term are warranted.

One of the most controversial aspects of genetic screening procedures is the use of the tests for fetal sex identification. Many parents need to know the sex of their child because of the possibility of sex-linked hereditary disorders. Some, however, utilize the prenatal screening tests strictly in order to discover the sex of the fetus. The debate over using fetal sex identification for selective abortion heated up in the 1990 California Democratic primary race for governor. Each candidate (Dianne Feinstein and John Van de Kamp)—not wishing to alienate huge blocks of voters—sought to straddle the fence on the issue. Under massive pressure from both pro- and anti-choice lobbies, the two candidates finally agreed that, yes, they found nothing wrong with the use of such screening by those who wished selectively to abort an unwanted fetus. One suspects, however, that the votes the candidates gained from their visibly opportunistic effort to please the majority of the voters may well have been worth less than their loss of political credibility among people who felt repugnance over the casual way the issue was handled. Selective abortion based strictly on the sex of the fetus is opposed even by many people who are otherwise unreservedly pro-choice.

Legally, a woman does not have to state her reason for early abortion. In the 1973 *Roe v. Wade* decision (reaffirmed since by the Supreme Court, but under assault once again in 1989–90), the courts protected any woman's right to decide, with the advice of a physician, to have an abortion. If the physician agrees that an abortion performed at that time would be safer than childbirth normally is (statistically assessed as sometime within the first trimester of pregnancy), the state may not interfere with the woman's decision. Only when the fetus becomes viable—that is, capable of life outside the womb—can the state prohibit abortion. With the advent of sophisticated neonatal facilities, this issue of viability has become more complicated than it was in 1973. But so long as the law says that a woman has the right to control her reproduction and has full rights of self-determination through the first trimester of pregnancy, abortion will be utilized for many reasons—some more and some less acceptable to persons other than the woman herself. Since the test results of amniocentesis are usually available only in the eighteenth to the twenty-fourth weeks of pregnancy—when the fetus is approaching or may have reached viability—many hospitals and physicians are declining to perform the procedure since they may end up with a live baby on their hands following abortion. Because late abortions are commonly performed only through induced labor (using either saline solution or prostaglandin) or dilation and evacuation (involving the psychologically stressful procedure of dismembering the fetus in the womb—a practice many physicians are unwilling to perform), the reality of our new ability to discover defects not long before birth has created an enormous moral dilemma for doctors. Says Dr. Richard Hausknect of New York's Mt. Sinai Hospital, "It makes us all schizophrenic. Nowadays we are asked to terminate a pregnancy that in two weeks doctors on the same floor are fighting to save."[9]

Happily, of the 1.6 million abortions performed in the United States in 1980, more than 90 percent were done within the first 12 weeks by the safe and simple procedure of suction curettage. Fewer than 13,000 abortions were performed later than the twenty-first week. Although only a relatively small number of fetuses survived these late procedures, the numbers are on the increase. Many hospitals—for both ethical and legal reasons—now refuse to perform abortions later than the twentieth week.

Fertilization in Vitro

Although not properly an issue of molecular biology or genetic engineering at this time (although it may be very soon), fertilization in vitro and the new era of the test-tube baby into which we have been ushered has its share of related ethical questions. The fertilization of an egg in vitro (literally, in a glass dish) is overall a rather simple procedure for the woman unable to conceive a child naturally. Once the complicated hormonal processes controlling the female reproductive cycle were understood, the actual steps in test-tube conception moved rapidly through development.

When the condition of the uterine wall is in its monthly state of readiness for pregnancy, an egg or, more commonly, eggs will be removed from the ovary by laparoscopy—a procedure requiring only a tiny incision into the abdominal wall—followed by aspiration. The eggs are placed in an environment conducive to fertilization and mixed with sperm. When an egg has been fertilized and has undergone cleavage, the tiny new zygote is then reintroduced into the uterus where, all things being equal, a normal pregnancy results.

Unhappily, all things are not always equal in attempts at in-vitro fertilization. Even under normal circumstances, conception is not that easy. Of each 100 eggs exposed to sperm through normal sexual intercourse, 84 are fertilized and only 69 actually implanted in the uterine wall. Thirty-seven of these survive to the sixth week of pregnancy, and 31 survive to birth. In the routine processes of everyday internal fertilization, therefore, at least 70 percent of the eggs are lost. The odds might be expected to increase enormously under conditions of in vitro, although for some women the procedure is their only hope for a successful pregnancy. In one study reported by Clifford Grobstein on 79 women who entered treatment, only 68 successfully underwent laparoscopy: 44 yielded properly mature eggs, with 32 cases of actual fertilization. Grobstein writes, "Four women became pregnant, of whom two carried the fetus to full term and two miscarried. . . . Moreover, the successful products of the procedure are still in their infancy, and it is possible that some long-term effects may yet be manifested."[10]

Utilizing in-vitro technology, British physicians announced in the summer of 1990 a new and successful screening system enabling them to weed out unwanted embryos and then implant those desired in the patient. Medical staff at Hammersmith Hospital in London have fertilized multiple eggs in vitro from a donor, grown them until each fertilized egg grew to eight cells, removed one cell from each embryo for testing to determine sex, and then (in the first successful test) discarded the males and implanted the females into the mother's womb. Twin daughters were subsequently born in a routine pregnancy. Scientists feel that the new technique holds most promise in determining genetic defects in the embryo at a very early stage of fetal development, doing away with the need for later and more dangerous fetal screening using amniocentesis or chorionic villi sampling. The enormously high cost of the procedure will certainly limit the availability of the test but, as one researcher noted, "This new screening process should have a huge social impact over the next two decades."[11]

Ironically, most women who are candidates for in-vitro fertilization have had to pay the double consequences of modern medical practice. Most request treatment due to damage done to their fallopian tubes earlier through the use of intrauterine devices prescribed initially to prevent pregnancy. Having already paid such a high price, they are then subjected to the invasive testing and massive expense of the in-vitro procedure, a process that often has to be repeated several times.

Given the impersonality of most modern medical practice, reproductive-system research seems almost geared toward eliminating woman entirely from the reproductive process. Successful in-vitro procedures are received more as victories of science than opportunities for thanksgiving. Indeed, a reproductive-system research continuum seems to be in the making. For a long time, there has been extensive research done on the artificial placenta (utilizing aborted but still temporarily viable fetuses). Efforts to culture the full gestation period within an artificial uterus are now being made. The final victory will be genetic alteration of the in-vitro fertilized egg—the genetic "therapy" now being touted by scientists all around the world.

For all of the promise offered to infertile couples by this technique, the ultimate social costs of the procedure must be measured. With limited health-care dollars available for research and development in this country, it would be unconscionable to spend the large sums necessary to fully perfect this procedure if it entailed robbing other more generally needed public-health services in order to impregnate a handful of women. In an era when government has retreated from providing necessary medical services to the poor and the aged and when school lunch programs for the needy are deemed "luxurious" by U.S. presidents, in-vitro fertility services can only be justified if private funds are found to pay the bill. Even then, due to the scarcity of sophisticated research facilities and trained staff, emphasis on programs like in-vitro fertilization may be only another medical robbing of the poor to provide exotic therapies for the more privileged. Given all the present uncertainty regarding the longer range well-being of in-vitro offspring, the human and the economic costs may yet prove to be incalculable. One can only hope that both hopeful parents and responsible medical personnel will see the wisdom in providing a secure future for some of the millions of unwanted children who need a family, rather than chancing the kind of procreational roulette each in-vitro fertilization occasions.

The Nature of Abnormality

More than one out of every 20 babies born in the United States today has a genetic abnormality— major or minor—of one kind or another. Each day, hundreds of parents face the terrible reality that even the wonders of modern science have not yet done much to solve the problems of genetic disease. Over the milennia of human history, natural selection has been our primary defense against the proliferation of defective genes. For good or ill, only the fittest survived. But medical technology has now changed all that. Once a relatively rare disease, Down's syndrome today accounts for one in every six cases of mental retardation, due both to medical intervention and to the increased number of older women choosing to have children. Most children afflicted with this disease now survive since, as one medical observer has said, "Medical science has reduced the premium on genetic fitness." And thus, really for the first time, an unprecedented moral dilemma has arisen. Are too many genetically defective people being allowed to survive? When is a life so hurtful to the individual, the family, or the society that it is truly not worth living? Given the need for at least some distributive justice in the delivery of health services, are the enormous sums required to maintain a severely retarded or diseased child warranted, in light of the needs of others not so handicapped? How does human society make the decision or develop criteria for deciding what is an unworthy life?

Putting aside the sometimes arcane arguments of the pro- and anti-abortion forces, all programs of genetic screening and prenatal diagnosis imply the inevitability of the decision to abort some fetuses. Ethicist Joseph Fletcher strongly advocates efforts to reduce to the fullest extent possible the risk of children being born with any kind of genetic deficiency.

> Our basic ethical choice as we consider man's new control over himself, over his body and his mind as well as over his society and environment, is still what it was when primitive man holed up in caves and made fires. Chance versus control. Should we leave the limits of human reproduction to take shape at random, keeping our children dependent on accidents of romance and the genetic endowment of sexual lottery. . . ? Or should we be responsible about it, that is, exercise our rational and human choice, no longer submissively trusting to the blind worship of raw nature?
>
> Producing our children by sexual roulette without preconceptive and uterine control, simply taking pot luck from random sexual combinations, is irresponsible—now that we know how to monitor against congenital infirmities. As we learn to direct mutations medically we should do so. This way it will be much easier to assure our children that they are wanted, that they were born on purpose.[12]

For many physicians—with all of the escalating concern of the medical profession to produce better and stronger individuals—assisting a woman to produce a "normal" child is both natural and sometimes psychologically required. For their own professional stakes and their own peace of mind, doctors need to delivery healthy babies. Inevitably, this defensive tendency places enormous pressure on parents to cooperate in having "healthy" children.

As noted in Chapter 2, the formal utilitarian ethic will always place the greater good of the society before the particular good of the individual. Operating from this kind of moral calculus, Fletcher suggests that there is no automatic right to the free exercise of procreation if such "rights become unjust when their exercise victimizes innocent children-to-be and the social fabric." This ethic basically assumes that humankind can define a standard by which to measure normality, that children not meeting this standard should never be brought into the world if such can be prevented, and that the standard should be backed up by the law of the state. Apart from anything else, the big problem with such genetic utilitarianism is the question of whether or not we are morally competent to develop absolute standards for human growth and conduct. While our images of human nature may be relatively sound today, it is entirely conceivable, as one of my students recently said, that the model for tomorrow's perfect human being might be that of the Marlboro man, Michael Jackson, or Miss America!

Arrogance on the part of our species is certainly nothing new. But trusting the contemporary model of Homo sapiens to determine our evolutionary shape for tomorrow may well be the most shortsighted thing we have ever done. Some changes in the gene pool may indeed prove to be advantageous. We must question, however, whether we possess the wisdom and foresight to evaluate and choose the basic changes we can be making. Medical ethicist Marc Lappe warns against this kind of utilitarian genetics:

> The dangers of such a proposal are so clear as to be self-evident: who determines the "positive standard"? Who (and what) determines the qualities that we collectively find so burdensome? A state policy? Should all developing fetuses with Down's syndrome be aborted? And what about a chromosomal variant of unknown significance?[13]

Our modern sense that we can somehow control our collective destiny and that, in spite of their lack of full understanding, our contemporary scientists and technologists can be trusted to do what is good must be seen as shortsighted in the extreme. With very few exceptions, the benefits to humankind as a result of most scientific advancement are equalled (and sometimes outweighed) by the disadvantages to our psychological, physical, environmental, and cultural well-being. Those who hope to program our genetic framework for the future too often ignore both the unknown and the demonstrable fact that even the simplest genetic deficiency is not easily measured in terms of its final impact on the individual. Environmental, social, and cultural impacts are as important in the development of the individual as the genetic constituency. We too easily generalize ethical universals from the empirical particulars to which we are currently indebted. Daniel Callahan of the Hastings Center has commented,

> It was counted a great advance of the modern mind when a bookkeeping God, with his minutely maintained ledger of bad and good deeds, was

noisily rejected. Yet here we are, beginning to keep our own books, and using them increasingly as a determinant in deciding whether or not defectives should be allowed the privilege of birth, and their parents the privilege of parenthood. Moreover, we seem to have forgotten the reason why the bookkeeping God was rejected—because it seemed eminently unjust, insensitive and outrageous that a scorecard be kept on human lives.[14]

This is not the place for an extensive discussion of the possible misuse of genetic information, but a few thoughts are in order. Already sperm banks are flourishing in this country, and Nobel laureates are storing their seed for the "benefit" of future generations. Word has it that eugenicist William Shockley has already made a deposit! Vance Packard in *The People Shapers* facetiously suggests that with the advent of sperm and ovum banks, prices could be determined per egg or ejaculate on the basis of the respective qualities of the donor. Arnold Schwartzeneger might be priced at $750, with an Albert Einstein going for up to $2,500—or perhaps just the reverse, depending on the genetic expectations of the purchaser! Here too, then, in our commodity-structured society, one will get what one pays for.[15]

Already, several major U.S. companies are using genetic screening programs as a condition for job placement. On the one hand, this seems paternalistic but proper as a means to safeguard the workplace. On the other hand, such programs could also be used as a sly alternative to cleaning up the workplace. Using genetics to sort out people—for whatever reason—has had a sorry history in the twentieth century. Genetic screening in the workplace should be subjected to very careful scrutiny as it becomes more widespread.

In the same vein, many more social abuses of genetic information may be evident in the future. In Chapter 11, we will see how the theories of the sociobiologists have been used to rationalize class, race, and sex discrimination. Subjective bias against persons of a different hue or cultural background can all too easily—given the tools of molecular genetics and an extensive genetic counseling program—be turned into medical practice or state policy. Those who consider such a statement to be simply alarmist forget history and the practice of our scientists and politicians in this century: genocide in Germany and Cambodia; the U.S. slaughter of the innocents in Vietnam; the development, use, and/or continued advocacy of chemical, nuclear, and biological weapons by several advanced industrial countries—all of which suggest the foolhardiness of blindly trusting in the wisdom of those who lead us.

Responding to the public controversy surrounding all these issues, the federal government has at least anticipated the impending move on the part of scientists from fetal therapy to the more arcane arena of gene therapy. In February 1984, the Recombinant-DNA Advisory Committee (RAC) of the National Institutes of Health established a procedure to develop recommendations for the oversight of gene therapy (that is, the introduction of a properly functioning gene to correct the effect of one that is defective). Many projects have been already submitted for review.

The hope is that such procedures will cure hereditary diseases that are caused by genetic mutation. The ethical issues related to gene therapy of this kind are numerous and vary in accordance with whether the projected treatment involves normal somatic cells or germ-line cells (the reproductive cells of sperm or eggs). The first kind of therapy (as in the injection of recombinant bone-marrow cells in the betathalassemia patients referred to earlier) would only affect the individual patient's health. However, germ-line repair (which might, for example, seek to correct the genetic disease of the potential offspring of two double-recessive betathalassemia parents) would go beyond the individual (the parents) and would affect the gene pool of the species itself.

Recombinant-DNA procedures in reproductive-cell biology have enormous possibilities for both positive and potentially destructive social change. The history of scientific and technological development suggests a tendency for those in control of either information or political power to use whatever has been developed, regardless of consequence to the population. As our ability to manipulate the genetic composition of our own children (and our society) grows in sophistication in the years ahead, the social pressures brought to bear on the new technologies will become ever more intense. The shape of current technology tends to determine options for the future. If we learn how to increase intelligence and the specific talents of individuals via genetic engineering (happily, a doubtful possibility), it will be very difficult to constrain those powers intent on utilizing the techniques to their own ends. Critics will no doubt be scolded and condemned for being scientific Luddites and for interfering with technological progress (as Nobel laureate James Watson did to his colleagues at Asilomar; see Chapter 7). As I have suggested throughout this book, however, it may be precisely that interference and criticism that is required if our species wants to survive long on Planet Earth!

None of this is to suggest that genetic research, screening programs, or counseling efforts should be discontinued. Options must be available when individuals are faced with a decision in which they might prevent the kind of needless suffering that some persons with massive genetic diseases experience. But programs directed toward developing ubiquitous social mechanisms to control behavior or to purify the species must always be either prohibited or very carefully monitored. It is not being alarmist to inform readers of the lack of any popular control mechanisms that would safeguard them from the often narrow self-interests of economic, political, and scientific decision-makers. Who determines the decision-making process, who profits from the decisions made, and what self-interests are involved in any major scientific effort are questions that cannot be ignored. Quality of life can never be measured in the simple terms of social utility or the ability to be productive according to established norms. While we can ethically make decisions to keep those who would suffer terribly from physical or mental handicaps from being born, such decisions must always be cautiously made. If life is a gift, then the refusal to accept that gift for whatever reasons of self-interest may well have unforetold consequences. Biochemist David Lygre has summed up the issue well:

> We should not presume that "normality," a term none of us can define adequately, is a prerequisite to a full and meaningful life. People are born with an enormous range of abilities and disabilities, and many "defective" people have not only experienced rich lives, but they have also made life richer for the rest of us.
>
> Perhaps physical perfection is incompatible with mental and spiritual perfection. We lose a sense of compassion, caring, and love if we exercise these qualities only when it is easy. Indeed, if we come to view defective people as unwanted intrusions who diminish the quality of our lives, the greatest pity will not be what is happening to them. It will be what has happened to us.[16]

Notes

1. Ruth Hubbard, "Human Embryo and Gene Manipulation," *Science for the People* 15, no. 3 (May/June 1983), p. 24.

2. Warren T. Reich, ed., *Encyclopedia of Bioethics* (New York: Free Press, 1978), p. 568.

3. M. Lappe, J. M. Gustafson, and R. Roblin, "Ethical and Social Issues in Screening for Genetic Disease," *New England Journal of Medicine* 286 (May 25, 1982), pp. 1129–32.

4. Ibid., p. 1130.

5. P. M. Boffey, "Panel Urges Preparations to Meet Big Demand for Genetic Screening," New York *Times*, February 27, 1983.

6. *Council of Europe Parliamentary Assembly Proceedings,* recommendation 934, Strasbourg, France, 1982.

7. S. R. Stephenson and D. D. Weaver, "Prenatal Diagnosis—A Compilation of Diagnosed Conditions," *American Journal of Obstetrics and Gynecology* (August 1, 1981), p. 319.

8. Laurence E. Karp, "The Prenatal Diagnosis of Genetic Disease," in T. A. Mappes and J. S. Zembatty, *Biomedical Ethics,* 2nd ed. (New York: McGraw-Hill, 1986), p. 499.

9. Dena Kleiman, "When Abortion Becomes Birth," New York *Times,* February 15, 1984, p. 14.

10. Clifford Grobstein, "External Human Fertilization," *Scientific American* 240, no. 6 (June 1979), p. 61.

11. Thomas H. Maugh II, "Birth Defects Weeded Out in a Test Tube," Los Angeles *Times,* July 30, 1990.

12. Joseph Fletcher, *The Ethics of Genetic Control* (New York: Anchor Press, 1974), p. 158.

13. Marc Lappe, *Genetic Politics* (New York: Simon and Schuster, 1979), pp. 118–19.

14. T. L. Beauchamp and L. Walters, *Bioethics* (Belmont, Calif.: Wadsworth Publishing, 1978), p. 582.

15. Vance Packard, *The People Shapers* (New York: Little, Brown, 1979).

16. David G. Lygre, *Life Manipulation* (New York: Walker, 1979), p. 69.

9

Bioethics I: The Rights of People

In a world with unlimited demand, finite resources, and enormous inequities in economic and political power, the question of who gets what and why—the historic problem of distributive justice—is at the heart of any system of ethics. Given the tradition in all societies that the well-placed or well-to-do always get the most and the best of everything, the question of how to deliver properly both the essentials required to maintain health (food, shelter, education) and needed health services must finally receive our attention. Distributive justice is at the very center of bioethics.

Though every social system from the beginning of time has given at least some form of lip service to the issue of fairness in sharing resources, practice has always fallen far short of the theoretical mark. Even in wealthy and powerful countries like the United States, the pretense of being able to effect equity in delivering the goods of society was given up long ago. The response of then U.S. Secretary of Agriculture Earl Butz during the 1974 World Food Conference in Rome to the request of poorer nations for more U.S. food aid classically states an unwritten distributional law. Representing both the U.S. government and the makers of U.S. food policy, Butz told the needy nations, "If you've got the money, we've got the food." In this chapter we will evaluate a number of environmental rights issues as they relate to people: equity and health care, health delivery services, and distributive justice.

Health Care and Medical Allocations

The dilemma of effecting distributive justice in the delivery of health-care services is particularly complicated. The Congressional Budget Office reported that, whereas in 1965 total health costs in the United

States were $41.7 billion or 6 percent of the gross national product (GNP), by 1982 some $322.4 billion (approximately 10.5 percent of the GNP) was spent on all forms of health care. By 1985, total health expenditures were $425 million. In 1990, it is certain that the total medical bill will exceed $500 billion, a figure representing almost 11 percent of the GNP. In contrast to our own profligacy in medical spending, the other major developed Western nations spend the following percentages of their GNP on health care: Sweden 8.8 percent, France 8.6 percent, West Germany 8.1 percent, Italy 7.6 percent, Japan 7.5 percent, Britain 5.9 percent.

In spite of the fact that this U.S. GNP percentage was substantially higher than the average of other advanced industrial countries (including those with socialized medical programs), the payoff does not appear to have necessarily helped the majority of the American people. The major benefits seem to have accrued to the medical profession itself. Per-capita health costs in the United States rose from $211 in 1965 to $1,365 in 1982 to approximately $2,000 in 1988. Only 40 percent of this total was underwritten by state and federal health-care programs.[1]

The much-maligned British medical system, for example, spends less than 6 percent of the national income on health. While the Thatcher government has cut overall health expenditures to the bone in that nation, still the National Health Service provides basic services to keep the vast majority of its people in good health. Robert Maxwell, a leading health analyst, studied ten Western-nation health systems and reported that, while the United States was highest in overall spending, it ranked ninth in the quality of health care provided. Britain, in contrast, was last in spending, but fourth in overall quality of health and the delivery of services.[2]

Life expectancies are lower overall for Americans than for citizens of almost any other developed country. Class and race factors loom large in this, with life expectancies for the poor and for minorities being at least ten years lower than the average of 70 for white males. Maternal deaths in the United States continue to be four times higher than in any of the Scandinavian countries. The urban and rural poor in many parts of the United States experience infant mortality rates approximating those of many Third World nations. The United States is currently ranked nineteenth in infant mortality, according to the World Health Organization (WHO). For a nation that spends almost twice as much on health care as many other "rich" countries of the world, the statistical data seem confusing. With all of our massive expenditures for health, it is shocking that so many other countries provide so much better care.

The infant mortality statistics are particularly troublesome since infant health is traditionally the best indicator there is of the general health of a people. It is quite amazing to realize that, in spite of the enormous medical spending in the United States, 18 nations around the world have lower infant mortality rates. The primary reason for the poor showing of the United States in infant health and survival when contrasted with the rest of the developed world is the high mortality associated with racial and class factors. While the middle and upper classes generally get as good care as can be found anywhere, racial minorities and the poor are far worse off. In 1987 the overall infant mortality rate in the United States was 10.1, per 1,000, who perished before reaching their first birthday (most of them dying in their first month of life). Black babies, however, had a death rate of 17.9 per 1,000. Hispanic infant mortality is at least as high as for Blacks, while the ratio for White newborns is only 8.6 deaths per 1,000 live births. These mortality figures result from the low birth weights of babies born to poor parents, due most often to inadequate maternal nutrition—the consequence of poverty and a generalized lack of adequate prenatal care. Sixty percent of infant deaths occur in babies with birth weights of under 5.5 pounds. The racial and class differentials in overall health care—including prenatal and infant care—are constant. Unhappily, they are routinely both expected and generally ignored by the health professions. Medical justice is indeed inadequately distributed in the United States.

One factor complicating the health situation is the disarray within the National Institutes of Health. Currently the largest medical research group in the world—financing research at hundreds of hospitals and universities (mainly in the United States, but also internationally) and supported by a budget of $7.5 billion annually—the agency is charged with protecting the health of people throughout the world (e.g., as the primary U.S. arm for AIDS research). Yet the NIH has (at the time of writing) been without a director since the election of George Bush to the presidency. In fact, the political test now required by the Bush administration for all senior medical appointments has led to a number of vacancies in key health administrative positions around the country. While salaries for major federal appointments in the field are poor compared to the private sector, the main stumbling block has been Bush's insistence that all senior scientists support the antiabortion "right to life" stance of his administration. Morale has been slipping for years within the NIH because of such moral litmus tests imposed by the political sector and because of a cutback in funding. Currently only 29 percent of approved medical research projects receive support from the NIH, because of budget decreases. Whether the Bush administration will be willing to compromise in order to restore the NIH to its former preeminence is doubtful.

Since medical care anywhere is essentially the end result of a production system that manufactures, markets, and distributes its product like any other consumer commodity, our bioethicist should be concerned with these strategic questions: What are the primary products of the U.S. health-care system? What might they be under a more ideal system? How should they be distributed? And since medical care by itself seems to be relatively ineffective in promoting overall health, some new priorities for conceptualizing what health care really means seem to be in order.

The U.S. Health-Care System

Health commentators frequently note that among the five variables that influence health—environment, lifestyle, society, genetics, and medical care—the last, surprisingly, is in fact the least important. While medical care is at times of major assistance, it is increasingly clear that attempting to equalize medical treatment may be one of the least effective ways to bring more equity into health-care delivery. Some form of compensatory justice, wherein the larger percentage of new expenditure is devoted to redressing the specific problems arising from past inequity in medical care, is at least part of the answer.

There is no doubt, however, that in certain areas the sophisticated U.S. health-care system has produced many advantages to the medical consumer. During the past 50 years, substantial control has been effected over many forms of communicable disease. Death rates from cardiovascular disease continue to fall—in spite of the fact that this combined category of chronic degenerative disorders remains our second largest killer. Above all, quite remarkable progress in the fields of biomedical research and technology can be seen. But our biotechnological record raises a great many concerns, as well—not the least of which involve the cost of such services, their availability to ordinary people, and the extent to which they represent a disproportionate percentage of a limited medical dollar.

There is the organ transplant field, for example. The first successful kidney transplant occurred in 1954. In many regards, this was an enormous success story for U.S. medicine. Today, the recipient of a cadaver kidney has a 60 percent chance of surviving at least five years, while a person receiving a kidney from a relative has an 80 percent five-year survival rate. The cost of extending such a program so that it can be generally available to everyone needing such assistance is highly controversial, however. Even when organs are available, transplants are terribly expensive; almost no one has the ability to pay their own way through the treatment. Yet it is estimated that up to 10,000 people are on the current waiting lists for new kidneys. In 1984, the cost of surgery alone for kidney transplants averaged $30,000, with the annual cost of medical maintenance running $5,000–8,000 per patient. Were every person needing such surgery to receive it, the total cost would be in the billions. Without some enlargement of the total health-care budget, such new expenditures would clearly have to be compensated for by reductions elsewhere. Whether or not such a medical robbing of Peter to pay Paul could be justified ethically is very doubtful. And the price of other organ transplants escalates enormously. Arthur L. Caplan from the Hastings Center's Institute of Society, Ethics, and the Life Sciences—reckoning with the fact that costs for some transplant procedures are in the hundreds of thousands of dollars—stated,

> Given the high cost of transplantation and the uncertainty over who will pay, it is not surprising that many people are currently being denied transplants solely because they cannot pay. Some hospitals refuse to operate on those who lack private means. . . . In today's constrained economic times such a policy [to underwrite governmentally all transplant costs] would be very difficult to expand to the newest forms of organ transplantation. With millions of persons potentially in need of transplantation now or in the future, a blanket reimbursement for the procedure would eventually bankrupt the Medicare and Medicaid programs.[3]

Inevitably, issues of the assumed social worth of a patient creeps in when life-or-death decisions regarding who shall receive donor organs are made by medical staff. In 1989, for example, 1,600 heart transplants were made in the United States, but 34,000 other people needing transplants died of congestive heart failure. As Caplan notes, "Poor people and those who lack insurance don't get referred for transplants. They wind up dead or in the emergency room."

This problem of the cost and quality of care ties into a number of public-health issues. At least some of our traditions of social justice and a number of our systems of public medicine imply a legal right to health care for all persons. As noted, the institutional problem of delivering on this assumption is enormous. Should this "right" be taken to include the most advanced biomedical services and the more exotic forms of life-extending therapies? Or should our social expectations be limited to preventive-care and health-maintenance services?

If we determine that each person has a basic right to health care, how do we determine what that care should be? Shall it, for example, be based on an adequate diet for all persons in the society? It is utterly clear that the best preventive medicine is adequate nutrition. Shall the society, therefore, universalize a medical "food stamp" program that will affirm the right of every individual to this requisite for maintaining good health? Who will determine what a system of health care based on the premise of "to each according to need" should be? Who will be responsible for aligning economic reality and medical priority with justice in the health-care sector in order to provide a decent minimum in services?

Distributive Justice

A primary consideration in the proper distribution of health services is precisely the question of what should or needs to be distributed. Since health services are organized on an ages-of-life pattern in which people become patients and are fit clinically into the various niches— fetal, newborn, pediatric, adolescent, adult, geriatric—it is difficult to escape from the assumption that medical service is the key factor in health maintenance and is thus the basis for any allocation of resources. Many of our personal expectations relating to health do conform to those special needs that are in part determined by age.

Social critic Ivan Illich points to another dimension of the health-care problem, however, using geriatric services as an example: "The demand for old age care has increased, not just because there are more old people who survive, but also because there are more people who state their claim that their old age should be cured. The industrial distortion [within the health professions] of our shared perception of reality has rendered us blind to the counterpurposive level of our enterprise."[4]

The anxious debate over priorities for health services and the role of government has become increasingly clamorous. And while this concern is important and must be addressed, it also signals, ironically, an increasing readiness on the part of the average person to forfeit personal autonomy to the professional healers. To equate good health with the availability of practitioner services is terribly wrongheaded. We do need good medical services, and they do need to be more equitably distributed. Far more important, however, is the personal willingness to assume primary responsibility for our own health and not simply entrust it to someone else. As Illich notes,

> Most of man's ailments consist of illnesses that are acute and benign—either self-limiting or subject to control through a few dozen routine interventions. For a wide range of conditions, those who are treated least probably make the best progress. "For the sick," Hippocrates said, "the least is best." More often than not, the best a learned and conscientious physician can do is convince his patient that he can live with his impairment, reassure him of an eventual recovery or of the availability of morphine at the time when he will need it, do for him what grandmother could have done, and otherwise defer to nature.[5]

Nonetheless, the question of distributive justice must still be faced. (The distribution of ill-advised services is a question all its own—the promotion of what may not in fact be the best medicine for the individual.) More than any other nation in the world, the United States has culturally decreed that medical services must be provided by the private, profit-oriented medical service sector, commonly called the "fee for service" system. In spite of the quite remarkable growth in public medicine in the past few years and the recognition—finally—by government (via Medicare and Medicaid, for example) that it bears some responsibility for tending to the health requirements of the citizenry, 60 percent of all medical payments today still go from private individuals to private medical practitioners. This contrasts sharply with the rest of the developed world, wherein virtually all medical services are public and compensation to the practitioner is made on a "fee for patient" basis. Since there is general agreement today that prevention is the best way to preclude the future need for even more exotic therapeutic techniques, it has become of major concern whether the funding for preventive health care should be the responsibility of the public or the individual.

For example, should what are oftentimes considered self-induced medical problems be exempted from coverage under either private or public care programs? Simple logic may lead some people to believe that those who smoke or drink to excess should be forced to pay either special premiums for health care or forgo treatment. Why should others be responsible for the care of those who knowingly engage in practices that most certainly lead to cancer or degenerative disease? However, this logic often ignores a more basic question directly related to the issue of distributive justice: How can any health system discriminate between the damage done to the lungs from air pollution and cigarette smoking? In fact, we could say that the illness related to "sinful" lifestyle is as much the result of governmentally approved social policies such as advertising and state subsidies for products like tobacco and the grains used to produce alcohol as it is of individual lifestyle decision. And if individuals who practice poor health habits are forced to pay additional costs for insurance because of their probable extra burden on the health system, should not those responsible for pollution emissions and other health-affecting practices bear the social cost of their production of ill health by special taxes to cover the cost of industrially induced illness?

Equity in the distribution of needed health services similarly demands informed decision-making in terms of both micro and macro allocations of the health-care budget. How much, for example, of the total budget of the state or nation should be devoted to health care? On what ethical basis are decisions to be reached between the competing and, unfortunately, necessary demands of the larger educational, police, defense, and other critical public-sector concerns? Once such overall determinations have been faced and decisions reached, how go about the problem of micro allocations? Which hospitals shall receive funds for computerized axial tomography (CAT) scanners, machines for kidney dialysis, surgical theaters for heart transplants, and state-of-the-art machinery for life-extending therapies? Since funding is never sufficient to enable all persons who might be helped by such services to actually receive them, how shall the determination be made as to who is "most needy"?

Should the vagaries of the market—of supply and demand and the ability to pay—continue to control medical services? Two examples illustrate the concern. Because of the financial risk to hospitals in maintaining emergency services (since many indigent people use these facilities), some hospitals in the Greater Los Angeles Area have recently closed their emergency rooms and in their place opened "sports medicine" clinics, whose young healthy clients are happy to pay for services rendered. At the other extreme, one of the most prestigious units for a hospital today is a cardiovascular and heart-transplant service. Notwithstanding their importance in overall cardiovascular research, heart transplants do get the headlines and do command huge fees. Accordingly, heart-transplant units have opened all around the country—even in smaller centers. Unhappily, since most services of this kind are only infrequently used in less populated areas, surgical staffs do not get the amount of practice required to develop and maintain their skills. Inevitably, then, a far higher percentage of patients die in such facilities than in the major transplant centers where surgeons' skills are better. In fact, some of the new centers have already closed because of the difficulty in maintaining them with a very small patient load. In any case, profit and prestige alike have contributed to a lessening of basic health services for many people in the society.

Despite the difficulty involved in determining health-care priorities, some humane formula must be developed to determine who are the least advantaged in the society, taking into consideration the factors of race, class, personal need, and the requirements for compensatory service. It is probably not possible for any nation to provide health care on an absolutely equitable and just basis for all members of the society, given the history of social and economic imbalance that obtain in every country. As the general level of well-being in a country increases, however, it is just that the greater percentage of that new sum of well-being be directed to those who have historically received the least. In U.S. society, the economic mechanisms of the market and its own criteria for efficiency serve as the primary distributive agent. Access to goods and services is granted indirectly via income or wages. The market system determines the allocation of such services in direct relationship to the relative scarcity of the service rendered. Thus, an equitable distribution is impossible within the mechanics of the market, and alternative redistributive methods must be devised so that those who cannot pay can nonetheless receive certain basic minimum life requirements.

Who Gets What?

Undergirding any consideration of all these economic realities is the necessity to think through the particular ethical theories as they apply to the distribution of scarce resources. Certain principles tend to stand out. The utilitarian concern for maximizing the general welfare is as close to an absolute in the delivery of health services as we shall ever find. A natural-law concern would suggest we focus on providing services that meet basic human needs and enable us to realize most properly our nature as human beings; that much is a given. The motivist requirement that we attempt to do good and that we do our best to treat people as ends in themselves is perhaps universal to any health-care delivery system.

Answers to the problems of medical-service delivery are not quickly discovered. The liberal society—concerned to at least some degree for the general welfare of most of its people—may determine that there shall be equal access to health care, with the only criterion being that of personal need. Immediately, however, the macro-allocation problem—the issue of limited resources—challenges the goal of equality and almost demands the establishment of priorities for different kinds of illnesses. This implies that the state may be forced to refuse its funding in certain kinds of health care. Whenever the withholding of care becomes necessary—for example, our earlier national experience when we had only a limited number of kidney dialysis machines for an ever-growing number of patients with renal failure, prior to the government's takeover of the dialysis program— we face ambiguities in making the decision about who shall receive care. The renal-failure/kidney-dialysis problem well illustrates the point. To end the difficult situation of forcing medical practitioners to choose who should die and who should live via the dialysis machine, Congress finally decided to underwrite the full cost of dialysis for any person requiring such services. The overall cost of this program now approaches $3 billion annually. Noble in intent and practice, the provision of such services nevertheless condemns other segments of society with equally serious but less well publicized illnesses to lower quality service. Even the increased expenditure for AIDS research is coming under criticism today from those who feel there are more urgent problems that the health-care system is not addressing. With a limited health-care budget, governments must prioritize their services.

Should the choice for patient care then be randomized so that everyone has an equal chance in a lottery of life and death? Or rather, should financial ability be the primary criterion for determining health care? Can the "value" of the person—that is, her or his social contributions made over a period of time—be factored into the decision? Does a parent with several children have priority over a single person, for lifesaving therapy? Should the issue of "prospects for success" in treatment be a factor, wherein only those patients with a fair chance of survival are given optimal treatment? Finally, if the patient has not received needed health care in the past because of class or race factors, should compensatory treatment be awarded when needed?

Further complicating the issue is the problem of health-care servicing in the context of macro allocations within the larger political economy. How should the priorities between expenditures for other valid social needs such as social services, child care, research and development, and job training be determined? Shall the defense establishment continue to have funding priority over all health and educational services? Should the priority be given to the general physical health needs of the population or to their mental health? How make the decision between the continuation of food stamps and family-planning services?

It may be—due to the escalating fiscal crisis of the state—that it should simply be understood that there can be no possibility of equal access to medical services for the whole population. In an era of limits, it may well be that the only guarantee that can be made in any society is for minimum family health care strictly related to health maintenance, with all other therapeutic and life-extending services made available only through privately funded research institutes and only on a fee-for-service basis. Although such a program would further institutionalize inequality at some levels, it would at least give the greater percentage of the tax dollar available for distribution in these sectors to those who most seriously need basic minimum services and where the actual payoff in terms of life span and consequent productivity would be maximized.

Although a variety of ways to provide distributive justice in health care exist, it appears that the options in advanced societies are essentially threefold. The first option is what Elizabeth Telfer has called a laissez-faire system of medical service. This would comprise a completely private system of health care such as that which characterized U.S. medical practice until the advent of Medicare and related state programs. Here, in rather primitive fashion, you get only what you can afford to pay for. The second option is the liberal or humanitarian system wherein tax-supported medical services are provided for the truly needy, with private forms of health insurance available for all others. This perhaps most closely approximates the existing U.S. system, except for the fact that the public-health safety net fails to catch a large percentage of people who need care.

Surprisingly, in addition to sections of the rural and urban poor who are unskilled at using the health care "system," many members of the lower to lower middle working-class population must also strictly fend for themselves. With too much income to qualify for public assistance but too little to pay the increasingly exorbitant fees of the medical practitioners, the taxpaying working class is one of the more medically deprived segments of U.S. society today. The third health-maintenance option would be a socialized medical program wherein a larger than normal percentage of the wealth of the society is preempted through taxation programs and then redistributed to provide basic health services for all the people. Most industrial-nation health programs now follow this basic system. While such programs do assure that catastrophic illness need not destroy the security of a family, their problems—depersonalized services, inefficient bureaucracies, an occasional overdependence on medical experts as people initially overload the system—often rival those of free-market medical servicing. Whatever the long-range options for the United States, the frugality of the Reagan–Bush expenditures in the health sector in the 1980s and the continued reign of a conservative Congress dictate that major changes in the U.S. health system are not on the immediate horizon.[6]

Coming from a religious/socialist tradition, this writer believes that the logically constructive aspects of traditional utilitarianism must be the major foundation of any contemporary bioethic. Two substantial advantages seem to accrue from the utilitarian formula. The first is the rather clear affirmation of the importance of human happiness and well-being. While many ethical traditions tend to offer moral absolutes or devotion to duty as the end goal of human life, utilitarianism properly understands that the human dilemma for most people is quite real and that any environmentally sound ethic able to lessen the burdens and maximize the satisfactions of the human journey for the greatest number of persons should be affirmed. Many modern psychologies similarly authenticate the importance of connecting the actual practices of real life with the ethical and value assumptions made by the individual. The ability to relate work and play, to be "self-actualized" as Abraham Maslow would say, and to connect private requirements and social needs are essential to the development of a healthy life.

The method of utilitarianism is here singularly constructive. It suggests rather clear and simple procedures for answering questions of personal need and social concern, and for the subsequent development of social policy. Most individuals and groups require operative guidelines and methods for ethical decision-making. An end goal emphasizing that actions should normally be directed toward the maximization of happiness and well-being for the greatest number of people—coupled with ecologically sound efforts to develop the social and political instrumentalities that effect such well-being—is the minimum common denominator for bioethical guidelines in any society truly concerned for the rights of its people.

Notes

1. Two popular articles dealing with the state of U.S. health care are Karen DeYoung, "Condition Critical," Washington *Post National Weekly Edition,* March 28–April 3, 1988; and Gregg Easterbrook, "The Revolution in Health Care," *Newsweek* (January 26, 1987).

2. Barry Newman, "Frugal Medical Service Keeps Britons Healthy and Patiently Waiting," *Wall Street Journal,* February 9, 1983.

3. Arthur L. Caplan, "Organ Transplants: The Costs of Success," *Hastings Center Report* 13, no. 6 (December 1983), p. 30.

4. Ivan Illich, *Medical Nemesis: The Expropriation of Health* (New York: Pantheon, 1976), p. 472.

5. Ibid. p. 474.

6. Elizabeth Telfer, "Justice, Welfare, and Health Care," *Journal of Medical Ethics* 2 (September 1976), esp. pp. 107–11.

10

Bioethics II: Staying in Control

Most of us would agree with the general principle that human beings should never be forced to conform to the will or direction of another person or group except insofar as such subjection might contribute to the individual's health or well-being, prevent harm to others, or better the social or ecological orders. Autonomy—our freedom from external restraint and the maintenance of control over our own existence—is universally understood as the final bastion of biological integrity. Death and taxes may be inevitable, but personal control over our minds and bodies is indispensable.

History, however, is—as much as anything else—a record of the attempts by powerful groupings within human societies to control and manipulate the lives and behavior of other people. Many of our primary social institutions—schools, political systems, religious groupings, the structures of law and order, and even sometimes the healing professions—have been based on the supposed need defined by one or another social class either to control or to modify the behavior patterns or attitudes of selected individuals or groups.

Bioethically, the related issues of autonomy, the right of informed consent, and social efforts to modify individual behavior intrude into every discussion and case study. Clearly, social order would be difficult without certain types of behavior management. Both external coercion and more subtle efforts at internal influence have always been used to maintain varying degrees of social order. Some are benign and absolutely needed, and some no more than thinly veiled efforts to maintain existing coercive relationships. In the process of raising children, for example, or in the subjection to discipline properly imposed by any learning process, individuals inevitably give up aspects of personal autonomy for their own long-range benefit, and submit to the intentions of others. Devising criteria for evaluating the relative good and bad in such efforts is a necessary part of bioethical investigation. Although we may not yet have fully approached an Orwellian version of 1984 or a Clockwork Orange determinism, certain ominous clouds lurk on the behavioral horizon. As a popular book on behavior control reported several years ago,

> There are now hundreds of men and women around the country using the new technology of behavior. They are manipulating the behavior of people in businesses, prisons, homes, public schools. They can untangle a homosexual, dry out an alcoholic, toilet train a youngster in half a day, turn a delinquent into a scholar. They say they have just begun. . . . No technology can amplify the . . . nightmare more than one that can turn a man into a puppet. The technology of behavior control offers this, too.[1]

Throughout history, the class relationships that have obtained in any society have always been reinforced by the subject/object dichotomy of power. To assure that those who dwell at lower levels of force and influence in the social orders will always be subject to the manipulations of those on top seems to have been the explicit political intention of most world leaders. The key to maintaining an autonomous life is for the individual to understand that she or he is a thinking, knowing subject who must fully participate (at least insofar as possible at any given time) in the decisions affecting the quality of personal and/or social life.

Any effort to limit the liberties of individuals and to reduce or impair autonomy must be subject to social constraints. Limitations on individual autonomy may at times be needed, but can only be justified by an appeal to culturally (and sometimes legally) approved *liberty-limiting principles*. These traditionally include the following concerns:

1. To prevent harm to others (the principle of private or public harm);

2. To prevent a major social offense to others that may limit their autonomy (the principle of offense);

3. To prevent self-harm (the principle of paternalism);

4. To provide otherwise unattainable service to the person constrained (the principle of extreme paternalism); and

5. To benefit others or the larger society (the utility or social welfare principle).[2]

As ethicists always point out, statements of rights and/or obligations also entail or presume statements of correlative duties and responsibilities. Although we may all agree that citizen A has certain rights, those rights may be impossible of attainment unless other people have been given or have assumed the correlative responsibility to help fulfill the rights of citizen A. It does little good, for example, to have protective rights structured into the law if the laws governing those rights are not somehow capable of enforcement. Similarly, there are different categories of rights. Those that normally exist in fact are legal rights, guaranteed by the ordering structures of the society. All other proclaimed rights are simply appeals to the values of society. Since legal rights encompass only a small fraction of actual and moral rights, however, the rights by principle alone are ultimately even more important than the formal legal rights and must be protected as carefully. Within the context of our bioethical discussion, these issues of rights and autonomy are closely related to the problems of individual consent to procedures—medical, biological, behavioral, environmental—that may limit liberty. It is to these concerns that we now turn.

Informed Consent throughout History

In an era when totalitarianism has become a reality in the consciousness and lives of hundreds of millions of people, increasing attention has necessarily been given to procedures that guarantee certain minimal human rights. That such procedures have been all too infrequently followed makes their establishment no less important. Particularly since the Nazi holocaust during World War II, the issue of the rights of individuals and the development of the legal apparatus to protect to the greatest extent possible the individual from unwarranted physical or psychological intrusion has received growing recognition.

At the heart of these discussions has been the issue of informed consent. In the medical field, for example, informed consent implies the granting of the fullest possible information about a projected medical treatment in order that the patient may have the necessary data on which to base a decision regarding alternatives. Since biological autonomy is such a key determinator of human sensibility, the issue of consent interfaces all of the other contemporary problems relating to therapeutic treatment. Unhappily, the application of the principle is not always quite so easy.

Although implicit in much of this century's medical practice, the

issue of informed consent was only fully raised to public scrutiny by
the Nuremberg war-crimes trial immediately following World War II.
In one of its primary segments, the trials focused on the medical
practices of the Nazis in their human experimentation programs.
Nuremberg is now considered to be the cornerstone of contemporary
thought in regard to human subjects research. However, it is interesting to note that pre-Nazi German medical codes were essentially just
as comprehensive as those formulated at Nuremberg. Yet these earlier
standards for the profession had no impact at all on Nazi medical
practices. It would be wise to remember that any systematized medical
ethic has its inevitable limitations. Those regulations that do not
reflect both the moral consensus of the practitioners and the values
of the larger society tend not to be enforced.[3]

Nuremberg did serve to recapitulate appropriate guidelines for
contemporary medical research and general practice. The even more
comprehensive Declaration of Helsinki prepared by the World Medical Association in 1975 deals more particularly with contemporary
biomedical issues and with some of the more complex issues in the
theory of informed consent—for example, when the patient is unable
to function as an autonomous individual, by virtue of physical or
mental impairment. What does seem clear is the need for a continual
updating of such ethical codes as practices in the healing professions
change.

While on the face of it the issue of informed consent seems obvious
enough—that we make decisions regarding biological autonomy
based on the fullest possible information—there are many problems
that nonetheless complicate the issue. For example, it is almost never
easy to determine when consent is in fact *informed* consent. For a
mentally competent but physically incapacitated patient, how much
detail on proposed medical procedures will actually inform rather
than confuse? A physician committed to past surgical habits may
honestly but ignorantly advise a woman with a breast cancer that a
radical surgical procedure is the only informed option possible. A
neighboring physician, better informed about the alternative procedure of "lumpectomy" (excision only of the tumor, followed by
postoperative radiation), may well be appalled that anyone would
advise a radical mastectomy in all such situations. Subjective factors
inevitably erode the ideal of informed consent.

In most societies today, documentation of informed consent is
required for all experimental procedures. In the first mechanical
heart transplant performed on Dr. Barney Clark, the consent form

turned out to be an 11-page document that was, in the view of one medical ethicist, "more notable for its length than its content." Although an advance in some respects over earlier consent forms for experimental procedures, even this highly visible incident of research procedure failed to deal with that important point at which a patient becomes incompetent to make further decisions about the treatment—or to give continually "informed" consent, in other words. The consent form signed by Dr. Clark essentially ignored the question of who would make those continuing decisions about his care if he could not make them himself. As almost everyone understands, informed consent is not a form but a process. Nonetheless, to the greatest extent possible, the form should reflect the process.[4]

Other aspects of the consent issue revolve around the degree of competence necessary to give consent to certain procedures and the problem of how to determine the voluntary nature of consent. For example, can a prisoner volunteering for an experimental procedure ever give full consent, given the subtle and overt pressures always weighing on the prison population? The matter of competence in consent becomes particularly difficult when applied to minors, to those not able to make decisions because of physical or mental impairment, or to broader public-health procedures affecting entire populations. In the United States, the general concern for informed consent was recently stated by the National Commission for the Protection of Human Subjects:

> The ethical conduct of research involving human subjects requires a balancing of society's interests, protecting the rights of a subject, and . . . developing knowledge that can benefit the subjects or society as a whole.

Attempts to regulate research on human beings has been largely limited to the four decades since Nuremberg provided a baseline document for such protocols. But it has not always been easy to enforce compliance with this new concern. Currently in the United States all funding by the Department of Health, Education, and Welfare (HEW) for research on human subjects falls under the HEW "general assurance" clause wherein the federal granting process provides compliance mechanisms. In spite of the regulatory apparatus, full compliance is still largely a matter of voluntary cooperation and self-regulation. At the University of California, Berkeley, for example, human-subjects and biological-hazards review boards—mandated under the HEW guidelines—have long been in existence.

Researchers are required to file the appropriate statements and forms validating that their intended research falls within the guidelines. The protocols are then reviewed by the appropriate review board and either approved or rejected. Once the paperwork is done, however, projects are rarely if ever subsequently reviewed, and individual researchers know that they have a virtual carte blanche to do whatever they might wish.

It is a long-established principle of law that a patient or a human subject has the right to refuse consent to medical treatment being offered. Without the consent of the patient, any imposition of treatment constitutes a legal instance of battery, for which the physician or institution responsible for rendering care can be held legally responsible. This legal guideline includes the right to refuse treatment for personal reasons. A long series of court cases tested this principle for those (like Jehovah's Witnesses) who refuse on religious grounds to accept blood transfusions. As Carl Weissburg and Jay Hartz have reported, "The right to refuse treatment—sometimes enunciated as the right to control what happens to one's body—has, in fact, been considered so fundamental that it has been held by some courts to have its basis in the constitutional right to privacy, first recognized in birth control and abortion cases."[5]

More politically complicated have been the research endeavors that use individuals from Third World cultures as subjects without any effort to elicit consent and with no intention of providing immediate benefit to the subjects. This has come to light most often in the testing of birth control devices (e.g., oral contraceptives and injections of the birth control agent Depo Provera in women in Latin America and South Asia). The demonstrated lack of respect or concern for persons from other cultures and the readiness by chemical companies to take advantage of such subjects as experimental guinea pigs has been demonstrated time and time again. Any use of poor, uneducated, institutionalized, or otherwise disadvantaged subjects to facilitate research that would otherwise be more difficult or more expensive is clearly improper. The issue of full, free, and informed consent must cut across all class and race considerations.[6]

Patients' Rights

In the recently popular film and Broadway play *Whose Life Is It Anyway?* a young sculptor raises the ultimate question of patients' rights. Permanently paralyzed from a spinal injury suffered in an automobile accident, the artist demands that he be released from the hospital, in full knowledge of the fact that without medical life-support systems he will die within a few days. Knowing that he can never again practice his profession, and unwilling to live a life of total dependency on others, he makes what to many others in the story appears to be the irrational decision to end his life. The medical practitioners, with the best of intentions, create a host of barriers to keep the patient under care. Finally, after obtaining a writ of habeas corpus, the young man is released from further medical treatment—recognizing that he will be unconscious in three days and dead in five.[7]

How far do the rights of patients extend? Is there or should there be a limit to our decision-making ability when it comes down to determining the time and procedures for our own dying? Although the case just described exaggerates the issue, it nonetheless raises a variety of quite real questions. Not all that long ago, illness and death were relatively uncomplicated subjects. Birth, in the first place, and also living in illness and dying were palpable realities of every day, neither to be welcomed nor hidden from view. We lived and died at home. The distinctions between healthy living, the process of dying, and death itself were absolutely clear. While health care of one form or another has generally been available throughout the ages, realistic people—hoping that the medical practitioners might be able to assist in some small fashion—understood the futility of assuming that much real help could come from the medical community. Far greater expectations were placed in the doings of the religious practitioners. Here, at least, there was an understanding of mortality, of "ashes to ashes and dust to dust."

For some of us, things are pretty much still the same. We know when we are healthy, become concerned when we are ill, and—in spite of all the death-evading efforts of a nervous society—rarely need to be told when we are dying. However, the quite remarkable advances in medical technology have raised a number of new considerations for many people—those who either require medical treatment or in any case, for differing reasons, are subjected to it. Although modern medicine has done rather little to increase overall life expectancy (since most improvements have been the result of better sanitation and nutrition—with thanks being more appropriately due to the managers of our sewage systems and to the economists than to the medical folk), it is possible today to prolong life artificially for extended periods of time. The dilemma of the young sculptor is thus not all that uncommon. Coupled with our Western tendency toward an almost absolute conceptual evasion and rejection of death, the problem often become acute. Lack of acceptance of this ultimate reality implies an inability to anticipate and prepare for it. Aging is considered a psychological problem rather than a biological fact, and grand efforts are made to postpone or "cure" the illness of death. In the process, a quite significant portion of the medical research-and-development dollar is expended to maintain the pretense that per-haps—if we just try hard enough—death, like polio, will simply disappear.

In another category of rights, the freedom of patients to have some control in choosing their own medical treatment has become an issue of importance. Medical critic Ivan Illich has reintroduced the Greek word *iatrogenesis* into the vocabulary of patients and practitioners alike. Suggesting a root cause for much modern illness, Illich says, "The medical establishment has become a major threat to health. The disabling impact of professional control over medicine has reached the porportions of an epidemic. *Iatrogenesis,* the name for this new epidemic, comes from *iatros,* the Greek word for 'physician,' and *genesis,* meaning 'origin.' "[8]

The issue is quite real. Because of the constant threat of malprac-tice, for example, the average medical practitioner today prescribes a variety of clinical treatments and tests that in earlier days would never have been considered. Extensive lab work has come to be seen not so much as a necessity in patient care so much as a protection from possible legal action in the future. As one young intern in a major metropolitan medical center recently stated, "Every time a patient comes in here complaining of a headache, I make him lie down and I do a spinal puncture. If they want to come in here and bother us with their headaches, let them have their spinal cords punctured. I'm not going to let anyone walk out of here with anything undiagnosed so they can sue me later. If they have a headache, just give them the works—we're here to protect ourselves, no one else."[9]

Notwithstanding that the critics of modern medicine sometimes take too broad a swipe, it is clear that the need to limit our overly professionalized and technologized health care is a real and growing issue within the social and political arenas. Perhaps the first step in affirming basic patients' rights and assuming more personal control and responsibility for our own health would be to demystify the forms of modern medical practice. The industrialization of medicine and the transfer of diagnosis and care to high-tech specialists and medical centers has ushered in an era in which the medical profession assumes all the responsibility for determining both what constitutes sickness and what shall be done to treat it. The first casualty of this takeover is the natural sense of autonomy that every individual should feel in physically taking care of her or his own body. There seems to be an ever clearer contradiction between the social decision to provide most people with unlimited medical services and the personal requirement that we lead autonomous lives and be the primary managers of our own health.

In *The Social Transformation of Modern Medicine,* medical historian Paul Starr of Harvard traces the changes in U.S. medical practice in the past two centuries and attempts to analyze the political and economic reasons for the visible change to the high-cost, depersonalized, corporate medicine we have all come to know and hate. Among a variety of other factors, Starr details the steps that were necessary in order for the profession to gain the kind of social sovereignty it displays today: restriction of access to the craft, the emergence of state and local medical societies dedicated to limiting competition, the formation of economic monopolies in the practice of medicine, physican control over hospitals, and the control over the subsequent mystification of developments in medical science.[10] "But," as one reviewer notes, "it is not the doctors who are the villains of Starr's book. Indeed, their grasp on American health care is quickly slipping. Rather, it is the so-called medical-industrial complex, the corporate ambulance chasers who threaten to turn health care into franchise businesses like MacDonald's or Burger King."[11]

It is noteworthy that the issue of self-reliant medical care has at least as much application to the developing world as to the health systems of the more "advanced" countries. Too much in the way of Western medical technology continues to be exported to deal with medical problems that have malnutrition—protein and caloric deficiencies—at their root. A variety of studies have shown that technological medicine has an essentially limited value (except to the entrepreneurs) in treating illness caused by undernourishment. The technological healers should be humbled by the realization that—throughout the world—gastrointestinal and respiratory infections open the gateways to infectious disease and higher mortality whenever nutrition is poor, *regardless* of the availability of medical care. Good nutrition leads to precisely the opposite—to improved health—even when no medical services are available.

This global mystification of medicine—with the transfer of most prescriptive rights of diagnosis and treatment to the medical professionals—has led to poorer health for most of us. It has also become a major intrusion into the basic rights of patients, preventing them from either knowing or helping to treat the causal factors in their illness and disease.

The readiness of the medical research community to devote huge sums for biomedical development—artificial hearts, complicated scanning devices—stands in stark contrast to the early indifference of the government and its initial unwillingness to fund research for acquired immune deficiency syndrome (AIDS)–related diseases. The fact that AIDS diseases first primarily affected members of the gay and certain immigrant communities carried a negative political clout. The federal government began its substantial funding of AIDS research only after nongays and nonimmigrants (heterosexuals, pregnant women, and babies) began to come down with it in sufficient numbers to provide a political base for efforts to resolve the problem.

This general concern for the rights of patients is directly related to the problems of autonomy and informed consent. Any bill of rights for patients in an era of highly specialized medicine must deal with several major concerns. The right of the patient to be free from any overt medical intrusion that may go against his or her will and medical self-interest must be recognized. Ultimately, the right of the individual to make decisions based on the best information relating to his or her medical self-interest must be honored, and the patient's own best judgment upheld.

The Right to Live or Die

In recent years, both private and governmental organizations have initiated a variety of efforts to deal more humanely with the needs of patients for whom death appears to be imminent. In 1976, California's landmark Natural Death Act became law. Since then, many other states plus the District of Columbia have passed similar "right to die" laws, with at least another 25 state legislative enactments now in various stages of approval.

The common denominator in all legislation now on the books is the provision of some mechanism by which the patient may direct the physician to cut off extraordinary life-sustaining procedures when death is near. Varying substantially in both intent and direction, natural death laws have thus far been not always effective, nor subject to easy application. The common provision that requires an updating of the "living will" a week or two before death has often complicated the procedure. There are still many legal ambiguities involved, and difficulties in coming to a humane interpretation of the laws. Eleven states have now enacted laws to protect physicians from any legal action that may be filed against them for failure to provide "extraordinary" care to such patients; this has alleviated some of the problems. Particularly troublesome are the instances when patients either change their minds subsequent to their filing of the living will or when there is a major change in their physical or psychological state. Clearly physicians should always discuss the details of any natural death provisions well in advance of the need to implement any such decision. Some living will provisos also call for the naming of a friend or family member with power of attorney to assist in matters of interpretation that might later arise.

Whether for good or ill, the Supreme Court of the United States in June 1990 sought to clarify the confused living-will situation. The Court began by affirming (with eight justices in the majority) that the Constitution guarantees the right of the individual to refuse medical treatment. The guarantee applies even if the patient is comatose, so long as the individual has earlier made it clear that, under specific circumstances (accident, terminal illness, and so forth), he or she chooses not to receive medical treatment. The Court then left it up to each state to determine how clear the intent of the individual should be and what kind of evidence should be required to give warrant to the intent. Unhappily, states vary enormously in their practices. Missouri, Maine, and New York require absolutely "clear and convincing evidence" before agreeing to a patient's earlier stated request. Other states accept even informal understandings of friends and family members in regard to the patient's desires. What seems to be the message from the Court, however, is that those who really want their wishes followed regarding refusal of "extraordinary" medical treatment in the event of a terminal illness must make their intentions absolutely clear in writing and by completing what is called a "Durable Power of Attorney for Health Care." In making such final plans, it is much better to be safe than sorry!

However, it has also become increasingly apparent that the right to die a natural death with dignity is not guaranteed by the filing of a living will, no matter how proper. Indeed, there are some cases in which natural death legislation coupled with a simplistic and idealistic view of the final days has made death even less dignified and more painful.

> Consider what sorts of death actually occur under the rubric of "natural death." A patient suffers a cardiac arrest and is not resuscitated. Result: sudden unconsciousness, without pain, and death within a number of seconds. Or a patient has an infection that is not treated. Result: the unrestrained multiplication of microorganisms, the production of toxins, interference with organic function, hypotension and death. If the kidneys fail and dialysis . . . is not undertaken . . . nausea, vomiting, gastrointestinal hemorrhage (evident in vomiting blood) . . . and convulsions. Dying may take from days to weeks.
>
> Narcotic sedation . . . may be partially effective in controlling pain . . . but this patient will *not* get the kind of death he thought he had bargined for.
>
> The crucial point is that certain conditions will produce a death that is more comfortable, more decent, more predictable, and more permitting of conscious and peaceful experience than others.[12]

In the current enthusiasm for the right to a dignified, natural death, there has arisen the sobering realization that a simplistic overreliance on patient autonomy can lead to cruel consequences. A clear understanding among patient, physician, and family well in advance can protect both the autonomy and the final ease and dignity that every person deserves.

Overall, wherever they are in force, the natural death statutes have generally provided comfort both to terminal patients desiring to be relieved of the often grotesque rituals of the biomedical deathdance; and to physicians who are thus removed (in actual practice) from subsequent legal action when deciding not to enforce extraordinary life-sustaining procedures to maintain an otherwise dying patient. On another level, physicians have neither a legal nor a moral obligation to provide any therapy that will not cure the disease or relieve its symptoms. The decision to withhold or limit treatment may arise from four different possible reasons:

1. It is reasonably clear on the basis of past medical experience that the treatment is futile.

2. It accords with the patient's wishes and represents the best possible informed consent of the patient.

3. It contributes directly to the quality of life of the patient by preventing unnecessary pain and suffering.

4. It provides relief from massive and unnecessary medical expenses. (Terminal cancer patients in this country can typically be charged \$2000–\$3000 per day for care in an intensive care unit suitable for their needs.)

A number of court decisions and the common law of the medical community have led in recent years to an increasing number of determinations to stop the life-support systems without waiting for a court order. Nonetheless, many physicians still hesitate to direct such actions. Some may refuse even to discuss the issues involved in their decisions. Legal advisers to medical practitioners and hospitals tend to give "safe" and conservative advice, counseling against any termination of life support without a binding court mandate. As some commentators have noted, however, such caution is often unsatisfactory for everyone: patient, family, physician, and hospital.

> Unfortunately, such advice is not always a satisfactory response to the problem from the point of view of the family. . . . Such advice, in many cases, causes the family and the hospital (and/or the physician) to become adversaries. Also, it imposes an enormous financial and emotional burden on the family and leaves the physician (who may agree that termination is medically appropriate) in a frustrated and untenable position. As the problem and costs involved become more frequently encountered, aggressive efforts may be taken by families to end their ordeal. Four factors have typically been considered by legal counsel in advising not to terminate life-support systems. These are: fears of (1) civil liability; (2) disciplinary action by regulatory agencies; (3) adverse publicity; and (4) criminal liability.[13]

Physicians' fear of criminal liability is the major deterrent to patients' rights in such cases; it is a primary reason for the decision to maintain the life of a terminal patient by artificial means. But observers are increasingly of the opinion that such legal concerns are largely unfounded. Given routine medical consultation, the concurrence of a second physician, and the agreement of the family, it is most unlikely that any showing of negligence could be demonstrated that might result in either civil or criminal action against an attending physician. As noted earlier, some states have now enacted legislation that specifically protects physicians from legal action in such cases.

For adults at least, the bioethical issue is simplified and moves appropriately to the area of the nature and meaning of death and the right of a patient to determine for herself or himself the action to be taken. Thus, on questions of living and dying, the well-being of the individual must be seen as the highest good of any treatment. Interestingly, the ideal utilitarian–motivist synthesis can once again be seen as an appropriate framework for reaching ethical decision. Persons are seen as an end in themselves, with the consequences of any particular course of medical treatment being the key determinant. Joseph Fletcher states the case:

> It is harder morally to justify letting someone die a slow and ugly death, dehumanized, than it is to justify letting him escape from such misery. This is the case at least in any code of ethics which is humanistic or personalistic, i.e., in any code of ethics which has a value system that puts humanness and personal integrity above biological life and function. It makes no difference whether such an ethics system is grounded in a theistic or a naturalistic philosophy. We may believe that God wills human happiness or that man's happiness is, as Protagoras thought, a self-validating standard of the good and the right. But what counts ethically is whether human needs come first—not whether the ultimate sanction is transcendental or secular.[14]

Most traditional debate on the right-to-die issue has focused on the sanctity rather than the quality of life. Proscriptions against passive euthanasia (i.e., caring for but no longer medically intervening with a dying patient) are often based on the attitude that life is too precious to allow for any acquiescense with a decision simply to "let the patient go." But such conservative advice rarely considers the actual well-being of the patient, particularly when the patient truly wishes to be let go. To be human is to be personally conscious, participatory in relationships with others, and—perhaps most important of all— desirous of living. Illness can remove one from the common plateau of humanness, however, through the tragedy of needless and unnecessary suffering. The ethics of simple biological life and the need to at all costs preserve it must at times give way to an ethics of the quality of life. As those of us who have been extensively involved with suffering and dying people come to understand, biological continuance in severe and totally debilitating illness and/or trauma is most often absolutely contrary to the social and psychological well-being of the individual. Apart from the growing hospice movement, which attempts to provide high-quality personalized care for patients with terminal illness, rather little attention has been given in the United States to the maintaining of quality in the most vital processes of living and dying. Quite apart from the matter of pain and suffering, Western thought has traditionally affirmed the rational function of human beings as being the primary and definitive characteristic of authentic human life. Although, as noted earlier, this needful dimension can be overemphasized in determining the quality of life, it is nonetheless a key determinant of humanhood. It is cerebration—the ability to think, reason, and be self-conscious—rather than simple brain function that determines the quality of life. Happily, today the legal "definition of death" in most states includes "brain death," the cessation of any brain activity as measured by scanning and monitoring instruments. Brain death is truly death, whether or not the body continues to function.

For the bioethicist, biological continuance is not an end in itself. Rather, it assumes the importance of integrating a number of values—measured either objectively or subjectively, as the individual may determine—in order that life may truly be worth living. When for good reasons (particularly in the biotechnological age) it is not, then the difficult choice to die should be ours to make. Increasingly, for people all over the world, personal health is as much threatened as environmental health. Ecoethics subsumes within it the concern for personal as well as planetary well-being.

Notes

1. Philip J. Hilts, *Behavior Mod* (New York: Bantam Books, 1974), p. 8.

2. Thomas A. Mappes and Jane S. Zembatty, *Biomedical Ethics*, 2nd ed. (New York: McGraw-Hill, 1986), pp. 31–32.

3. Carol Levine, "Research Ethics before Nuremberg: German Doctors and Nazi Law," *Hastings Center Report* 14, no. 2 (April 1984), pp. 2–3.

4. George J. Annas, "Consent to the Artificial Heart," *Hastings Center Report* 13, no. 2 (April 1983), pp. 20–22.

5. Carl Weissburg and Jay N. Hartz, "Doctrine of Consent Poses Questions in Terminating Life Support System," *Health Law Review* 12 (October/November 1979), p. 38.

6. Ibid. p. 140.

7. For recent case studies of the same type, see the *Bioethics Letter* 3, no. 11 (November 1982).

8. Ivan Illich, *Medical Nemesis: The Expropriation of Health* (New York: Pantheon, 1976), p. 3.

9. Marcia Millman, "Patients' Rights: How Much Should Doctors Tell?" *New West* (January 17, 1977), p. 30.

10. Paul Starr, *The Social Transformation of American Medicine* (New York: Basic Books, 1983).

11. Alan M. Brandt, "The Ways and Means of American Medicine," *Hastings Center Report* 13, no. 3 (June 1983), p. 43.

12. M. Pabst Bettin, "The Least Worst Death," *Hastings Center Report* 13, no. 2 (April 1983), pp. 14–15; emphasis in original.

13. Carl Weissburg and Jay N. Hartz, "Legal and Ethical Risks Make Doctors Hesitant to Stop Life Support Systems," *Health Law Perspectives* (1984), p. 64.

14. Joseph Fletcher, *Humanhood: Essays in Biomedical Ethics* (New York: Prometheus Books, 1979), p. 149.

11

The Selfish Gene

Ever since the advent of Darwinian evolutionary theory, the debate over the relative importance of nature and nurture in human development has been going strong. Does heredity or environment play the dominant role in individual achievement and in social progress? More importantly, is cultural development—in particular, the growth of ethical value systems—simply a consequence of selfish genes seeking their own betterment? Do we, as males and females within particular ethnic groupings, have anything at all to say about the roles we will play in society or are our actions simply the predetermined casting of some cosmic genetic dice?

During the past two decades, the emergence of the school of sociobiology has lent fresh fuel to this old fire. It will be my intention in this chapter to explore whether or not the claims made by the mainstream of sociobiology—a trend proposing a new kind of positivist biological and genetic determinism—have any kind of scientific or sociological validity.

In his groundbreaking and highly controversial book *Sociobiology,* Harvard ethologist Edward O. Wilson defines the field of sociobiology as "the systematic study of the biological basis of all human behavior,"[1] If its proponents can indeed prove that biology by itself is the basis for all human behavior, then our perspectives on ethics, social behavior, and the values we have institutionalized over the millenia must significantly change. If in fact genetic information is the only effective force in shaping individuals and societies—as the sociobiologists claim—then our sense of present and future will have to be quite different from those familiar and now somehow innocent images of a meaningful life envisioned by the various ethical and religious world views that have emerged in human history.

As a social theory, sociobiology is largely patterned on the principles of Darwinian natural selection. Viewing evolution as little more than the survival of the fittest in a competitive natural order, socio-biology pushes all behavior back to a kind of genetic game of craps. Orthodox neo-Darwinism has always argued that the key construct in evolution is to be found in the fact that the developing organism (the phenotype) is rigidly and absolutely determined by the genetic infor-mation (the genotype) programmed into it at birth. It affirms that the process of natural selection is a perfect architect, constructing organ-isms through trial and error in ways that will enable them to meet the problems they will face in particular natural environments, and maximizing their reproductive fitness. Thus, each physical character-istic is simply a product of natural selection operating on behalf of the particular organism. But, as biologist Stephen Jay Gould has said in reflecting on the fact that evolutionary theory must inevitably have a certain "zoocentric" core wherein all animals conform to certain biological principles, "the zoocentric view can be extended too far into a caricature often called the 'nothing but' fallacy (humans are 'nothing but' animals)."[2]

Indeed, for the past decade or more, there has been a major break in the traditional reliance of evolutionary theorists on neo-Darwinism, a rigidly determinist theory that has special appeal to sociobiologists. Newer theories hold that the genotype is not solely responsible for animal development, but that the environment also plays a major role. Adaptive abilities are not fixed at birth. Before evaluating the main trends in sociobiological theory, we shall take a look at this newer perspective on evolution.

Darwinian theory—the intellectual underpinning and beginning point for all serious evolutionary research and analysis, including conservative developmental doctrines like sociobiology—has always maintained that physical traits can be inherited but never acquired through nongenetic contact with the environment. In this view, species play no role whatsoever in shaping their own genetic destinies. Condemning all alternative theories (like that of the French biologist the Chevalier de Lamarck who affirmed that species characteristics can arise as much from an organism's response to immediate survival needs as to longer and more incremental genetic change—one ex-ample of the more immediate response being the thickened callouses on the knees and rump of the ostrich to make sitting more comfort-able), strict neo-Darwinists insisted that species variation occurs only through the chance connections of natural selection. As biologist Gordon Taylor has said,

Darwin believed, in the last resort, that the environment determined the way its occupants would evolve, whereas Lamarck, who believed that the creatures chose their environment, left the course of evolution open to free and individual choice. These two views foreshadowed the political controversy which was about to flare up between Marxism, which claimed man could change his social environment and hence himself, and those Christians who held that God has preordained each man's role in life.[3]

The traditional theory of natural selection, with its description of only gradual and imperceptible changes in species development over eons of time, is being forcefully challenged these days by mathematicians, paleontologists, and molecular geneticists who seem to have proven that natural selection alone cannot account for the enormous and complicated changes one notes in animal evolution. The "punctuated equilibrium" theory of Stephen Jay Gould—that "evolution moves in fits and starts rather than by slow, steady change"—is increasingly accepted within the scientific community and again contradicts the basic assumptions of the sociobiologists.

In his current book *Wonderful Life,* Gould suggests that in fact evolution works more by accident than by slow inevitable progress. While Homo sapiens is certainly unique, there is nothing in the laws of nature that somehow directed evolution on an upward spiral toward the production of human beings. Declaring that "we're all just lucky to be here," Gould thinks the mass extinctions that have affected other species (e.g., the dinosaurs) could just as well have eradicated us.[4] The "creative" evolutionists of not so long ago who (especially Teilhard de Chardin) affirmed that evolution has always been somehow intentionally geared toward the production of its most important species—human beings—were too much influenced by religious enthusiasm and too little by a recognition that God might have an interest in the intrinsic value of other creatures, as well.

Thus, the old Darwinian understanding seems too narrow and, in fact, one-dimensional to provide for the splendid multiplication of species and specialized characteristics that we see all about us. According to some critics, mathematical theory alone refutes the claim that genetic change through natural selection brought about all the diverse forms of life on Earth.

It is our interpretation that if "random" is given a serious and crucial interpretation from a probabilistic point of view, the randomness postulate is highly implausible and that an adequate scientific theory of evolution must await the discovery and elucidation of new natural laws.

Thus, to conclude, we believe that there is a considerable gap in the neo-Darwinian theory of evolution, and we believe that it cannot be bridged within the current conception of biology.[5]

As proponents of the newer scientific evolutionary theory suggest, our own animal history has probably been too short for things like the complicated chemistry of the blood or the subtleties of the eye to have occurred through chance. The laws of probability seem not to admit of such manipulations, even over millions of years. Other factors must be at work. Jeremy Rifkin notes,

The more researchers penetrate the inner workings of embryological development, the more convinced they become that other forces besides genes are at work fashioning the organism. The emerging consensus is that the genes are subordinate in the developmental process and that the solution to the problem of development lies at the cellular and intercellular level rather than at the genetic level.[6]

Overall, then, neo-Darwinism—the formal theoretical tool of sociobiology—seems simply too rigid to explain the majesty and mystery of life. Granted, the creationists are utterly in error. Evolution has certainly taken place, but most assuredly not in the way that evolutionary theorists have postulated for at least 100 years. Gordon Taylor lists more than a dozen validated scientific challenges to the formal determinism and the biological rigidity of traditional evolutionary theory and, by implication, of sociobiology. The more important include facts related to the following concerns:

• The suddenness with which new species have developed, and the lack of fossil remains from the periods during which the Darwinists say the slow evolution had to have taken place;
• The suddenness with which new life forms "radiated" into numerous variants;
• The suddenness of the many species extinctions (95 percent of all species that have thus far evolved), and the lack of any clear scientific reasons for these extinctions;
• The occurrence of parallel evolution in which the same basic physical structures have evolved in different places and under quite different circumstances;
• The occurrence of negative evolutionary momentum wherein some characteristics continue evolving even at harm to the species; and

• The apparent failure of some species and organisms to develop at all.[7]

The new revolution in molecular genetics (aspects of which were reviewed in Chapters 7 and 8) has, ironically, produced a kind of evidence Darwin could not have known for those apparently sudden and rapid evolutionary developments that Darwin critics cite. Modern scientific data seem to support such rapid evolutionary transformation and contradict the traditional hypothesis of natural selection. The simple fact that genetic segments from different species can now be recombined to make new life forms suggests at least the strong possibility that such recombinations of genetic stuff may have occurred naturally between species throughout evolutionary history. Such changes would account for what seem to have been quantum leaps in the development of many organisms. The new genetics reveals a plasticity in the gene structure that may continue to transform evolutionary thinking.

Those sociobiologists who persist in their dependence on the old inflexible theory of the absolute genetic predetermination of behavioral characteristics (e.g., that men are men and women are women and we had better not tamper with genetically ordained role behavior) must now reckon with the fact that some acquired characteristics have probably always been heritable. Evolutionary change moves much more rapidly and more flexibly than was once assumed. If genes are only expressed when the cellular environment calls for them to be expressed—rather than in accord with some genetic gamble—it makes little sense to say (as does E. O. Wilson) that in the social realm all ethics and cultural development are occasioned strictly by genetic tendencies.

The newer understandings provide a base of optimism for human development. If information flows into the genome as well as out, it carries with it the possibility of a more positive social adaptation for our species. As the new genetics is showing us day by day, the specific environment (chemicals, geographical location, chance mutation, and sudden environmental need) can alter the phenotype—sometimes rather quickly. Information does seem to move toward the genome as well as out from it, and adaptation appears to be an adjustment to new modes of life and changed environments as well as to the genetic information encoded in the reproductive cells. As species, we are most certainly no more than what we are. But what we are is not simply the consequence of some cosmic arbitrariness in nature, but also of shorter range needs and requirements of the species. There is still room for free choice and, for humans, cultural and ethical development in response to need.

Sociobiology

The remainder of this chapter will assess the efforts of contemporary sociobiology in applying a probably outmoded view of evolutionary process to the understanding of modern human behavior. Attempting to explain, for example, the oft-studied paradox that animals—while genetically programmed, it would seem, to exhibit a primary concern for their own self-interest—may nonetheless occasionally evidence altruistic behavior, sociobiology raises the critical question of whether or not all "ethical" behavior—including that of Homo sapiens—is not biologically foreordained. In speaking to this issue, E. O. Wilson states,

> As more complex social behavior by the organism is added to the genes' techniques for replicating themselves, altruism becomes increasingly prevalent and eventually appears in exaggerated forms. This brings us to the central problem of sociobiology: how can altruism which by definition reduces personal fitness, possibly evolve by natural selection? The answer is kinship: if the genes causing the altruism are shared by two organisms because of common descent, and if the altruistic act by one organism increases the joint contribution of these genes to the next generation, the propensity to altruism will spread through the gene pool. This occurs even though the altruist makes less of a solitary contribution to the gene pool as the price of its altruistic act.[8]

Wilson and most sociobiologists think of altruism as a biologically unique and ultimately selfish inclination that leads to actions beneficial to other individuals or groups but always at some shorter range cost to the actor. While altruistic behavior never has intentionality behind it, it almost always has within it some form of biological payoff. Why should human animals in their "natural" state demonstrate such actions as a result of which they may sacrifice some immediate satisfaction for an unknown general good? Because (drawing on the sociobiologists' animal-to-human parallelisms) those who were concerned only for their immediate self-interest or well-being—who, for example, could not be bothered to protect clan or family or group—

would probably leave fewer descendents, due to the overall weakening of the community. More importantly, there would be less chance for survival of their genetic material. Since we have only one way of passing on the genetic material in our DNA—that is, through reproduction—it is quite natural that we should wish to maximize the number of our direct descendents and, by affirming kinship ties, assure the continuance of some of our genetic stuff at least indirectly. Thus, genes that promoted only those tendencies toward maximizing personal well-being—ignoring the concerns of kin—would be less likely to survive than genes with other more pragmatic and altruistic interests. Even ethics of the "you scratch my back and I'll scratch yours" variety have benefits that far surpass immediate satisfaction. Truly "selfish" genes, according to the sociobiologists, will promote tendencies that increasingly enable the individual to evidence concern for kin (the most characteristic form of altruism) and for the larger group (the community, the tribe, the nation). This process then makes possible the kind of reciprocal altruism where the individual shows concern for another either in the hope of sometime receiving something in return, or simply out of a concern to further the well-being of the other person. All such "moral" actions are said to have genetic self-interest at their base.

We will return to Wilson's "central theoretical problem" of altruism when we consider the possibility of an evolutionary ethic later in the chapter. Of central significance to us here, however, is that, in this new form of biological predestination, all the traditional virtues of our species—unselfishness, conscience, love—seem utterly unrelated to any intentional effort on the part of individuals or groups to further either happiness or the greater social good. All virtue results simply from the transmission of controlling genes. As Richard Dawkins notes, "Much as we might wish to believe otherwise, universal love and the welfare of the species as a whole are concepts which simply do not make evolutionary sense."[9]

This controlling view of the sociobiologists, based more on social assumption than on empirical study, is both disturbing and surprising. Stretching theory to the point of absurdity, some contemporary sociobiological analysts have attempted, for example, to explain away the significance of rape in human society by suggesting this is a characteristic that has been genetically selected for over the millennia. All animal behavior, they argue, tends to maximize fitness and inevitably selects for maximum contribution to the well-being of the species and for the production and survival of the largest number of offspring. Rape is thus said to satisfy both an erotic and a reproductive need. But the theorists who biologically justify rape ignore its social and cultural base and that it is not a form of sexual practice, but a form of violence. Stephen Jay Gould says,

> Sociobiologists are often fooled by the misleading external and superficial similarity between behaviors in humans and other animals. They attach human names to what other creatures do and speak of slavery in ants, rape in mallard ducks, and adultery in mountain bluebirds. . . . Such an old, old story. We hold a mirror to nature and see ourselves and our own prejudices in the glass. . . . [faltering] in the *hubris* of arguing that evolution undertook its elaborate labor of some 3½ billion years only to generate the little twig that we call *Homo sapiens*.[10]

None of this is totally new, however. Certain of our Western intellectual traditions (mainly idealism) have inspired a readiness to posit superficially mechanical views of humans and nature. René Descartes suggested a working metaphor in 1644, saying, "I have described this earth, and the whole visible world . . . as if it were a machine in the shape and movements of all its parts."[11] But in a terse critique of this mechanistic antecedent of sociobiology, Harvard biologist Richard Lewontin states,

> What has happened [since Descartes] is that, in the minds of natural scientists and a large fraction of social scientists as well, the world has ceased to be like a machine, but instead is seen as if it were a machine. Cartesian reductionism, which regards the entire world of things as, in fact, a very complicated electromechanical device, is not simply the dominant mode of thought in natural science, but the only mode to enter the consciousness of the vast majority of modern scientists. It is no exaggeration to say that most scientists simply do not know how to think about the world except as a machine.
>
> The demonstration that living organisms in all their aspects (with the exception of the human conscious mind) could be explained as a mechanical system was at the heart of Descartes' argument for a clocklike world.[12]

Those who criticize this Cartesian *redux* in modern determinism believe that overall the new sociobiology reflects such a world view and simply furthers the movement toward a new and more sophisticated version of the social Darwinism that characterized much sociological theory in the late nineteenth century. During this period, sociologists like Herbert Spencer attempted in rather primitive fashion to apply the basic principles of evolutionary theory and natural selection to the analysis and evaluation of human social conduct. In his influential book *Social Statics,* Spencer launched a movement in which the "struggle for existence" and the "survival of the strongest" became slogans through which explanations could be found for all patterns of injustice in modern society.[13] Like the population theory of the Reverend Thomas Malthus a century and a half earlier, Spencerian eugenics was used to justify the existing class relationships in the society and to exempt the rich from any responsibility toward the larger social order. If all of our frailties are determined by genetic construction, how foolish to criticize the status quo!

The misery of the "lower" orders and the suffering of the oppressed were understood by Spencer (and implicitly affirmed, one suspects, by much modern sociobiology) as simply the inevitable by-products of an evolutionary process in which the strong would always rise like cream to the top of the social order and those less fit would be genetically directed to serve the stronger or else be destroyed. Any interference with this evolutionary struggle was seen by Spencer as evil. From this primitive hodgepodge of misunderstood science and ultraconservative social theory came the pseudoscience of eugenics. This now largely discredited system of selective human breeding was intended, by at least most of the social Darwinians, to create a new master race. That twentieth-century fascism approved and incorporated Spencerian ethics and eugenics into its social theory should not be surprising. The implications of Spencerian thought were tailor-made for application by totalitarian systems.

While it may be true that some modern sociologists have downplayed the importance of heredity in human social development— viewing the human consciousness as little more than a wax tablet of the mind on which the social order carves its instructions—the dangers of biological determinism still lurk within the study of society, posing a vastly greater threat to the survival of the species than ever before. Any effort to reconstruct a neo-Spencerian eugenics—or to do social analysis from the assumptions of that theory—turns the science of social relationships into just another branch of molecular biology. Eugenics and any extension thereof place automatic biological constraints on the possibility of our doing social good. If all is in fact biologically foreordained, then it is both presumptuous and foolish to be overly concerned about community action or the greater well-being of society. Criticizing this modern version of the mechanistic world view, Lewontin describes the new tendency thus:

> Cartesian biology objectifies organisms. They are seen as the passive consequences of internal and external forces, genes, and environment. Organisms are objects, the internal and external forces the subjects. What [our hoped for] dialectical biology attempts to do is to break down the alienation of subject and object, to insist on the interpenetration of gene, organism, and environment. . . . Organism and environment are both in a constant state of becoming, mutually determining each other. . . . It is not that a whole is more than the sum of its parts, but that the parts themselves are redefined and re-created in the process of their interaction.[14]

True, contemporary sociobiologists—albeit tipping often in the direction of a formal and rigid determinism—rarely draw the same conclusions from their theory as did the old social Darwinists. Though their statements in defending their stance seem to contradict their research conclusions, many heartily resent being cast within the determinist net. Pointing to his total work, for example, E. O. Wilson reminds us that he first provides comparative studies of animal social behavior and then only suggests that there are many parallels in behavioral development between lower and higher animal species. Exploring the development of altruism in animals, Wilson draws out the animal-to-human connections that reflect an unusual movement beyond immediate self-interest in certain actions, and that thus appear to have genetic origin. Always in this theory, however, altruistic behavior—whether in primates or humans—is considered to serve the genetic tendencies and patterns of kinship. Sociobiology rejects any kind of cultural or spiritual "ethical" progression. Notwithstanding the protest of its advocates, in sociobiology there seems no alternative to the biologically mechanistic and determinist view of the nature and destiny of our species.

For Wilson, all human values and systems of ethics are thus essentially the result of genetic development. Behavioral patterns and social structures alike are seen as no more than organs of the body, and as extensions of the genotype. Bouts of creativity or hostility, tendencies either toward homo- or heterosexuality, the failures of entrepreneurs, or the miscalculations of workers—all are simply outcomes of genetic programming. One of the most controversial aspects of the theory is in its regarding of social sexual roles as being genetically determined.

In the film *Sociobiology: Doing What Comes Naturally*, Wilson's colleague Robert L. Trivers bluntly states, "The sexes are biologically programmed or wired to behave the way they do. . . . Most aspects of human behavior including ethical systems and moral values are biologically determined."

In perhaps the most crucial section of Wilson's authoritative text *Sociobiology*—the concluding chapter titled "Man: From Sociobiology to Sociology"—he criticizes the social conventions that for some time have credited cultural variation with playing a major and often dominant role in the social and environmental context. Stating that we need a discipline of anthropological genetics in order more properly to evaluate human behavior, Wilson criticizes the more holistic biologies of persons like Theodore Dobzhansky, who has said, "Culture is not inherited through genes, it is acquired from other human beings. . . . In a sense, human genes have surrendered their primary role in human evolution to an entirely new, non-biological or superorganic regent, culture."[15]

Escalating his opposition to the cultural evolutionists, Wilson suggests that the time has come for ethics to be taken away from the realm of philosophy and "biologized." He rejects the belief that the human mind can have any direct consciousness of right and wrong (doing away with both Platonic and Cartesian epistemology in one fell swoop), or that it can utilize logic in the development of particular rules for social conduct. Rejecting all forms of social voluntarism or the ideas of social contract as traditionally formulated by European liberals like Locke and Rousseau, Wilson defends his belief that genetic transfer and the functioning of "the neural machinery of ethical judgment" can be the basis for understanding any form of human conduct today. Wilson believes there can be no truly relevant sociology until science develops "a full, neuronal explanation of the human brain. Only when the machinery [of the brain] can be torn down on paper at the level of the cell and put together again will the properties of emotion and ethical judgment become clear." Affirming that a real ethic cannot be developed other than as a consequence of genetic transfer, Wilson states,

Stress can then be evaluated in terms of the neurophysiological perturbations and their relaxation times. Cognition will be translated into circuitry. Learning and creativeness will be defined as the alteration of specific portions of the cognitive machinery regulated by input from the emotive centers. Having cannibalized psychology, this new neurobiology will yield an enduring set of first principles for sociology. To maintain the species indefinitely, we are compelled to drive toward total knowledge, right down to the levels of the neuron and the gene. When we have progressed enough to explain ourselves in these mechanistic terms . . . then the social sciences will have come to full flower.[16]

In spite of the sometimes strident and cheerleaderish quality of these pronouncements, it is only fair to note (as we have above also) that Wilson and others like him regularly protest what they consider to be the false accusations of critics in reviewing their work. They denounce the extremists who prophesy that this new biological determinism will open the door to a reenactment of the Spencerian sterilization laws (once operative in 20 U.S. states), restrictive immigration policies, and the kind of eugenics that led to the gas chambers of Nazi Germany. Wilson says that he "regrets and resents this ugly, irresponsible, and totally false accusation." It is perfectly clear, however—even accepting sociobiology's protestations of innocence—that social theories based on some notion of the biological superiority of one class, race, or sex have historically been used by those who would profit politically from their application. No doubt, Wilson and most modern genetic absolutists do not intend to reinforce the existing jeopardies of race and class. That their work can be (and often is) used to further such ends is nonetheless undeniable.

Toward an Evolutionary Ethic

Notwithstanding the foregoing criticism of the more absolutist biological determinists, the process of natural selection in evolution has played a significant role in the development of human culture. The genetic struggles that warred it out over the ages paved the way for those capacities required for the acquisition of certain human values. Evolution has conferred on humankind a wondrous assortment of special endowments: consciousness, subjectivity, educability, sensitivities to self and others, the talent to develop and use systems of language. None of these exist independently of biological evolution; cultural evolution cannot be viewed as completely separate from genetic development. Such an affirmation of our collective hereditary indebtedness must also define the limits, however, to what at first glance may seem like a more than partial dependence on the role of biology in social development.

The systems of philosophical reflection and ethics that have developed over the millenia of human history—those special characteristics that distinguish our species from all the others—are essentially the product of human wisdom developed through experience. At the same time, it is only fair to say that some critics do protest too strongly against the excesses of sociobiology and refuse to include any kind of evolutionary insights in developing a sound bioethical system. Ethicist Peter Singer states the rationale for a "both/and" approach to genetics and culture in value formation.

> My own view, which reflects my consequentialist position in ethics, is that all who think about ethical issues should draw their conclusions on the basis of the best information available. When well grounded biological theories are relevant to an ethical decision, they should be taken into account. The particular moral judgments that we end up making may reflect these theories. For this reason, it is perfectly true that philosophers, along with everyone else, should know something about the current state of biological theories of human nature. To ignore biology is to ignore one possible source of knowledge relevant to ethical decisions.[17]

Recognizing our kindred biological indebtedness, we must then move on, however, to affirm that our special human characteristics are now as much the product of human culture as of genetic predisposition. No one would deny how remarkable and complex is the genetic pool from which we all spring. Yet genetic transmission occurs only once in every human life. And determinative though it certainly is in some areas, genetic control is much less constant an influence than the enculturation that is a regular and never-ending fact of human existence. Human consciousness, which can rightly be understood as the culmination of an evolutionary process, is still as much a social phenomenon as a biological one.

As we anticipate a most difficult collective future for humankind—including the almost certain prospect of a number of environmental and social crises unprecedented in human history—it is critical that we not succumb to the kind of genetic fatalism that only shrugs its biological shoulders at what some predict will be an unhappy ending for our species. Human ethics, our values and moral sensibilities, must continue to be utilized in seeking solutions to the new dilemmas we shall face. We do not have to wait (nor would it be reasonable to do so) for genetic transformation to reshape our social and ethical systems.

Ethical behavior, therefore, has more than a utilitarian and evolutionary/adaptive function. Bioethicist George H. Keiffer has postulated the need for what he calls an "evolutionary ethic." Affirming that we must weigh the relative importance both of biological evolution and of cultural development and innovation in the development of specieswide moral and ethical systems, Keiffer notes that

> Systems of ethics are the product of human wisdom and the experience of human beings living together and not of the expression of human genes. Though a rational system of ethics cannot be independent of evolution, neither can a system of ethics be derived directly from evolution. The prevailing view of those that have studied the question is that although the potential for developing an ethical system is the outcome of evolutionary processes, meaning and value are culturally determined.[18]

These issues, then, go beyond those normally proposed by ethicists. If the observation of many experts is correct—that the survival of the species is totally dependent on present-day human conduct—the relative arguments of determinists and culturalists (the nature versus nurture debate) may be critical to that survival. R. W. Sperry, professor of psychobiology at the California Institute of Technology, explains the importance of the issue this way:

> I tend to rate the problems of human values Number One for science above the more concrete crisis problems like poverty, population, energy or pollution on the following grounds.
> First, all these crisis conditions are man-made and very largely the products of human values. Further, they are not correctable on any long-term basis without first changing the underlying human value priorities involved. The more strategic way to remedy these conditions is to go after the social value priorities directly rather than simply waiting for the value changes to be forced by changing conditions.[19]

Sometimes, it is the general arrogance of the determinists that requires a commonsense kind of mellowing before any holistic cooperation between the two sides can occur. (The recalcitrance of some culturalists has been admitted above.) Hard-line determinist Richard Dawkins has been forced to relativize his usual stance with an interesting affirmation of biocultural development. Stating that a new kind of evolutionary force may have appeared on the planet, Dawkins describes this new reality as "still in its infancy, still drifting clumsily about in its primeval soup but already achieving evolutionary change at a rate which leaves the old gene panting far behind." The new medium, suggests Dawkins, is the soup of "human culture." He originates the word *meme* to describe this emergent unit of cultural transmission.

> Examples of *memes* are tunes, ideas, catch-phrases, . . . ways of making pots or building arches. Just as genes propagate themselves in the gene pool by leaping from body to body via sperms or eggs, so *memes* propagate themselves in the *meme* pool by leaping from brain to brain via a process which in the broad sense can be called imitation. Whenever conditions arise in which a new kind of replicator can make copies of itself, replicators will tend to take over and start a new kind of evolution of their own. Once this new evolution begins, it will in no sense be subservient to the old. Biologists have assimilated the idea of genetic evolution so deeply that we tend to forget that it is only one of many kinds of evolution.[20]

Even E. O. Wilson has been known to contradict his primary line.

> The evidence is strong that almost all differences between human societies are based on learning and social conditioning, rather than heredity."[21]

But this occasional relativizing of an otherwise absolutist position seems contradictory and more intended to ameliorate criticisms of sociobiology than to incorporate new data into the theory. The apparent appeal of a generalized biological absolution to the ambiguities of human behavior and culture is politically dangerous since it is too quickly affirmed in the popular consciousness. Simplistic solutions to the dilemmas of human existence are often captured by propagandists (e.g., the promotion of creationist theories by the Moral Majority) and/or the media and quickly transformed into what is taken to be truth by those unacquainted with the facts. On the positive side, however, sociobiology calls to mind the unforgettable reality that we are, as Homo sapiens, the end product of a long history of genetic evolution. It can provide an authentic new dimension in understanding the ethical behavior of human beings. To ignore our evolutionary history may be to doom our future. Only, the "circle of altruism" is both wider and less biologically ordained than that proposed by the determinist. As Peter Singer says, the circle "has broadened from the family and tribe to the nation and race, and we are beginning to recognize that our obligations extend to all human beings."[22] The ecoethicist lives within an even wider realm, and recognizes that the ethical responsibility extends beyond humankind to all of the natural world. Including a sense of such universal altruism as a reality in the human condition represents a quantum leap in ethical theory from that of the selfish gene.

The danger in even the moderate forms of sociobiology, then, is the limitation implied in their vision and prospectus for the human race. There is an inevitable tendency lurking within them to distinguish between those who are biologically more or less select. We can ill afford today those sociobiological shortcuts that have created such social havoc in our recent past. It is now more important than ever before to differentiate between that science which serves—albeit not intentionally—particular political and social end goals, and that which is dedicated to easing the human condition. The consequences of some of these "neo-Cartesian" forms of science can be no more ignored than the consequences of any other wide-scale human action. As bioethicist Joseph Duffy notes,

> These consequences may include dramatic changes in our own sense of what is possible with respect to the determination of human behavior, the manipulation of human genetics, and the alteration of life forms. What is possible is a matter of scientific discovery, of knowledge and technology. Its limits are yet to be determined. But beyond what is possible, there is another question to ponder: what is desirable. The answers to that question are more definite, more problematic, more closely related to choices about what we value, what we cherish as the most important and critical aspects of human life.[23]

Sociobiology has presented us with one explanation for the development of ethics in human society. We can profit from listening to its proponents. It cannot tell us, however, what we should do to maximize our human potential. It seems, instead, to limit that critical sphere of moral and ethical action that we will need if our species is to develop the social options and the new societies required for survival in what promises to be a most uncertain and likely very dangerous future. A whole new set of hard ethical choices has been created for people today by virtue of the many recent developments in the biological and physical sciences. On top of this, our choices are now more difficult because we have the power to do more good and to do more harm than ever before. Caution is critically warranted in our evaluation of any emergent ethic, particularly one rooted in such a questionable science as sociobiology.

Notes

1. Edward O. Wilson, *Sociobiology: The Abridged Edition* (Cambridge, Mass.: Belknap Press, 1980), p. 4.

2. Stephen Jay Gould, *Hen's Teeth and Horse's Toes* (New York: W.W. Norton, 1983), p. 242.

3. Gordon R. Taylor, *The Great Evolution Mystery* (New York: Harper and Row, 1983), pp. 53–54.

4. Stephen J. Gould, *Wonderful Life* (New York: W.W. Norton, 1989).

5. Murray Eden, "Inadequacies of Neo-Darwinian Evolution as a Scientific Theory," in P. Moorehead and M. Kaplan, eds., *Mathematical Challenges to the Neo-Darwinian Interpretation of Evolution* (Philadelphia: Wistar Press, 1967), p. 109.

6. Jeremy Rifkin, *Algeny: A New Word—A New World* (New York: Penguin Books, 1984), pp. 164–65.

7. Taylor, *Great Evolution Mystery*, pp. 137–38.

8. Wilson, *Sociobiology*, p. 3.

9. Richard Dawkins, *The Selfish Gene* (Oxford, U.K.: Oxford University Press, 1976), pp. 2–3.

10. Gould, *Hen's Teeth*, pp. 242–45.

11. René Descartes, *The Principles of Philosophy* (Boston: Kluwer, 1984), art. 203; originally published in 1644.

12. R. C. Lewontin, "The Corpse in the Elevator," *New York Review of Books*, January 20, 1983.

13. Herbert Spencer, *Social Statics: Or the Conditions Essential to Human Happiness* (New York: D. Appleton, 1866).

14. Lewontin, "Corpse in Elevator," p. 37.

15. Theodosius Dobzhansky, "Anthropology and the Natural Sciences—The Problem of Human Evolution," *Current Anthropology* 4 (April 1963), pp. 138 and esp. 146–48.

16. Wilson, *Sociobiology*, p. 300.

17. Peter Singer, *The Expanding Circle: Ethics and Sociobiology* (New York: Meridian Press, 1981), p. 68.

18. George H. Keiffer, *Bioethics: A Textbook of Issues* (New York: Addison-Wesley, 1979), p. 21.

19. R. W. Sperry, as quoted in ibid., p. 32.

20. Ibid., p. 208.

21. E. O. Wilson, *On Human Nature* (Cambridge, Mass: Belknap Press, 1978), p. 48.

22. Singer, *Expanding Circle*, p. 120.

23. Joseph Duffy, *An Introduction to Hard Choices*, Office of Radio and Television for Learning, Boston, 1979.

12

The Social Sources of Environmental Values

Too infrequently do we ask ourselves the important question, How is it that we develop our particular philosophies of life, our ethics and our morals? Perhaps sociologists and novelists are better aware than sociobiologists and philosophers of the truth that cultural history and personal experience are more important in determining individual values and life directions than abstract ideas. In spite of Plato and the essentially normative idealist tilt in Western intellectual history, experientially based awareness precedes the mandate of the a priori for most of us. In real life, practice influences theory more than the reverse. C. Wright Mills precisely sums up our situation in trying to find some solid ground with telltale traces that there is a rich lode of environmental values lying just below. "Neither the life of an individual nor the history of a society can be understood without understanding both. The sociological imagination enables us to grasp history, biography, and the relations between the two within society. That is its task and its promise."[1]

Tom Wolfe in his novel *The Bonfire of the Vanities*—an accurately troublesome dissection of class, racial conflict, and life values in New York City—reminds us that life is always played out in history.[2] The largely Black and Hispanic culture in the Bronx, and its consequent ethic, is inevitably and qualitatively different from that of the WASP culture on Wall Street and in the suburbs. Although in both ethics and politics we may think of our own lives as essentially nonhistorical, such is never in fact the case. Our values are to a very large extent the consequence of actions and events in the past that now shape our individual personality and our social credos.

For most people, then, social-cultural experience is enormously more important in the development of environmental values than ideas by themselves. Certain environmental educators believe that the environmental ethic is largely conditioned by outdoors experiences and occasional wilderness adventures.[3] But actually, major historical forces seem to be the dominant factors in this regard.[4]

The best way to underscore the importance of social-cultural forces in value formation is to listen to real people discussing these matters. Therefore, the balance of this chapter is largely a summary of the personal reflections (oral and written) of university students in an environmental ethics class at the University of California, Berkeley, in the spring of 1988.[5]

There seem to be at least two major dimensions to the value impact of social-historical forces on ecoethics. The first is how we understand the self in relation to the larger society. The second is reflected in the tensions arising from the inevitable conflicts that emerge as we work out our personal ethic within the larger historical setting.

Person/Society Influences

Every person fits either more or less comfortably within the social stratifications of the larger society. What is one's family position within the social order? How have the historical forces within and outside of the society (industrialization, urbanization, immigration, the division of labor in the society, depressions, wars) affected the self-understanding of the individual in relation to nature? Living as we do in class society, how do the particular characteristics of class (privilege or disadvantage) affect our moral valuations?

Which were the cultural values transmitted by our family and/or the larger social orders? How were such values reinforced, reinterpreted, or rejected in our contacts with the institutional areas of church, school, work, and politics? What are the expectations held by self and/or family relative to our career and personal life goals?

Tensions emerging from the acceptance or rejection of cultural values affect the development of the moral sensitivity. What are the conflicts experienced between the individual's goals and ethics and those of the major social institutions of the society? In what ways do all of these factors affect the individual's personal life ethic? As one person notes,

> I must look first at the values of my family. This is because . . . the family's views work as a filter through which we view society and the world's events. This filter, however, often distorts reality!

That we are essentially a nation of immigrants has profoundly affected environmental values in the United States. To assess the impact of possibly inheriting "immigrant values," people in the environmental ethics class conducted a self-survey exercise. Many of the students were planning an environmental career. They were asked simply to list the dominant values that they felt would be regularly reinforced in the immigrant family situation, either by parents or grandparents. Common factors noted were:

- The work ethic of parents and grandparents;
- The United States as the new promised land (and almost always defended as such, in spite of the social contradictions that often made life difficult for the immigrants);
- The respect for land—"our Mother"—on the part of peasant or agricultural worker immigrants;
- The universality of hard times economically, and the negative impacts of the Great Depression;
- The absolute centrality of the family;
- The constant concern for upward mobility, with the transition for the immigrants most often leading from peasant class to factory worker, then to middle class, and occasionally to upper-middle-class and upper-class levels;
- The double insulation experienced by most immigrant families: (1) social-religious and ethnic insulation in the first generation, and then (2) economic and cultural insulation from their own people of the privileged ones who finally make it economically;
- The demographic trend of a rural-to-urban shift, both geographically and socially.

However, the most sophisticated analyses of these social-institutional impacts came from those who had actually experienced them—the institutionalized racism, sexism, anti-Semitism, and classism. Historically those persons who have been most seriously involved in trying to change the status quo were those who had something to gain from such a change. Being at the higher levels of class privilege seems, ironically, to lead people in one of two quite separate directions: either to a kind of serene acceptance of what is (because what is is pretty nice), or else to a sense of the individual's radical discontinuity with institutional values (perhaps because of the increased time and leisure available to think critically about equity and justice). The overall impacts of social and economic class are thus critical factors in shaping the emerging ecoethic.

The Person versus the Society

Most of us find it difficult to analyze the nature of our own conflict and tension with the larger society. That such tensions are reflected in our understandings of self, neighbor, and nature are inevitable, however. And—in spite of an almost universally expressed antipathy toward "theory"—those few students who in fact attempted to incorporate some form of ideological base (religious, political, cultural) within their life experience seemed better able to define the nature of conflict and contradiction in their own lives and in the society, and to see their way through these dilemmas.

The issues of economic class and family lifestyle seem more important than others in the formation of the environmental ethic. Responding to questions posed about the ethical impact of the overall socialization process, individuals in this socio-biographical survey spoke of certain primary influences. After describing her "ruling class" family, one student said,

> My environmental philosophy was shaped by three main factors: (1) my family position in the social structure, (2) the physical and cultural environment of my country, (3) life in the city environment. The fact that my family belonged to the upper-middle class allowed me to escape the city and go into nature, where I found peace and joy. Because of economic privilege, I had contact with the mountains, the woods and the lakes and learned to respect and love nature.

Speaking of her industrialist father who more than anyone else attempted to expose her to nature, she noted,

> Although he was an integral part of the very system he abhorred, he always felt a conflict between the requirements of his job and his personal desires and inclinations. In spite of his being "part of the problem," he had a strong sense of the "wrongs" humanity was inflicting upon nature. Since I was a kid, he taught me about pollution, he showed me illegal discharges on the side of the roads and how entire hills once covered with woods were now a black desert because of arson to clear the way for real estate speculation. He knew what societal values should be but vocational restraints kept him from acting on them.

Compare this with the reflections of an engineering student of Philippine ancestry who spent most of his early life working in the agricultural fields of California.

> My personal philosophy and ethics, environmental and otherwise, are derived from strictly economic considerations. I have no qualms about exploiting nature. . . . We will be fine for many generations. Resource depletion is not our problem. It is the problem of some unfortunate future generation. I feel absolutely no sense of duty to future genera-tions. The benefit of those here and now should be of more concern than the welfare of people who do not exist.

Describing his childhood in agricultural labor camps where daily he saw "agribusiness raping the land" and the racist attitudes displayed by farmers toward farmworkers, he says:

> I now see land as a means to an end and I want to grab my piece of the pie. Those who don't have it, want it. And when money is synonymous with happiness, environmental concern takes a backseat. I do not foresee a time when I will become involved with either deep or shallow ecology groups . . . and I don't give a flaming horse's ass about tropical rainforests. The values instilled in me by my parents are egocentric and homocentric. Their ideas regarding my future are all self-centered with upward mobility as the main agenda. They never have told me either directly or indirectly to be kind to animals.

A recent "upper class" immigrant from Italy stated,

> By living in the U.S. I was confronted with the fact that each specific society provides us with a "mental grid," a cultural matrix through which we organize reality. As I discovered that my cultural coordinates were different I became more aware of them. One of these differences is the way Europeans view society as a class structure, organized and moved by economic and political forces, while Americans in general place much more emphasis on the individual and identify the existence of potent psychological factors as primary determinants of motivation.

Another student reflected on his family's enormous wealth and its impact on his own environmental values.

> I have always seen an intrinsic value in nature and nonurban environ-ments. My family is relatively ecocentric except that because of our history we have completely accepted the idea that we will be able to solve

our problems as a nation and as human beings. There is a belief within my family that progress is never ending which stems from our strong sense of family history and our hopes for the future. My family's class privilege has obviously had an impact on our ecological values. . . . Material advantage has enabled us to pursue such interests. Ultimately, however, I understand that my primary loyalty must be to my class, to my family, and to my fulfillment of their expectations for me.

In a somewhat different vein, a student from a working-class background continued this theme:

I now understand what my sociology professor was talking about when he said that the relative affluence of the 1950s in the U.S. correlates directly to the emergence of a national social conscience in the 1960s. His rationale is that with economic security, the individual can rise beyond the single-minded preoccupation with one's own needs and begin to concern himself with the unmet needs of others.

Summing up the basic contradiction between economic concern and ecological consciousness expressed by most of the students, one woman said,

The biggest contradiction of all is that on one side I hold values of justice, harmony, and ecological balance, and on the other I am a privileged member of the most privileged country on earth, most contributing to political instability, social inequality and depletion of natural resources. I thrive in the very system I abhor. I see no easy solution to this paradox since I am not ready to let go of my privileges if these are not replaced by new sociopolitical realities that would make such a sacrifice meaningful.

Another woman noted several psychosocial factors of class origin that can affect value formation.

The expectation of future social and economic security gives one a sense of time in the long term. Ethical obligations to future generations makes sense to me. Being able to lift their heads from the grindstone means the upper strata of society can afford more maturity of vision and feel an investment in more distant goals. It also gives a better perspective on how quickly some environmental situations, for example, the loss of rainforests, are occurring.

Personal economic security also contributes to my (and many people's) attitude towards the earth as its caretakers. When the world is your oyster, you feel more like extending yourself to protect and care for it than if your situation is one of scratching and clawing for everything you have with the possibility that it may be taken away at any time. Not being in a state of personal crisis helps me care about the rest of the world.

But the bad part of this husbandry attitude is a desire to defend what is important to *my* interests, even at the expense of other groups. It's much easier for me to care about saving my environment from being spoiled than to care about enhancing the economic situation of other classes. Having economic options allows the socially privileged to advocate things that might impose hardships on those without such a range of choices.

Many persons involved in this survey also recognized the extent to which certain kinds of cultural isolation and insulation contribute to a generalized indifference to nature values. This applies both to those who were raised in urban ghettos, where any kind of contact with nature was unusual at best and a threat at the worst, and to those who grew up in the suburbs. One woman stated,

The suburban oasis in which I grew up removed me from any daily contact with the natural world. This middle-class phenomenon actually contributed to my sense of awe even in the "wilds" of Bakersfield's bellowing, drill-covered oil fields. While the tract homes of our neighborhood possessed green lawns and colorful flowers that contrasted with the brown fields owned by Shell, they lacked the teeming rabbit, bird, and coyote life, the snakes and lizards and pretty rocks of the oil fields. Living in tract housing projects . . . made the oil fields seem a wonderland. For me, at least, the suburbs were so sterile that suburban dwellers felt more of an "unnaturalness" with nature than city dwellers.

Women rather easily made the connection between a sensitive concern for human beings and a proper respect for both self and nature.

I see a strong connection between the way we treat our bodies and the way we connect with nature. As a society we view our bodies as something to be dominated, to use and abuse, as a means to pleasure or a source of pain, always to be controlled by the mind, the real "I." We operate the same instrumentalization over nature: We want to control it, dominate it, use it to our satisfaction. Nature, like the body, is "it" separate from the "I." I learned to incorporate and integrate my physical part into my image of the self. I have learned to listen to my body, to decode its messages and to acknowledge that it has an intelligence of its own. The separation between spirit and matter then appeared as a false dichotomy. On a parallel level, the line between the living and the nonliving became blurred, bringing me to a different approach toward nature. Is a river alive? Is a mountain? In the same way that I recognized an intelligence of the body, I acknowledged the existence of a parallel kind of intelligence of the planet itself.

The oppressive reality of the social formatting of females by family and institutions led another woman to say that

I judge it important for me as a woman to stay away from marriage and childbearing. Women have been defined for centuries by their marital status and by their roles as mothers and I recognize the power of the family institution as it is today to lock females into a patriarchally defined role. The search for a new earth and a new society means the creation of new roles and cultural possibilities.

Reflecting on the impact of dominant patriarchal attitudes in the society and their connection with nature values, one woman stated,

I was always a tomboy growing up, and viewed the masculine values of physical strength, machoism, and competition as superior to feminine values. I now see that this attitude resulted from living in a patriarchal society which values physical strength and masculine qualities. This focus on masculinity was reinforced regularly by my family. I always felt that my father was sexist and favored my brother over me and my sisters. It took time for me to learn the contrary values of sensitivity and respect for nature. My later emphasis on spiritual rather than physical strength was a very different message than the one I received from the society around me.

Describing her parents as "feminists," another woman said,

The single factor which has probably had the greatest effect on my environmental values is my mother's infertility. Instead of artificial insemination . . . as a solution to their childlessness they chose adoption. There is an important value which is present in the adoption of a child and that is unselfish sharing. We are not individuals on this earth but members of a large family of creatures which includes all animals and plants. My parents saw a child in need and opened their home and hearts to welcome her. From the unselfishness of my parents I have learned to give freely and openly. I have expanded on this idea and now realize the right to life of all animals and plants. I better understand now how the political, social and economic history of my family has shaped my environmental ethics and values.

The normative value of the work ethic for immigrant families and their descendents seems to be almost universal.

> The imprints that growing up during the Depression left on my father can be seen through his hard work ethic, his pursuit of higher education and his thrift. My family's economic history affects my environmental ethics because of the clash between economics and environmental concerns which anyone who is interested in preserving our environment must confront. My father is presently a big land developer who fights zoning commissions and city councils, disregarding the environmental effects of his projects because he wants to make money. His socialization made any other outcome almost inconceivable.

One woman, detailing the life history of almost all members of her family as "plagued by hardships and poverty," described the change that occurred in her father as he became a successful oil developer.

> Now he believes that the underprivileged should fend for themselves. He feels no social responsibility to think about the consequences of resource exploitation. Given his impoverished past, however, I find this new indifference to nature as a simple reflection of his personal economic history. I doubt if anyone who has been reduced to a life of severe survival subsistence, affected by a series of unpredictable environmental catastrophes (e.g., the Dust Bowl in the 1930s), would think of nature as being fragile.

Reflecting again on the predominant value of the acquisition of material things and the relative indifference within certain immigrant communities to other larger and "leisure time" pursuits, the grandson of European immigrants said,

> My grandparents felt an impulse to save, not so much for future consumption, but rather just for the sake of saving. There was a great emphasis placed not upon the accumulation of wealth per se, but rather on the expression of a middle-class work ethic. Work was not viewed as a means to an end, as expressed in contemporary American culture, but rather as an end in itself.

Although many other socialization factors (religion, education, cultural isolation) were considered to be of importance in the development of these students' environmental values, class understandings emerged as paramount in the analysis. Socio-biographical reflection of this type highlights the impact of social and cultural forces in the determination of significant aspects of the individual's environmental ethic.

Being aware of one's formative social history is no guarantee of personal involvement in the shaping of either an ecological perspective or a new vision of reality. Without it, however, such tasks remain forever impossible. As we move now to a consideration of global dilemmas (war and species extinctions) and alternative strategies for change, we are reminded that both theory (deep ecology; nonanthropocentric value formation; ego-, homo-, and ecocentric ethics) *and* the socialization process of the individual in the midst of complex social orders inevitably and sometimes paradoxically combine to provide the framework for development of an ecoethic.

Notes

1. C. Wright Mills, *The Sociological Imagination* (New York and London: Oxford University Press, 1967), p. 1.

2. Tom Wolfe, *The Bonfire of the Vanities* (New York: Farrar, Straus, and Giroux, 1987).

3. Although very little has been published on the origins of environmental values, a common tendency has been to focus on environmental education, particularly the outdoor and wilderness aspects of such efforts. An example of this is Thomas Tanner's "Significant Life Experiences: A New Research Area in Environmental Education," *Journal of Environmental Education* (Summer 1980), pp. 20–24. While recognizing the importance of such experiences, the evidence from the socio-biographical survey referred to in this chapter suggests that sociological conditioning rather than ventures into nature tends to play the dominant role in development of the environmental ethic.

4. The author taught an environmental studies class to minority honors high school students on the Berkeley campus for six years. Most of these students (more than 200 over the six-year period) were from downtown urban areas of San Francisco, Oakland, and Richmond, California. None of them had ever experienced a serious outdoor or wilderness experience. During field trips into the Sierra Nevada Mountains, the students found it virtually impossible to be relaxed in a wilderness setting. A lifetime in the urban ghetto had distanced these otherwise highly sensitive young people from the forest and made environmental education in that setting very difficult. Many of the students were terrified by forest insects and apprehen-

sive about "wild creatures" invading the campground. Understandably, they extended the urban lifestyle into the forest—complete with carefully selected school clothing and ghetto blasters. In time, many did overcome some of their conditioning. But for most of these young people, the best approach to environmental education turned out to be not the nature experience, but rather an exploration of urban environmental dilemmas. The environmental ethic had to be seen as absolutely relevant to their everyday life experience and practical in terms of day-to-day life in the city. Although the wilderness experience was exemplary in a limited way, it had to be applied as a case study of what could and should be considerations in the nation's economic development. Before the economy of nature could be understood, the issues of air and water pollution, waste management, and urban congestion had first to be explored. Only then would the example and the intrinsic value of wilderness sometimes be understood.

5. The author is much indebted to Dr. Jerry W. Sanders, who formulated the basic structure of this socio-biography in a world order course at City College of New York. Dr. Sanders' method is described in Barbara J. Wein, ed., *Peace and World Order Studies: A Curriculum Guide,* 4th ed. (New York: World Policy Institute, 1984). Fifty graduate and undergraduate students on the Berkeley campus of the University of California participated in the 1988 survey, "The Social Sources of Environmental Values."

13

Ecoethics and Modern War

Ever since nation-states began using organized warfare as an ultimate lever of state policy, efforts have been made by Western philosophers, scholars, and statesmen to analyze both the nature of war and its relative propriety at particular moments in history. In the 2,300 years since Aristotle first proclaimed that war may on occasion be a necessary evil, a never-ending effort has been under way to formulate both the criteria for beginning a war (the *jus ad bellum*) and the rules for the actual conduct of the war (the *jus in bello*).

These efforts have been essentially twofold. Intellectuals, most often within the religious communities, have sought to philosophize on how it may be possible to limit war. Others—most often the generals and politicians—have been concerned about developing an ethic to justify the wars that are the inevitable and often desired results of their accumulations of national or regional power.

In an attempt to deal with both of these issues, the concept of the "just war" was born. Since the Western nations whose scholars and thinkers were called on to develop the apologetic for the just war were traditionally Christian nations, it was quite natural that much of the serious reflection on the issues of war and peace was conducted within the Christian theological community. Significantly, during the past 50 years, philosophers and theologians alike have tried to recapture the conceptual apparatus of just war thinking as a way of reflecting on the nature of modern warfare. Of primary interest in recent decades have been the renewed justification of wars that are defensive in nature (à la Reinhold Niebuhr) and—of far greater historic importance for ordinary people living in the last decade of the twentieth century—new discussions on restraint in the conduct of war. Efforts to clarify these issues in the Roman Catholic church (from Vatican II to the current bishop's crusade against nuclear war) have been particularly notable. As James T. Johnson suggests,

If the just war tradition represents . . . the fundamental way we in the West think about the justification and the limitation of violence, then regular and continuing systematic moral analysis of its contents is absolutely necessary, both to clarify what we think and to correct mistaken ways of reasoning. . . . The existence of this tradition, recognizable and discrete over time . . . testifies that the study of moral values is a practical enterprise rooted in community, not an undertaking belonging to the realm of the abstract.[1]

Just War Theory Revisited

It goes without saying that war has always been a standard way of dealing with either external or supposed internal threats to established power. Some form of just war theorizing (i.e., development of a rationale for the entry into and the conduct of the war) was necessary for the reasons suggested above: to mystify the actual causes of the war when the warmaker was clearly acting only out of a disproportionate kind of self-interest; and to develop a kind of moral calculus that could be applied both to limit and to restrain the scope of the war and the actions of the combatants. Since it is likely true that the ultimate biological ethics issue today is the one that emerges from the nature of modern warfare—particularly nuclear war—it is important to note at the outset the general outlines of traditional just-war thinking. The essential framework of just war theory describes the conditions that are required (moral, philosophical, political) before any particular war can be justified and sanctioned by the dominant value system (normally, the state and/or its supportive religious apparatus). Just war theory attempts to describe the relationship between morality and politics—most particularly, politics in the context of the use of force.

The formal criteria for the just war were slowly enunciated over many hundreds of years. Aristotle, in his concern for order and his insistence that the state formally acknowledge and affirm controversial aspects of its own policy, stated clearly that war may sometimes be necessary. But if it is to be "just," it must be formally approved by state authority and must be understood never as an end in itself. Since everyone understands that peace is the necessary precondition for the development of the higher human qualities, a war can be a just war only if it leads to peace and order. Having been a general himself, Cicero (102–43 B.C.) enunciated the Roman view of just war and, ironically for this warmaking nation, began to spell out the just war principles in more detail. There must be a just cause for entry into war. The only real justification can be self-defense. The state must offer a formal declaration of war if the war is to be legal. Even when these first conditions are met, there is always a subsequent need to define good procedures in warmaking so as to limit its harmful effects.

Augustine (354–430 A.D.) later enlarged the moral circle of just war thinking. Since Christians are called to peacemaking—not warmaking—the decision to go to war should be strictly in obedience to either the will of God or some formal lawful authority. The good intention of the authority in sanctioning the war must be made clear. Unhappily, this rather broad understanding of the conditions wherein war might be legitimized later provided so-called Christian nations with all the justification they needed to undertake military ventures like the Crusades, which for several centuries caused untold suffering throughout the world. And Augustine's suggestion that war could always be undertaken to "abolish vice" gave an essential carte blanche to any self-defined Christian leader wishing to engage in hostile action against another nation or group.

As it developed, just war theory formally legitimated war only when it was seen as a positive means of achieving some particular political or social goal. The just war can never be simply a war of aggression; it requires some overarching purpose or function in order to receive moral sanction—for example, the claim of the Allied Powers in World War II that their military efforts were being carried on "to make the world safe for democracy." Preconditions for the declaration of a just war have historically included these factors:

1. There must be a just *cause* for the war, including some explication of the aims of the conflict. Just causes traditionally involve issues like protecting innocent people, defending against aggression, or restoring the rights that have been wrongfully denied a people or wrongfully taken from them. Such appeals to justice are phrased, whenever possible, in language that transcends immediate political conviction and prejudice and that can appeal to the prospective supporters on national, religious, or class lines.

2. The *means* must be seen as appropriate to the just end sought. Is the war waged in accord with some generally approved standard of conduct? Is it waged by a sovereign state and has that state formally declared a state of war to exist? Is military force used only when

nonmilitary efforts have proven themselves to be ineffective? Is there a reasonable chance of victory, that the military force used will in fact redress the existing grievance?

3. The principle of *proportionality* must always be affirmed and maintained. Are noncombatants given maximum protection? Are the methods of warfare strictly controlled to ensure that the machinery and weapons of the conflict do not get out of hand? Are all of the means of force proportional to the end goals sought?

Thomas Aquinas recognized that, even when all of the factors noted above are observed, evil may nonetheless result from what seems in every way to have been a justly intended war. Accordingly, he offered some additional precautions: that the good intentions be made clear to all observers; and that, in the overall calculus, the evil inevitably resulting from the use of violence be made truly secondary to the positive effects of what the war will accomplish. Aquinas understood that just war theory would always be somewhat compromised, and that its intention must be more to limit war than to justify it.[2]

Since the beginning of World War II, there has been an emphasis within these traditions on the importance of further reflection concerning the special nature of modern war. The newer revisionist schools in just war thinking have been dominated by theologians whose perspectives directly speak to contemporary warmaking realities: Reinhold Niebuhr, Paul Ramsey, and the post–Vatican II consensus within the Roman Catholic church. In addition, Michael Walzer, Douglas P. Lackey, and James T. Johnson have provided thoughtful secular analyses on the application of just war theory to modern warfare.[3]

One principal exponent of a renovated just war theory (although he refrained from ever describing it as just war theory) was Reinhold Niebuhr, professor of theology at Union Theological Seminary in New York. Rejecting much of the pacifist humanism of the post–World War I era, Niebuhr in the 1930s affirmed the perspective of "Christian realism"—namely that, since force and politics will always be linked, political relevance directs that some formal conceptual accommodation be developed to deal with that reality. In *Moral Man and Immoral Society,* Niebuhr distinguishes between the relative moralities of individuals and of "collectives" and declares that good social intentions rarely eventuate in good political actions. When confronted by evil political force, good action will not necessarily be noncoercive.

The differences between violent and non-violent methods of coercion and resistance are not so absolute that it would be possible to regard violence as a morally impossible instrument of social change. It may on occasion be the servant of moral goodwill. And non-violent methods are not perfect proofs of a loving temper.[4]

Speaking from within his understanding of religious "realism," Niebuhr reminded his audience that divine love is neither necessarily nor often revealed in the ordinary affairs of states and nations. In an altogether imperfect world, the pursuit of justice may at times require supporting a just war. This doctrine served liberal Protestantism well during the decade surrounding World War II. Even better than Augustine served Rome with his just war philosophy did Niebuhr's doctrine serve the United States in its conflict with Hitler's Third Reich. In quite a positive sense, Niebuhr's Christian realism acted in that particular situation as a needed "civil" religion—an intellectual and moral calculus providing ethical warrant to the state for its actions.

Highly critical of the liberalism reflected in doctrines of moral and social evolution (such as the social idealism of John Dewey), Niebuhr indicated that war may well prove to be a moral necessity in times of international stress. Viewing Europe from the United States in the 1930s, Niebuhr hedged his counsel to democracy's statesmen that violent means may be acceptable in the quest for peace with counsels of restraint in the use of power. But in a world where good people are constrained by evil social and political forces, moral optimism is impossible unless good people using evil means for proper ends overcome bad people with generally evil intentions.

Niebuhr thus represents in himself the two poles of traditional just-war theory: the development of a justification for engaging in a particular war; and the reminder that everything must be done in between times either to prevent the war or else to monitor its conduct carefully. Interestingly, Niebuhr—so strongly condemned by the radical pacificists within his own religious tradition—became himself a nuclear pacifist, rightly believing that the application of the principle of proportionality in the conduct of war could never under any circumstances permit the use of such genocidal weaponry.[5] Any use of nuclear weapons would only bring on injustice far greater than the situation that the weapon was intended to correct.

The Catholic doctrine of just war has been as politically self-serving throughout history as that of the Protestants. Who can forget the image of the Catholic bishops blessing the guns of Franco in the Spanish Civil War? But Catholicism has been more adaptive and more uniformly cognizant of the changing developments in the conduct of war than most other religious groups. In one sense, the ethical reflections of Catholic philosophers are especially significant and perhaps influential, since they speak not so much as individuals but often for the church itself. All too frequently, antiwar theorizing can end up in the limbo of personal opinion. In any case, since the great warmaking nations of the Western world have been Christian, and often Catholic, it is appropriate that Catholic thinking (and on occasion its dogma) should reflect the changing realities of power in the politics of force. Although Catholic doctrine was actually relatively quiet throughout the centuries on the issue of the legitimation of war—with the church too often simply acquiescing with the dictums of particular state policy—the emergence of modern warfare with all of its accumulated horrors has provoked Catholic scholars into a serious reconsideration of the issue. As James Johnson has noted,

> The special evils of contemporary modes of war have formed a major theme in Roman Catholic thought on war for the past century. Revulsion at the very nature of such war sets a tone maintained in Catholic teaching during this entire time. Just as, in the Middle Ages, it was a peace movement within the church that produced the first halting steps towards an ecclesiastically sanctioned just war doctrine, so this reaction against war in the late nineteenth and twentieth centuries has contributed to the rediscovery of just war tradition as a source of moral guidance.[6]

Pope John XXIII's 1963 encyclical letter *Pacem in Terris,* which again legitimated the concept of defensive war, provided further elaboration of the difficulty of keeping proportionality a viable concern under the conditions of modern war. As Pope John said, "In this age which boasts of its atomic power, it no longer makes sense to maintain that war is a fit instrument with which to repair the violation of justice."

And while some commentators feel that the overall tone of recent Catholic teaching simply continues the traditional just-war allowance for the defensive war—including the possible use of nuclear weapons—the types of limits affirmed by Vatican Council II and other recent statements are most certainly of a kind that falls little short of outright condemnation. As spokesmen at Vatican II said, "Any act of war aimed indiscriminately at the destruction of entire cities or of extensive areas along with their population is a crime against God and man himself. It merits unequivocal and unhesitating condemnation."[7]

Even more strongly, Pope Paul VI's 1965 address to the United Nations recognized the impossibility of utilizing traditional theory to justify the use of nuclear weapons in modern warmaking: "Suffice it to recall that the blood of millions of men, that countless and unheard-of sufferings, that useless massacres and fearful ruins have sealed the pact uniting you, with a vow which must change the future history of the world: never again war, war never again!"[8]

More recently, the enormously controversial efforts of the U.S. Catholic Bishops' Conference in developing a pastoral letter that totally condemns any use of nuclear weapons and calls for a bilateral nuclear freeze are in line with this properly revisionist and now anti-nuclear just-war doctrine of Catholic scholarship. As the final draft of the bishop's pastoral letter stated in May 1983:

> Once we take into account not only the military advantages that will be achieved by using [nuclear] means, but all the harms reasonably expected to follow from using it, can its use still be justified? Do the exorbitant costs, the general climate of insecurity generated, the possibility of accidental detonation . . . , the danger of error and miscalculation . . .—do such evils . . . deriving from the arms race make the race itself a disproportionate response to aggression? Pope John Paul II is very clear in his insistence that the right and duty of a people to protect their existence and freedom is contingent on the use of proportionate means.

Pope John Paul II later elevated John Bernardin, archbishop of Chicago and a key figure in preparing the letter, to the rank of cardinal. Earlier Bernardin had felt the wrath of the Reagan administration for his forceful opposition to U.S. nuclear-weapons policy. Indeed, the president's attempt (as reported in the newspapers) to muscle the U.S. bishops into ceasing their nuclear criticism by sending former CIA Director General Vernon Walters to Rome to put pressure on the pope seems to have misfired. Sensing a typically crude U.S. power play, the pope refused to meet with the general. All in all, this new awareness on the part of the church with regard to the reality and the horror of nuclear war, and its rediscovery of just war theory, have added a new dimension to contemporary opposition against the destructive apparatus of modern warfare so cherished by the major military powers.

Related to the general concerns of just war theory is the issue of general as opposed to particular objections to war. Most philosophical reflection on war deals with the question of particular opposition— that is, the special circumstances that make a particular war relatively more good or evil than some other war. However, in terms of state policy, nations have never been able to deal with the question of particularity. Laws governing rules of conscription, for example, always state that—when conscientious objection is even permitted— COs must affirm opposition to all war, rather than a more selective objection to a particular war. The reasons are clear. While nation-states may be sufficiently liberal to listen to the general voices of conscience, particular objections raise special problems that are more difficult for the advocates of national policy to handle. The history of the selective service system in the United States during the Vietnam era is a case in point. General conscientious objection to war was affirmed as a sometimes acceptable reason for assigning the inductee or GI to alternative rather than military service during Vietnam. However, the draftee who said "I would have fought against Hitler but I am morally opposed to participation in this *particular* war" was refused any CO status. Such selective and particularized morality— long a characteristic of just war thinking—may well become a larger issue in the future as more and more persons called on for military conscription may *selectively* oppose participation in wars that encompass the possible use of nuclear weapons, chemical and biological weapons, or the techniques of "limited intensity" warfare against smaller political targets (such as the U.S. use of limited-intensity conflict in Grenada and Panama). Hopefully, some understanding of the principle of proportionality will inform the judgments of the conscripts if not of the political leaders of the nuclear superpowers.

The Dilemma of Nuclear War

This brings us more directly to an issue of overwhelming importance, both in the area of ecoethics and in any contemporary moral calculus of the just war: the use of nuclear weapons. Deliberately obfuscating the issue, the political leaderships of both East and West have intentionally blunted any common understanding of the absolute terror of nuclear war. The human and ecological consequences of such modern warfare need restating.

In addition to the vast stores of strategic and tactical nuclear weapons in the world today, Soviet submarines alone have more than 300 megatons of nuclear warheads targeted at U.S. cities and military installations. The United States has a far larger megatonnage aimed at the Soviet Union. Altogether, the "advanced" nations of the world have almost 60,000 nuclear weapons of various types, sizes, and descriptions ready for use: 34,000 are owned by the United States; 24,000 by the Soviet Union; 1,000 by Britain; and several hundred apiece by France and China. India, Israel, South Africa, and possibly other nations are also nuclear capable. Under Reagan military policies, the United States alone manufactured 17,000 additional nuclear warheads in eight years.

Other statistics further illustrate the growing problem of attempting to apply the old just-war theory to modern warmaking capacity. The United States' strategic nuclear plan now includes 40,000 targets worldwide, including 60 in Moscow alone. Eighty percent of Soviet cities of 25,000 population are now targeted by at least one U.S. nuclear weapon. Most probably there has been a Soviet quid pro quo. Although the United States finally ratified the Biological Weapons Convention in 1975, that pact—while prohibiting the possession of biological agents that have no peaceful or protective use—does allow research into antidotes and biological defenses. In effect, this serves to keep the door open on continued research in all of the arcane pathways of chemical and biological weapons. Every three days a military satellite is launched somewhere around the world. Of the 2,725 satellites launched between 1957 and 1981, as much as 70 percent were for strictly military purposes. More than 18 million full-time military personnel now man the world's armies. More than twice that number work as civilians for the military establishments. Sixty percent of the world's 60,000 combat aircraft are controlled by NATO and Warsaw Pact nations. The Soviet navy is the largest in the world, with more than 1,200 major fighting ships. The United States runs a close second. The nations of the world operate more than 3,000 foreign military bases and installations. Twenty-one countries send military advisers and assistance to other nations. Discounting the possibility of defense expenditure reductions due to the cooling of the Cold War and the democratic changes now under way in Warsaw Pact nations, the United States alone intends to spend $1.4 trillion for its armed forces and weapons systems in the 1989–93 period.[9]

Physicians for Social Responsibility, the U.S. branch of International Physicians for the Prevention of Nuclear War (their organizational names suggesting with classic scientific detachment that nuclear warfare is "contraindicated"), sponsored two national conferences in 1980 to remind the health professions of "the medical consequences of nuclear war." The group presented statistical profiles on the consequences of low-level nuclear attacks on Boston and San Francisco, illustrating the absurdity in thinking that any concept of proportionality can be applied to warmaking in today's world.

One 20-megaton nuclear weapon (one of the more than 50,000 warheads now in existence) exploding at ground level in Boston would destroy all the buildings within 15 miles of the blast center. Blindness occasioned by retinal burning would be the fate of all human and animal life for distances exceeding 40 miles from the epicenter; 2.2 million immediate fatalities would occur, with millions of other persons severely burned, blinded, or otherwise seriously wounded. Radiation sickness would kill many of the wounded within a few weeks. Water and food sources for thousands of square miles around would all be destroyed or so badly irradiated as to render them worthless. Medical facilities and services would be almost completely wiped out. Moving the Boston scenario to New York City would increase the immediate fatalities to 10 million. In the much smaller but more compact San Francisco Bay Area, the same 20-megaton bomb would kill 1.9 million persons and seriously injure another 874,000. The number of casualties from third-degree burns just in the city of San Francisco would require 10–20 times the capacity of all burn-care centers in the entire United States. All animals and many insect forms in the general area would be blinded either from the ultraviolet radiation loosed through the destruction of the ozone layer or from the blast effect. This would kill them in short order. Thus, virtually the entire biosphere would be massively disrupted by this incremental but rapid disordering of the Earth's plant and animal connections.

> Over the first two to four weeks after the attack, thousands of short-term survivors will die of radiation sickness. The problem of mass infection is particularly ugly. Even assuming that a fire storm conveniently incinerates 500,000 of the dead there will remain 300,000 or more decomposing corpses [for every one megaton of blast] in the Bay area.[10]

But even this vision of the holocaust is a minimally unreal projection. For in fact, instead of one 20-megaton attack, it is estimated that in an all-out assault the United States will undergo 6,559 megatons of nuclear attack throughout the entire nation.

> Moments after the attack, 86 million people—nearly forty percent of the population—will be dead. An additional 34 million . . . will be severely injured. Fifty million additional fatalities are anticipated during the shelter period, for a total of 133 million deaths. 60 million Americans may survive.[11]

Happily, the negotiations begun in earnest in 1988 to limit intermediate-range nuclear forces (the INF Treaty), the mutual forces reductions now under way in Europe, and the continuing discussions for reduction in the strategic-weapons stockpiles have been the most assuring developments since the end of World War II that the nuclear genie may yet be put back in the bottle. The world's more conventional warring continues to expand, however. Twenty separate wars were still under way in 1989: Angola, South Africa, Mozambique, Uganda, Ethiopia, Sudan, Chad, Lebanon, Afghanistan, Sri Lanka, Burma, Cambodia, Vietnam, Indonesia, the Philippines, Peru, Colombia, Nicaragua, El Salvador, and Guatemala. In 1987, more than 250,000 people died in these wars. Nerve gas—commonly known as "the poor man's A-Bomb"—made a dramatic comeback in the Iraq–Iran war. And chemical/biological weapons systems continue to be developed in almost every corner of the world. In the face of such an overwhelming threat to all living things, to perpetuate the operative dualisms of much philosophical and religious thought—the separation of nature from human history, and our accompanying antinature anthropocentrism—is to define a new form of the demonic in the structures of human thought and action.

Throughout this chapter, I have referred to the two primary political functions of just war theory that seem to make it as relevant today as ever—not so much in stopping war, but in causing policymakers to think carefully about either beginning or defending war. First, the theory recognizes the fact that, in the affairs of people and nations, conflict will be an ever-present factor. Accordingly, it endeavors to present some operative rules of the game that should apply before nations in fact take the step of going to war over disagreements. Second, it posits some moral theorems by which the actual conduct of the just war is to be judged. Whether or not it has ever been truly effective in preventing war, the just war calculus has regularly called on rulers and generals to exercise more caution than they otherwise might. And it provides a baseline set of moral standards whereby citizens can at least try to make political and military leaders live up to their own principles. Moreover, it has at least indirectly led to efforts by both nations and international agencies to develop reasonable "rules of war," through the development of a variety of international covenants.

The very nature of modern warfare, however, makes just war theorizing more difficult than ever before. The traditional doctrines are concerned not only for the justification of war, but for its consequences. Today, the consequences of war are perhaps more certain than ever. Granted, with nuclear weapons, the potential impact—for example—of genetic injury and of biospheric ecological disruption is almost impossible to predict exactly. But one thing is for sure: The impact will be totally unprecedented and catastrophic beyond any of our wildest imaginings.

And this is exactly why bioethicists need to rediscover for themselves the traditional arguments. By applying the norms of the just war—civilization's traditional method of acknowledging war's horrendous evil—it becomes impossible under any philosophical or moral formula to justify the use of modern nuclear weaponry. The elements in the theory—the safety of noncombatants, the greater good that shall accrue as a result of the war, the need to use proportionate means of warfare relative to the ends sought—all logically and morally mitigate against any effort to rationalize the use of such weapons. The effort to make moral opponents live up to their own political or ethical principles—the real point of just war theory—is never without merit. Accordingly, just war theory needs to recapture its rightful place in the national debate. Nuclear war pacifism is a logical and linear outgrowth of the application of just war theory today. Ultimate limits of some sort must be set by supposedly rational people and reasonable governments in their relationships with hostile antagonists. That nuclear weapons of any sort transgress such reasonable limits should now be clear to everyone.

However, the moral and political opinions available to those who would utilize the just war theory are not uncomplicated. For all of us, nonviolence, nuclear pacifism, and the condemnation of all forms of war are at least penultimate necessities. In spite of Niebuhr's reminders that violent means may sometimes serve the causes of justice, there are those who will opt for absolute opposition to conflict in the affairs of nations—a contemporary radical pacifism. Others, perhaps less sanguine about the possibility of achieving the ideal but nonetheless believing in the absolute need to limit the means of war, will argue that the strengthening of conventional military forces constitutes the only realistic and the only moral alternative to nuclear war. Bioethically, both options are viable.

> The real challenge held out by the contemporary rediscovery of just war thought as a source of moral wisdom is to develop such more discriminating, more proportionate means of warfare. In the present context, this implies more reliance upon conventional forces (even with the moral difficulties posed by some conventional arms) . . . and upon the physical separation of military installations from centers of civilian population.[12]

The great dilemma is that these options to nuclear war—formal pacifism, or increased reliance on conventional weaponry—are politically unpopular, budgetarily hard to sell (there being more "bang for the buck" in nuclear weapons), ideologically complicated, and virtually impossible to effect under existing systems of political and economic control. The latter and seemingly sensible appeal to conventional arms could lead to alternative weapons systems—chemical and biological, for example—that may historically prove to be as devastating as those they were intended to replace. A world-famous molecular geneticist recently told one of my classes at Berkeley, "If you think nuclear weapons are something to be afraid of, you should see what the genetic engineers can do! Their devices can even be more destructive." Besides, as noted in Chapter 3, the necessary social and economic development of the Third World is being disrupted by the arms trade; sales of even the most sophisticated conventional weapons to the developing world are on the rise.

The bioethical imperative thus seems to be twofold. On the one hand, it is worthwhile to remind political leaders constantly of the just war calculus—and of the impossibility under this historic moral code for any modern war to be justified. More particularly, however, it is now imperative to work for total global disarmament and—especially in the United States and the Soviet Union—for unilateral or multilateral nuclear disarmament as a requisite for survival. In fact, important new voices are being heard in the United States, joining the plea for nuclear disarmament. Physicist Freeman Dyson's impressive proposals in *Weapons and Hope* detail possibly workable scenarios to bring the arms race under control. Of most importance, Dyson suggests that, if he were running the United States, he would rid his country of nuclear weapons by unilateral disarmament and "accept the risks of leaving the Soviet Union as the only major nuclear power in the world." This would entail "a shift to non-nuclear strategy," rather than a continuance of an "offense-dominated balance of nuclear terror as the ultimate basis of our security."[13] Great-power developments for arms reduction stimulated by changes in the strategic-arms doctrines of both the Soviet Union and the United States make Dyson's proposals actually realizable as we enter the last decade of the century.

Peace philosopher Jonathan Schell in *The Abolition* argues that the traditional peace and nuclear-freeze movements have not gone far enough. Our primary task, Schell says, is to find "a way of abolishing nuclear weapons that does not require us to found a world government, which the world shows virtually no interest in founding." Furthermore, he proposes that the nuclear powers "agree . . . to drop their swords and lift their shields toward one another instead" by abolishing nuclear inventories, but maintaining the capacity for their production. If some form of fixed lead time for nuclear rearmament could be negotiated, then "the capacity for rebuilding nuclear weapons would deter nations from rebuilding them and then using them, just as in our present, nuclear-armed world possession of the weapons themselves deters nations from using them."[14]

The challenge to ecoethics in raising issues that concern protecting the world from both nuclear and conventional weaponry is how to make that which is morally preferable also politically possible. Political and military leaders must somehow come to understand that nuclear deployments have not brought security over the years, and that—whatever may be the sophistication of their "defensive" systems—nothing can guarantee immunity from nuclear annihilation. Continuing this nuclear arms race not only brings us closer to global catastrophe, it guarantees a continuance of global debt, a reconcentration of power into ever fewer and fewer hands, and a psychological posturing by top leaders that in itself threatens both sanity and survival. Should we determine that complete solutions to the moral dilemmas of war are not possible, we must at least do whatever we can to fight against the outbreak of any new war and allow our attitudes and behavior to be informed by thinking people who have experienced unresolvable problems in the past. As Albert Camus reminds us,

We are faced with evil. And, as for me, I feel rather as Augustine did before becoming a Christian when he said: "I tried to find the source of evil and I got nowhere." But it is also true that I, and a few others, know what must be done, if not to reduce evil, at least not to add to it. Perhaps we cannot prevent this world from being a world in which children are tortured. But we can at least reduce the number of tortured children.[15]

Notes

1. James T. Johnson, *Just War Tradition and the Restraint of War* (Princeton, N.J.: Princeton University Press, 1981), p. 329.

2. Thomas Aquinas, *Summa Theologica*, vol. 2, bk. 2, q. 40, art. 1, in *Great Books of the Western World*, vol. 20 (Chicago: Encyclopaedia Britannica, 1952), pp. 578–79.

3. See Michael Walzer, *Just and Unjust Wars: A Moral Argument with Historical Illustrations* (New York: Basic Books, 1977); Douglas P. Lackey, *Moral Principles and Nuclear Weapons* (Totowa, N.J.: Rowman and Allanheld Publishers, 1984); and Johnson, *Just War Tradition*.

4. Reinhold Niebuhr, *Moral Man and Immoral Society* (New York: Charles Scribner's Sons, 1960), p. 251. Originally published in 1932.

5. Paul Ramsey, *The Just War: Force and Political Responsibility* (New York: Charles Scribner's Sons, 1968), p. 211.

6. Johnson, *Just War Tradition*, p. 339.

7. Walter M. Abbot, S.J., ed., *The Documents of Vatican II* (New York: Guild Press, 1966), pp. 294–95.

8. Pope Paul VI, "Never Again War," *United Nations General Assembly Minutes*, 1965, p. 37.

9. Michael Kidron and Dan Smith, *The War Atlas: Armed Conflict—Armed Peace* (New York: Simon and Schuster, 1983).

10. H. Jack Geiger, "The Illusion of Survival," in Ruth Adams and Susan Cullen, eds., *The Final Epidemic* (Chicago: University of Chicago Press, 1981), p. 180.

11. H. L. Abrams, "Infection and Communicable Diseases," in Adams and Cullen, *Final Epidemic*, pp. 192–94.

12. Johnson, *Just War Tradition*, p. 366.

13. Freeman Dyson, *Weapons and Hope* (New York: Harper and Row, 1984).

14. Jonathan Schell, *The Abolition* (New York: A.A. Knopf, 1984).

15. Albert Camus, "The Unbeliever and Christians," in *Resistance, Rebellion, and Death* (New York: A.A. Knoff, 1961), p. 73.

14

All God's Creatures

Of the more than 1 million animal species now existing in Earth's biosphere, only one—our own—has claimed as a birthright the privilege of dominating (and when it seemed to be necessary, slaughtering) any or all of the rest. No doubt, at one level, there has been good historic rationale for this practice. Our ancestors faced the struggles of life right alongside every other of Earth's animals, and perhaps understandably practiced many of the common brutalities of competitive survival. In later years, though, our social and religious practices tended by and large to reinforce those earlier habits by teaching us to have contempt or, at most, tolerance for all nonhuman species (see Chapter 1 and 2). We have routinely assigned to the birds of the air, the fish of the sea, and all the rest of Earth's creatures simply an instrumental value—a use value—so that nothing would stand in the way of our doing with them as we might wish. However strong the past may be, though, we must necessarily raise the question today as to whether or not such practices are correct.

It will be the thesis of this chapter that all animals have certain natural rights, are moral subjects in a genuine albeit different sense from Homo sapiens, and belong within our general sphere of ethical concern. Although the primary concern here is with the moral question of rights, a brief overview of the way human beings have traditionally treated other species is needed to set the context.

Each year, billions of animals—all with the ability to feel pain and to suffer—are used as food by our dominant species. Furthermore, in the United States alone, more than 60 million animals are killed each year in biomedical research. On the consequentialist level, some of this slaughter of the innocent may perhaps be justifiable.

Animals are used in about 60 percent of all biomedical research in the United States. In the past year, for example, scientific history was made when new genes were added to mouse embryos to produce a genetically altered mouse. A 1980 Nobel laureate in medicine won his prize for using skin grafts and tumor transplants in mice to advance knowledge of the human immune system.[1]

But other forms of "research" are much more questionable. The following is a sampling from experimentation that has recently been conducted at the University of California: Female Rhesus monkeys are confined in restraining chairs for extended periods of time, to determine whether the resulting stress disrupts their menstrual cycles. Dogs have their penises mounted in plexiglas molds with a steel pin inserted through the attached portion of the penis, to determine nerve response. Animals are infected with meningitis—the treatment for which is already known—and are studied, with no therapy, until they die of the disease. Other research at the University of California, Davis, has included: radiation killings of beagles, preceded in most cases by radiation-induced bone injuries, jaw fractures, painful tumors, and shock; spinning chickens in a centrifuge until paralysis and death occurs; severing of the spinal cords of dogs, followed by masturbating them to determine sexual reactions; and inducement of fatal eye ulcers in pigs. None of these experiments resulted in any significant or relevant findings.[2]

This chapter will look more closely at the related issues of using animals for food and for research, the question of whether or not animals have any natural rights (and if so, whether they should ever have equal rights with human beings), and finally the dangerous extent to which plant life is being genetically simplified today—a matter that may ultimately be far more important than the animal rights issue. We conclude with a review of the number of plants and animals now extinct and the long-range problem of endangered species.

Moral Rights for Animals?

Is it likely that God takes no delight whatever in the more than 1,000,000 other living things on this planet, yet does delight in, derive value from contemplating, the one human species so lately emergent on this planet?[3]

However one may deal with some of the assumptions in that question—whether one believes in God or in some larger ordering reality within the natural world—it is both a logical and an ethical necessity to understand that all living things have some form of intrinsic value and that they exist for reasons other than simply to serve the needs of our own most adaptive species. As we peruse the evolutionary charts and note the enormous similarity in neural development between human beings, primates, and whales and porpoises (among many other animals), how can we still insist that all the billions of years of biological development have been no more than a mere preparation for the advent of Homo sapiens? Even the most innocent of us are aware of the interrelationships that stand out so clearly within the natural orders. Not only poets understand the beauty of that whole which is nature, and others than biologists know the truth in the certain ecological law that everything is connected to everything else.

Our dilemma seems actually quite simple. Either much of our use and appropriation of animals for food and for medical research is unethical, or we had better come up with some philosophical justification for the absolute dominance that our own species exercises over all others and the manner in which we now treat these "lower" orders. This brings up the question whether our species is entitled (essentially for our own convenience) to mold the needs of other animals to our own and even to proceed with the deliberate elimination of hundreds and thousands of other species. For one tiny minority to claim such a vast birthright requires, from this writer's perspective, either very wide-scale and insidious ethical sophistry or else the creation of a whole new set of myths to justify the existing practices. Neither option seems morally responsible. Since human actions are now rapidly transforming all the ecological relationships of the planet, it is time to face the fact that some of our most accepted human social customs inflict large-scale suffering and the intentional although often ignorant extermination of species. As philosopher Charles Hartshorne puts it,

> To say that the human species is more important than other species suggests the question, how *much* more? Can we, even if only in the vaguest way, quantify the answer? One human person is "of more value than many sparrows," but is one person of more value than an entire species of bird?
>
> There are those who say that, since human beings are radically superior to nonhuman individuals, it is hypocritical or absurd to shed tears over ill-treatment of subhuman creatures, while ignoring the well-

being of many human beings, the poor or the ethnic minorities. This argument seems to be at its strongest if the ill-treatment in the sub-human is only of individuals. But the issue is not so clear if it is a question of species, threatened wholesale by slaughter or by habitat destruction.[4]

Thus we come to the moral rights of nonhuman beings and of our obligations to them. At issue is the extent to which they in fact belong—with all of the implications arising therefrom for our personal action and conduct—within our own sphere of ethical concern. It is my assumption that the principles we affirm as the intrinsic rights of human beings should not differ in substance from those that we are called on to apply to other creatures. Foremost among these are the rights to freedom from suffering and from confinement and constraint. Our own basic animal right to life assumes the correlative right for others of freedom from unnecessary torment.

Ethicist Peter Singer (whose thoughts and overall perspective on animal rights are reflected throughout this chapter) has found the root of the problem to be what he calls our human tendency toward "speciesism"—our assumption that the only concepts of value are those relating to our own species. Speciesism is a reflection of that common and seemingly imprinted bias or prejudice that groups of individuals within some species exhibit toward members of other groups. In his important book *Animal Liberation,* Singer suggests that "supporters of liberation for Blacks and Women should support animal liberation too."[5]

For the practical ethicist, however, the extension of value does not imply that the treatment of individuals within different groups or species must always be exactly the same or that they must necessarily have the same rights. "The basic principle of equality does not require equal or identical *treatment;* it requires equal *consideration.* Equal consideration for different beings may lead to different treatment and different rights."[6]

In Chapter 1, we noted briefly some of the current concerns in the ecoethical debate about egalitarianism in the human–nonhuman animal relationship. If intrinsic value is affirmed for nonhuman creatures, does it follow that such creatures should be accorded the right to pursue their own evolutionary destinies? If so, would this not have a devastating impact on our behavior toward nonhuman living communities? Those of us who are concerned for effecting some form of a deeper ecology may wish to affirm a sense of connection and integration between human beings and nature, for what Arne Naess calls "biospherical egalitarianism." While we can agree that in principle all animals have an equal right to live, we in practice must place this kind of functional egalitarianism within the context of everyday survival, understanding that the rule applies only when there is no absolute conflict between the survival of the higher and lower animals. As ethicist Warwick Fox notes,

> The deep ecologist who is "thoroughgoing" in confusing ecological egalitarianism in principle with ecological egalitarianism in practice is forced into the position that they might as well eat meat as vegetables since all organisms possess equal intrinsic value. In stark contrast to this is the comment by Alan Watts that he was a vegetarian "because cows scream louder than carrots."
>
> Deep ecology does itself a disservice by employing a definition of anthropocentrism which is so overly exclusive that it condemns more or less any theory of value.[7]

We know in fact that absolute equality between humans and the plant and animal worlds is impossible. Unhappily, our killing and exploitation of certain other parts of the creation are inevitable. Nonanthropocentric value theory is a requirement for an ecoethic; but the view that there is absolute equality between all living beings, *if applied in practice*, would make the survival of the human species impossible.

This does not, however, diminish the importance of a nonanthropocentric ethic. The utilitarian philosopher Jeremy Bentham once affirmed,

> The day may come when the rest of the animal creation may acquire those rights which never could have been withholden from them but by the hand of tyranny. The French have already discovered that the blackness of the skin is no reason why a human being should be abandoned without redress to the caprice of a tormentor. It may one day come to be recognized that the number of the legs . . . or the termination of the *os sacrum* are reasons equally insufficient for abandoning a sensitive being to the same fate. What else is it that should trace the insuperable line? Is it perhaps the faculty of reason, or perhaps of discourse? But a full-grown horse or dog is beyond comparison a more rational, as well as a more conversable animal, than an infant of a day or a week or even a month old. But suppose they were otherwise, what would it avail? The question is not, can they *reason*? nor can they *talk*? but, *can they suffer*?[8]

The issue, then, is not so much that of equal worth as that of the unnecessary infliction of pain. This writer, for one, assumes that the life of a self-aware, communicating human being capable of rational thought is more valuable, during a conflict for survival, than the life of a creature without such capacities. However, in no sense does this higher value carry with it the right to kill indiscriminately. Much of our rationale in destroying other creatures has had to do with our own convenience. Ethically, however, convenience does not constitute necessary moral justification for practices leading to the suffering of other creatures. After all, in this context as in others, social custom can often be used to camouflage what is in fact no more than evil intent.

Interestingly, in spite of all the incontrovertible proof to the contrary, children in our society are still too often taught that animals do not really feel pain as humans do. In fact, mammalian vertebrates have nervous systems not dissimilar from our own. They clearly feel just as much physical pain as humans do. The sensory organs of most animals are far more acute than those in most humans—sure biological indication that their nervous systems are at a high level of quality and sensitivity. As Singer and others have reported, studies show conclusively that animals are also capable of suffering emotional injuries like fear, anxiety, stress, and rage; and they regularly show these feelings in ordinary situations. More importantly, those of us who have lived with house pets know experientially about the intense feelings they can exhibit.

Although psychologists once quite casually dismissed the idea that higher levels of consciousness might exist in animals, responsible researchers nowadays use this fact as the starting point for much of their work. International conclaves like the Dahlem Conference in Berlin in 1981 draw evolutionary biologists and neurologists from around the world to share their findings on consciousness within the subhuman animal world.

> The view that mind and consciousness, like intelligence, are graded phenomena, different for different species, . . . underlies the conclusions of the Berlin conference. The old . . . question about the validity of ascribing consciousness to creatures other than ourselves can be replaced with more precise experimental questions about the sensitivity, intelligence, and experience of animals. We need not ask whether animals have intelligence, or language, or emotions, but rather what intelligence, what kind of language, and which emotions.[9]

Animal Experimentation

Given our growing realizations about the sensitivity and consciousness of animals, experimentation utilizing live subjects should always have at least some worthwhile purpose in terms of the advancement of science and human understanding. Many organized research activities involving animals have no such function at all. Since there are very few regulatory mandates that cover animal experimentation, there is little that stands in the way of even those research projects whose highest intentions seem to be that of tormenting animals. One area of special concern to us must be the kind of work being done on primates—apes and monkeys. Because primates are so neurologically and anatomically close to Homo sapiens, their behavior most resembles our; the inclination to use primates in research is thus very strong. Since the social and psychological attitudes of primates (as well as their nervous systems) are also so much like ours, this kind of research must be the most suspect of all.

Far from being relevant to the well-being of the research animals themselves, some of the most common primate reseach has nothing to do with even finding out information that may benefit the human species. On the Berkeley campus of the University of California, researchers in the psychology department have recently become involved in a major project (funded by the National Institutes of Health) to study the mechanisms of color vision in human beings. Perhaps this research may be of some value to people at some point in the future. But to aid their research, the scientists screw a stereotaxic device into the brains of kittens and Macaque monkeys, enabling electrodes to be inserted directly into the brain tissue in order to study certain problems of visual response. After experimentation, the animals are killed. Like so many other instances of scientific curiosity involving animal experimentation, this research seems more directly concerned with satisfying the psychological needs of the experimenters than with producing medically significant knowledge. Other abuses of animals have also been discovered on this campus in the past decade, by both private and government veterinarians—exploratory surgery on animals by untrained students as part of their on-the-job training; the use of sick and suffering animals in research; overcrowded and unsanitary animal housing facilities; and the constant illegal acquisition of animals for experimental use. Happily, in part because of the publicity occasioned by past abuses, a major new animal-care facility has been erected on the Berkeley campus.

While most researchers do take care to minimize the suffering of laboratory animals, some in industry and on university campuses are little more than voyeurs of animal experimentation—doing research with little scientific justification. Their actions have created a climate of criticism and censure, affecting even many needed research projects involving animal subjects. Given the circumstances of our chemical age and the necessity to test dangerous drugs and chemicals before exposing humans to them, there is a growing need for more and more serious research on matters relating to human and environmental health and welfare. Some of this research will inevitably involve animal testing. The writer has for many years been part of an effort to pursuade the U.S. government to undertake the large-scale epidemiological tests that might determine the health consequences to the almost 3 million U.S. soldiers and an equal number of Indo-Chinese nationals who were exposed to tetra-chloro-dibenzo-dioxin (TCDD) in the Agent Orange defoliants used by Americans in the Vietnam War. We know anecdotally of birth defects, cancers, and genetic damage done to many people by the use of these phenoxy herbicides. Some limited primate testing *may* be required if we are to discover the exact nature of the health problems that these millions of people face. And again, all of the current research related to the development of an AIDS vaccine involves early testing on chimpanzees. But even careful and humanely conducted animal research will now be increasingly difficult to justify, given the terrible conditions obtaining at many private and university animal research labs around the country.

Happily, some alternatives to traditional forms of testing—not requiring animal subjects—have been developed. Biochemist Bruce Ames at the University of California, Berkeley, has developed a technique to determine both carcinogenicity and mutagenicity in chemical compounds by culturing bacteria and then observing the effects of the compounds upon them. The "Ames test" resolves many problems. It is cheap. More important, it overcomes the traditional problem in animal testing of not being able to expose a sufficient number of generations of a particular species to the test material and adequately determine its cancer-causing or other health effects. Computer simulations can now also substitute for many of the earlier techniques in animal research. Recognizing these developments, 50 members of Congress recently sponsored legislation introduced by Representative Frederick Richmond of New York requiring that up to

50 percent of federal funds now earmarked annually for animal studies be recircuited to other forms of research.

Bentham's main argument for animal rights—that of the capacity of an animal for suffering—can never be forgotten. Recognizing that some animal research will perhaps forever be required, we must proceed according to certain basic guidelines and precautions, as enumerated above: requiring a more humane treatment of research animals, in the first place; and substituting other research methods that do not require animal subjects, for most traditional work. A basic reconception of such work also calls for the total elimination of any laboratory research involving primates, excepting under the most extreme and unusual circumstances.

Animals for Food

While many of us can easily agree with the moral injunctions against the needless use of animals for research, the issue becomes far more complicated (as Peter Singer has so carefully noted) when it moves to the realm of our dinner table. The use of animals for food obviously far exceeds all other kinds of animal killing. Hundreds of millions of livestock and billions of chickens are slaughtered for food each year in the United States. The chicken in every pot is the final step in a daily process of inhumanity to animals. Most of us (with the occasional exception of people like my friend who insists on personally killing every animal he and his family eat) are normally shielded from the bloodier and less delectable aspects of our dining routines. As research animals deserve certain rights, so too do those domesticated creatures whose sole reason for being is to produce food for humans require certain protections.

In fact, they receive nothing of the kind in the factory farms of contemporary food processing. Peter Singer and a host of other commentators document the tragic reality. Hundreds of thousands of cattle are today penned up in feed lots—standing all day confined in their own filth, and inoculated regularly with antibiotics and other drugs to prevent disease—in order to maximize both profits to the entrepreneurs and the tasty fat content of the meat. Broiler chickens are placed in windowless sheds with no possibility of movement during their entire lives. They are kept in darkness to prevent the cannibalism that would otherwise occur in such overcrowded conditions. Full-grown broiler chickens are normally allotted only a 6 × 12-

inch living space. Suction pipes are used to transport live birds to cartons for shipment. Laying hens live just as much packed together— five live birds in an 18-inch-square cage. The noise, stench, and squalor of poultry production can be overwhelming.

Factory-style pig raising does little justice either to this intelligent creature or to its human patron. Advertisements for the new pork-producing "bacon bin" proudly advertise that the hog so raised never sees daylight from birth to slaughterhouse. Brood sows are routinely kept in 2×6-foot stalls for virtually their entire lives, going from pregnancy to suckling and back again. One device common in Europe and now being introduced in the United States is the "iron maiden," a frame that permanently immobilizes the sow so she will not roll over and injure her offspring.

Veal, the flesh of young calves, is both a delicacy and an example of one of the *worst* kinds of maltreatment of animals. Since milk cows are normally kept pregnant to maximize milk production, their male calves are traditionally taken from them and immediately killed to provide the delicate flesh so prized by gourmets. As Peter Singer notes,

> Now using methods first developed in Holland, farmers have found a way to keep the calf longer without the flesh becoming darker or less tender. This means that the veal calf, when sold, may weigh as much as 325 pounds instead of the ninety odd pounds that newborn calves weigh.
>
> The trick depends on keeping the calf in highly unnatural conditions. If the calf were left to grow up outside . . . it would begin to develop muscles, which would make its flesh tough. So the specialist veal producer takes his calves straight from the auction ring to a confinement unit. Here . . . he will have rows of wooden stalls. Each stall will be 1 foot 10 inches wide and 4 feet 6 inches long. The stall will have no straw or other bedding, since the calf might eat it, spoiling the paleness of his flesh. Here the calves will live for the next 13–15 weeks. They will leave their stalls only to be taken out to slaughter.[10]

Similar techniques are used in the production of rabbits and turkeys. Excepting those few countries like Australia and New Zealand where animals are normally range fed, even the adventures of lambs in the pasture may soon also be changed to the artificial life of the livestock charnel house. More efficient ways are being developed to prepare them for our dinner tables. Anyone who has ever visited livestock slaughterhouses—particularly those that conduct a religiously prescribed ritual killing wherein the stunning of the animal before slaughter is prohibited—will understand the horrible routines behind the eating practices of the majority of people in the United States and much of Europe.

As noted earlier, Western religious traditions have exacerbated the problem of humanity's latent antagonism to the natural orders and its relative indifference to the suffering of nonhuman animals. The universal "no" of Judaism and both Protestantism and Roman Catholicism to any suggestion that God might be concerned about other orders than the human is clear throughout history. The heirarchical ordering of the creation, as reflected in our biblical and theological traditions, provided the ideological base for an ethical instrumentalism relative to the conduct of humans toward the plant and animal worlds.

Whereas Catholic theology was never quite so antinaturalist as Protestantism became, the bias against any manifestation of concern for animals was clear even in the very early centuries of the Christian era. From the time of the first proclamation of the gospel, it was more than 1,500 years until the church substantively criticized cruelty to animals. In the thirteenth century, Thomas Aquinas laid out the historic position of the Christian tradition in accord with the ethical norms of his time.

> It matters not how man behaves to animals, because God has subjected all things to man's power, . . . and it is in this sense that the Apostle says that God has no care for oxen, because God does not ask of man what he does with oxen or other animals.[11]

During the Middle Ages, the practice of experimenting on animals became quite common in the new effort to learn about anatomy. Descartes and other scientists regularly affirmed that such practices were acceptable since animals could feel no pain. Experimenters at a religious seminary in the seventeenth century are described as follows:

> They administered beatings to dogs with perfect indifference, and made fun of those who pitied the creatures as if they felt pain. They said the animals were clocks; that the cries they emitted when struck were only the noise of a little spring that had been touched, but that the whole body was without feeling. They nailed poor animals up on boards by their four paws to vivisect them and see the circulation of the blood which was a great subject of conversation.[12]

Given our traditional hostility even toward contrary members of our own species, it is perhaps not surprising that such indifference and downright cruelty toward animals should have developed over the years. The treatment we have afforded nonhumans is different only in quantity—not quality—from the abhorrent practices to which we have subjected our own brethren. Clearly, however, animals should in fact be seen as having certain intrinsic rights and values; we are morally mandated to safeguard these rights as much as we possibly can.

For some people, the best remedy to the ubiquitous maltreatment of domestic animals will be found in following a meat-free diet. And certainly there is no better way, in either practice or theory, to extend a kind of protection to animals never before experienced in human history. Short of such abstinence, however, most people will respond most effectively to the situation by engaging in self-education and then assisting others to understand both the nature and history of human maltreatment of animals. This will provide enormous relief to those creatures great and small who share this planet with us.

All Flesh Is Grass

Every beginning ecology course opens with a scientific reaffirmation of the statement that "all flesh is grass." Food chains originate when solar energy is captured by plants in photosynthesis, thus making possible all other higher forms of life on Earth. Human life could probably continue even with massive interruptions in the cycles of animal life, but it would last no time without the support of plant life in all its abundance and variety. The Bible here is quite correct. All life, indeed, begins as grass.

Yet our newspapers and journals regularly carry reports on how humankind is simplifying its agricultural ecosystems. Green revolutions and high-technology agriculture have led to an increased dependence on agricultural chemicals that now threaten both the current levels of food production and, in some cases, our human health. Everywhere, domestic plant strains are being genetically simplified to produce (sometimes) greater short-term yields. In the process, however, our food plants are becoming dramatically more susceptible to insects and disease. Before World War II, more than 30 strains of wheat were grown in Turkey; today, one strain is dominant. This genetic simplification can provide simple short-range solutions to the need for an increase in cereal production, but always at the risk of enormous future disruptions in the ecological balance. The more long-range requirements for diversity and strength within our global ecosystem is routinely ignored in today's world.

Indeed, the global threat to wild plants and animals receives almost no popular attention. But the record of extinction in the past few hundred years is remarkable by any standard. Over the past 2,000 years, we have exterminated about 3 percent of the globe's mammal species. During the past 375 years, hundreds of species of birds and other animals have become extinct. In the past 150 years alone, mammal extermination has increased 55-fold. If these exterminations continue to increase at that rate, experts predict that in about 30 years all the remaining 4,062 species of mammals will be gone.[13]

More than 100 plant species have been lost completely in the past 100 years, and a total of 23,000 plant and animal species are now considered either endangered or threatened. Those who suggest that this reality should not cause us any concern because extinction and evolution are parts of the natural process forget that, for the first time, the rate of species extermination now far exceeds the rate of species formation. As Paul and Anne Ehrlich have put it, species are the rivets in the Spaceship Earth. Intentionally popping any of these rivets—unfortunately a standard practice of industry, government, and thoughtless private people today—must be seen as both stupid and dangerous.

Ecologically, the point is well taken. While no one understands precisely the collective and interconnected roles that the different species perform within Earth's ecosystems, species diversity is routinely acknowledged to be a major contributing factor in the strength and stability of ecosystems. The more species present, the greater are the survival possibilities for all. Even the sociobiological ethologist E. O. Wilson of Harvard has clearly stated the biological implications of the extinction of species:

> The worst thing that can happen—will happen in the 1980's—is not energy depletion, economic collapse, limited nuclear war, or conquest by a totalitarian government. As terrible as these catastrophes would be for us, they can be repaired within a few generations. The one process ongoing in the 1980's that will take millions of years to correct is the loss of genetic and species diversity by the destruction of natural habitats. This is the folly our descendants are least likely to forgive us.[14]

Some of the tales of extinction in our day bear repeating here. Both naturalist John James Audubon and author Mark Twain described in the early nineteenth century how passenger pigeons would blacken the sky in their migrations. But tens of millions were killed each year in the latter part of that century, and the last passenger pigeon finally died in the Cincinnati Zoo in 1914. The 60–100 million American bison that roamed the plains in 1870 were reduced to 22 animals by 1885. Sixteen subspecies of grizzly bear, six of wolves, and dozens of other mammals were exterminated during the same period. Chief Seattle reminded the white man of one irrefutable aspect of an ecoethic:

> If I decide to accept your offer to buy our land, I will make one condition. The white man must treat the beasts of this land as his brothers. I am a savage and do not understand any other way. I have seen a thousand rotting buffaloes on the prairies left by the white man who shot them from a passing train. What is man without the beasts? If all the beasts were gone, men would die from great loneliness of spirit.[15]

Any responsible system of biological ethics will affirm that all animals have certain basic rights and must necessarily be accorded certain protections. No longer can we ourselves tolerate our traditional Western exploitation of subhuman animal life, and of the plants that form the basis of all life forms and ecological systems. Neither animals nor plants are simply instrumentalities to be used for whatever we feel appropriate. They are more than simply means to human ends. They are part of the creation—perhaps a more important part than Homo sapiens. Bioethicists must understand that it is time to end the burden of the beasts!

Notes

1. James Gorman, "Burden of the Beasts," *Discover* (February 1981), p. 22.

2. Kate Gallagher, "Animals at Berkeley: Inside Campus Research Labs," *Daily Weekly Magazine* (October 15, 1982).

3. Charles Hartshorne, "Subhuman Rights," *Environmental Ethics* 1 (Spring 1979), p. 50.

4. Ibid., p. 57–59; emphasis in original.

5. Peter Singer, *Animal Liberation* (New York: Avon Books, 1975), p. 1.

6. Ibid., p. 3; emphasis in original.

7. Warwick Fox, "Deep Ecology: A New Philosophy of Our Time?" *Ecologist* 14, nos. 5–6 (1984), p. 200.

8. Jeremy Bentham, "Introduction to the Principles of Morals and Legislation," ch. 17, in *Library of Classics,* vol. 6 (Indianapolis: Hafner, 1948).

9. Robert C. Solomon, "Has Not an Animal Organs, Dimensions, Senses, Affections, Passions?" *Psychology Today* (March 1982).

10. Singer, *Animal Liberation,* pp. 122–23.

11. Thomas Aquinas, *Summa Theologica,* vol. 2, bk. 1, q. 102, art. 6, in *Great Books of the Western World,* vol. 20, (Chicago: Encyclopaedia Britannica, 1952), p. 297.

12. Singer, *Animal Liberation,* p. 209.

13. Lee Talbot, as quoted in Anne Ehrlich and Paul Ehrlich, *Extinction: The Causes and Consequences of the Disappearance of Species* (New York: Random House, 1981), p. xvii.

14. E. O. Wilson in *Harvard Magazine* (January/February 1980).

15. Chief Seattle, "The Great Chief Sends Word," in *Chief Seattle's Testament* (Leicester, U.K.: St. Bernard Press, 1977).

15

Perspectives on Environmental Change

Almost from the moment the first English settlers stepped ashore in Virginia and New England, they were involved in organizing for social change. We know of the early struggles: for religious freedom, for civil liberties, for economic justice, and for independence from oppressive rulers. Leadership in these early "movements" was initially from the bottom up, with the people most concerned and active in seeking solutions inevitably selected to lead the particular struggle. In addition to their work within the political arena, there have always been organizers during our three and a half centuries of history who focused on certain key issues. Foremost among these have been class, race, sexual equality, civil liberties, and the role of the people in the conduct of war. The goals of each organizing group, although rarely fully realized, have been consistently imbued with the modern ethical ideals of freedom and justice for all. Those dealing with the inequities of class—poor people's organizations, union organizers, unemployed worker's councils—necessarily hoped that the economic pie would be increased both in size and quality, with larger portions allocated to those traditionally left out or receiving only small shares. The racial struggle—from the fight against slavery to the demand for equal rights before the law—has been visible in this country since the first slaves were brought to Virginia in 1619. The movement for women's rights—in the workplace, in the polling booth, in the home, in the freedom to choose for themselves what is right and appropriate in their personal life—has enlisted perhaps millions of American women since the colonial days. And a substantial minority of the people has always been involved in the moral struggle during times of war to redefine the meaning and scope of the just war for their own period of history. In spite of the Bill of Rights and our other constitutional guarantees of civil liberty, each generation has been forced to redefine the nature of freedom and independence for themselves. The struggle for justice has been a constant battle.

Our history, then, is a reminder of the absolute requirement in a democratic society that concerned people work in their communities, and when necessary take to the streets, to repair injustice of any kind. In my own life, changing social values have forced me on three occasions into the position where I had no option but to work as an organizer: part-time in the civil rights movement in the 1950s and 1960s; full-time in the antiwar movement during the Vietnam era; and as both a personal and vocational priority since 1971 in the struggle for ecological awareness and health. Many people reading this book will have had similar experiences.

The Environmental Movement

Although since Colonial times there have been efforts made at environmental organizing (effective enough to have created restrictions on timber cutting in Pennsylvania during the seventeenth century), the modern environmental movement emerged from two distinct trends: (1) the arguments between "preservationists" and "conservationists" in the late nineteenth and early twentieth centuries; and (2) the post–World War II, postconservationist concern for an environmentally augmented "quality of life."

Preservationists—perhaps best exemplified by the legendary John Muir—believed that, to the greatest extent possible, natural resources should be preserved as they are, both because of their own intrinsic value and for the enjoyment of future generations. The preservationist movement fought for the establishment of national parks and opposed the ongoing efforts of the timber and mineral industries to exploit nature. They shared a philosophical framework remarkably similar to that of the transcendentalists in New England. Romantic and idealist, they believed that God was immanent in both nature and the human being. Nonetheless, serious efforts must be undertaken to protect and preserve the natural orders. With Ralph Waldo Emerson and Henry David Thoreau, they were individualistic and emphasized self-reliance in personal life and integration of the self with the natural world.

Conservationism—reflecting what was later called "the gospel of efficiency"—sought to apply the best and most modern management techniques to the human care for and use of natural resources.

Gifford Pinchot, the first director of the newly established U.S. Forest Service—while espousing the beauty and grandeur of nature—called forests "a manufacturing plant for the production of wood." These new conservationist philosophers of natural resource "management" were essentially scientists: foresters, hydrologists, plant pathologists, and the like. Their goal was never the formal exploitation of nature (although this sometimes occurred), but rather the promotion of a careful and planned utilization of the resource base. Today's advocates of sustainable development might be startled to discover how similar their agenda is to that of the conservationist leadership in the era from 1890 to 1920 in the United States.

While the preservationist/conservationist struggle is still under way, it is fair to say that the management view of the conservationists has, unhappily, been the hands-down winner. With increasing populations, accelerated demand for every natural resource, and diminishing global supplies of raw materials, the emphasis on good management is increasingly important. At the same time, the preservationist concern for setting aside parklands, maintaining wild and scenic territories, protecting old-growth forests, and limiting destruction of rainforests is more important today than ever before. The protection of species—plant and animal—from exploitation and extinction is an ecoethical priority. With changing demands and increasing pressure, environmentalists must today accept the double imperative of fighting both the preservationist and the conservationist battles.

The new industrialization in the United States that began during World War II set in motion a train of environmental disturbances that elicited the concern of people other than the well-to-do who had fought the preservation and conservation battles. Before World War II, there had been a modest flurry of interest over pollution of the air and water, and some regulations had been passed to enforce limited environmental controls on both state and federal levels. With the new postwar reliance on petrochemicals and the use of toxic materials in manufacturing, however, came a new dimension and sense of urgency in environmental organizing. For the first time, a generalized fear about public health—the pollution of the workplace, the effects of hazardous waste, poor air and dirty water, the effects of pollution on children—began to take shape. Since 1960, the environmental movement has been shaped more around such quality-of-life issues than over the traditional natural-resource use concerns.

A simple characterization of the past three decades of environmental history in the United States might look like this: The 1960s was a time of increasing popular and governmental concern over *quality-of-life* concerns (those that immediately affect one's physical health and well-being); the 1970s, the period of *environmental regulation* when the emergent health and conservationist concerns were reflected in dozens of new environmental laws, policies, and regulations (the cornerstone being the National Environmental Policy Act—NEPA—of 1969–70); and the 1980s, the reactionary response to the preceding decade as symbolized in the Reagan administration's hostility toward the ecology movement, inaugurating the decade of *environmental indifference*.

Beginning with the passage of NEPA, the 1970s saw enormous progress in the escalating fight against pollution and environmental degradation. Laws were passed on every level—local, state, and federal—to begin the long-neglected cleanup of the outdoor environment and the workplace. It was now understood that continued reliance on state initiatives to control pollution would forever be ineffective and that national standards would be required if effective and universally applicable environmental regulations were to be enforced. Other victories not related to governmental regulation were commonplace, also. One good example is the popular struggle against nuclear power. The antinuclear movement reached its zenith at the fortuitous moment when demand for electricity in the nation was being reduced from a 7 percent annual growth rate to just over 2 percent. The public-safety concerns about nuclear power and the change in forecast on electricity demand saw the last contract for a U.S. nuclear plant signed in 1978, with more than 100 other plants—some almost completed—either cancelled or mothballed. With the last nuclear plants in the United States now to be completed by 1995, and with current generating-plant life expectancies estimated to be no more than 30 years, it is safe to say that the era of using nuclear power to produce electricity will be finished in this country by the year 2025. Overall, the impact on the nation of environmental activism in the 1960s and 1970s was enormous. Things began to change for the worse, however, with the inauguration of Ronald Reagan as president of the United States.[1]

Reagan-era Environmentalism

Some critics note that the environmental movement may have sown the seeds of its own slowdown in the 1980s by virtue of its assault on industrial pollution. The demand for cleanup—and that industry accept some of the social costs of its own polluting activity—represented a threat to the industrial status quo that was little understood when the Earth movements were flowering in the early 1970s. As Daniel Faber and James O'Connor have noted,

> Environmental action and legislation had the unintentional effect of raising the cost of capital and reducing capital's flexibility with respect to its power to appropriate and capitalize nature. By the mid-1970's, the movement had constituted itself as a social barrier to capitalist accumulation, contributing to declining profits and stagflation, as well as to the internationalization of capitalist production. As a result, large corporations and other capitalist interests which were loosely or tightly regulated by . . . government mobilized politically with the purpose of restructuring the state and the economy which, in turn, weakened the environmental movement itself. The result was the Age of Reagan, the credit driven boom of the 1980's, and a deepening environmental crisis and social crisis within the environmental movement.[2]

I disagree with this overemphasis on the power of the environmental movement in restructuring U.S. capital in the 1970s. I also disagree with the implication that, given this supposed result, environmentalists should have moderated their assault on industry. It is certainly true, however, that the overall impact of the movement—both through its grassroots efforts and its pressure brought to bear on the movers of government policy—was enormous.

Perhaps the generally positive environmentalism of government during the 1970s will be seen later as an historic anomaly, and the Reaganite reaction seen as a more traditional and predictable approach. The decade of the 1970s produced quite a remarkable array of positive programs for both ecological and public health and safety. Conservative economic and political forces had no option but to respond to what were perceived as threats to their well-being. Although the Clean Air Act of 1970 (since revised on several occasions) was estimated by the Council on Environmental Quality (CEQ) to have saved at least 14,000 lives in its first few years of operation, it was roundly condemned by groups like the Business Round Table and by President Reagan, who publicly stated on many occasions that no concern for environmental quality should be permitted to interfere with corporate profits.[3]

Some of the threats to industry from environmentalism were imaginary. As we will shortly note in more detail, unemployment was substantially lower in 1986 than it would have been without the new environmental programs. At least 1 million new "environmental" jobs were created in the 1970–80 period. But an official, long-range government concern for ecological health was simply not in the cards. Neither is it likely today unless (or until, rather) things get really bad at home.

Both the lessening concern for the environment manifest in the closing years of the Carter administration (due less to intention than to budgetary crisis) and the outright assault on environmental quality under Reagan are fully consistent with U.S. economic and political tradition. To expect much more than we have been reluctantly given by government relative to environmental protection would be seriously to misread the basic tendencies of U.S. political and economic history. Much of the hope of the environmental movement during the 1970s and 1980s, for example, focused on the courts and the possibility of applying legal remedies to ecological insults. And the courts have indeed provided a number of protections from the worst abuses of pollution and land-use planning. But it is also true that such efforts are generally out of step with the more traditional role of the courts in the United States—which has been to protect the rights of private property as carefully as individual rights. Since the primary cause for both pollution and natural resource exploitation has been the economically inevitable effort of industry within a market economy to maximize profits, the court can hardly be expected over the long run to take actions that would be inimical to the welfare of the system of industrial production operative throughout the country.

The proper role of government—executive, legislative, or judicial—in interposing itself between the rights of private property and the rights of individuals and the community has always been controversial. Since the prospects are remote for any near-term structural change in government that might allow more long-term concern for ecological health, it is important that environmentalists understand some of the basic social and economic limiting factors that face government in such instances. While strategies for environmental action must take full advantage of the legislative and legal processes, we must reaffirm that the major hope for any longer range and substantive environmental progress is from the pressures that mass-based, popular, grassroots organizations can bring to bear on policymakers. We cannot expect legislators to initiate actions that threaten the welfare of the power brokers of the corporate state without being pushed every step of the way by the people.

From the very beginning of the organized environmental movement, government has been trying either to join it in order to control it, or to co-opt its leadership. Remember: It was Richard Nixon who supported with rhetoric and then financially underwrote many of the events of the first Earth Day in 1970.[4] Granted that this was little more than an effort to distract attention and divert leadership from the anti–Vietnam War movement, it did establish a pattern—reinforcing the already visible politically moderate, populist, and anti-ideological stance of most environmentalists. One critic of the "middle-class bias" within the environmental groupings early on stated, "If we take its proponents as seriously as they wish to be taken this [movement] is a diversion from politics as such . . . providing a nonpartisan rallying point . . . leaving to the present power brokers the task of directing the nation's destiny."[5]

This analysis has proven to be both right and wrong. It quite completely underestimated the impact of the movement on industrial and governmental power in the United States, as documented above. Although theory and practice are most effective when closely linked, the nonideological environmental movement powerfully impacted the nation during the 1970s. But other troubles were on the horizon as the Reagan era began. As social ecologist Murray Bookchin noted in 1980,

> To speak bluntly: the coming decade may well determine whether the ecology movement will be reduced to a decorative appendage of an inherently diseased anti-ecological society, a society riddled by an unbridled need for control, domination and exploitation of humanity and nature. . . . Ironically, the opening of the eighties, so rich in its promise of sweeping changes in values and consciousness, has also seen the emergence of a new opportunism. Many self-styled "founders" of the [environmental movement] have become . . . "managerial radicals"—the manipulators of a political consensus that operates within the system in the very name of opposing it.[6]

In an article I wrote in 1980, this author pointed out the fact that the cutting edge of the movement was passing from those who understood the commonality of concern among organizing activists everywhere—environmentalists, liberationists, people struggling in their own ways against war and poverty and classism and racism and sexism—to the more privileged managers in government bureaucracies, conservationist environmental organizations, and the universities. This tendency accelerated in the 1980s. Perhaps the best example of this was the 1986 decision made by Friends of the Earth—originally one of the most grassroots-oriented environmental groups around—to oust founder David Brower and move the organization's headquarters from San Francisco (which may be the "grassroots" capital of the United States) to Washington, D.C., in order that its lobbyists might have more direct access to the springs of power. While both are needed—skilled and articulate spokespersons to meet policymakers on a relatively even footing *and* grassroots groupings who remember that it is the people on the local level who are impacted the most by ecological degradation—the movement clearly split in the 1980s over which emphasis should have priority.

The Ideological Rifts

It is no secret that there are real ideological differences in the environmental movement today. These differences are reflected in the approach to issues as well as in the structural form of the organizations. The Sierra Club, with essentially middle-class members who fight polluters through the courts, is different in style and substance from the Environmental Project on Central America (EPOCA), whose members fight environmental battles through their identification with the particular struggles of oppressed peoples. Both differ markedly from Earth First!, which totally condemns the bureaucratization of the movement and its effort to affect policymakers and which is absolutely committed to an anarchic, antihumanist, monkey-wrenching approach to ecological activism.

Not surprisingly, Third World and working-class people have had little interest in involving themselves with the standard-brand ecology groups that are perhaps rightly perceived as having little concern for or sense of identity with the problems of working people. (Parenthetically, it must be noted that the response of workers to the environmental elitists in the early 1970s was little different from the response of workers to today's Earth First! organization and its stated indifference to the welfare of working people.) Too often an apolitical environmentalism can be a diversion from the important task of evaluating the shape and posture of the future struggle against the wielders of social power. And few advocates of the mainstream political tendencies—the free-enterprisers and the socialists—have been up to the task of matching practice to theory in the environmental context. Apologists for the market cannot escape from the fact that capitalism sees nature as essentially no more than one of the means of production. Socialists historically ignore the natural world completely in their belief that nature has unlimited reserves if only properly and scientifically managed.

It is also true that, in the modern world of bureautechnocracy and immensely diffused decision-making, even the clearest ideologies tend to lose their distinctiveness rather quickly. Modern social organization tends both to resent and to discount conceptual clarity. Intention and ideology are like chunks of raw meat fed into the sausage grinder of worldly action. What comes out in the end seems so very different from what went in at the beginning. This makes it all the more important, however, that grassroots environmentalists construct sharply focused political and social guidelines as the basis for their organizational work. Ideological clarity does not mean (as critics like the Fabers and O'Connors on the left or the Earth Firsters on the right seem to believe) that theory becomes the sole motivating factor for practice. We know today that massive theoretical and formally ideological frameworks most often get in the way of mass-based organizing. As writer-activist Daniel Berman said in criticizing a formally socialist approach to environmental organizing, "The open 'socialists' in our Bay Area Committee on Occupational Safety and Health group initiated a discussion which lasted until 11:30 one Friday night which managed to drive away the labor unionists who had been looking for help on concrete health struggles within their plants and unions. Once again, when you started talking about 'socialism' the organization turned into a world series of the U.S. left."[7]

On the contrary, ideologically sensitive environmental organizers must first be concerned for the development of common-sense kinds of guidelines. Who should control our natural resources, and how should that control be organized? How does an organization go about coalition building? What should be the minimal (not the maximal) grounds for joint political action? What are the primary and inescapable social goals around which strategies should be built? What are the organization's priorities for education and action? How is it possible to utilize the strengths of the organization and minimize its weaknesses? Can there be a normative ecoethic that will guide day-to-day activities? As community organizer Saul Alinsky used to tell students in his organizing seminars, "Serious organizers establish early on who they can work with. They are clear about identifying potential friends and likely enemies." Without relative clarity of purpose, such identifications become virtually impossible.

In a more profound fashion than ever before, ecology has emerged as a truly "subversive science," calling into question not only the scientific and technological virtues of the day but also the underlying values of the entire society. As always, the questions of ethics—the development of systematic frameworks for analysis and action—and the setting of standards for our work are best dealt with by ordinary people facing up to the realities of survival in their own time. While governments can sometimes help to define such questions, they can rarely do much to implement a viable ethic in the national consciousness. Environmental activists should find some comfort in the fact that power does ultimately rest with the people so long as the people are prepared to work toward effecting the needed changes that governments tend to ignore.

Environmentalists may find it uncomfortable to have to think about reformulating their ideology within the movement as well as devising a new standard of self-criticism. Those persons who are essentially content with the existing economic and political orders may resent the suggestion that we take our conceptual starting points more seriously. What seems incontrovertible, however, is that many symptoms of the malaise of the age—undifferentiated patterns of growth, underdevelopment in the Third World and overdevelopment in the West, poverty and disease, militarism, inequities in the global production and distribution systems, the double disadvantages of race and sex—all stem from the same social causes as the ecocrisis. No one of these problems can be solved apart from sound political and economic analysis and the development of creative strategies for action. People who wish to foster a more politically mature environmentalism will not content themselves with simply joining the nearest conservation group. They may properly do this, but they will also become increasingly impatient for the more "nonreformist reforms"—those efforts which both challenge and seek to resolve the contradictions and structural imbalances in the social order that have led to environmental and other major social problems.[8]

The old idea in the United States that the pursuit of private gain will inevitably result in benefit to the society at large is—in spite of the "me first" attitude that has characterized the Reagan–Bush years—the refuge of only a relatively small coterie of true believers. Those of us who feel, for example, that more public involvement in resource management policy is a requirement for ecological survival need to make our starting points clear. This does not mean having to endorse the entire ideological positions of either the left or the right.

It is too easy for comfortable reformists who do not challenge the social status quo to construct postrevolutionary fantasies, forgetting about the tough but necessary job of organizing people. It is perhaps even worse for nonreformists to say that established power is so entrenched that the very best we can do is work out modest compromises with those who despoil. Neither option will do nature much good nor properly illustrate the Gaia connections between ecology, economics, and ethics.

As we begin the third decade since Earth Day in 1970, we may see both a continuation and a reinforcement of some of the negative trends of the past 20 years; bureaucratic co-optation of environmental leadership, efforts to focus simply on single issues without understanding the need to link environmental issues to other social problems, and ever more direct assaults on those environmental programs that in some way threaten the profits of U.S. industry. If such undoing can push us back to our roots, however—to local organizing, to the building of powerful community coalitions, to the development of broadly conceived social strategies and careful delineation of first principles—then the government opposition to ecological health that we have known during the Reagan–Bush era may be successfully survived, after all.

The Global Movement of the Greens

For more than 20 years, the global ecology movement has been enhanced by the persistent effort of the European Green parties to impact party politics in a number of countries. The Green coalitions came together around the belief that the various citizens' movements throughout Europe (antinuclear, feminist, antiwar and prodétente, environmentalist) required more formal avenues of political expression than simply through their own organizations (a longtime concern in the United States, as well). Under the multiparty, proportional representation basis of the parliamentary system, minority candidates can run for office and often be elected. And in fact, Green candidates have been elected to office in (what was) West Germany, Belgium, Holland, and within the Parliament of the European Economic Community (EEC).

Apart from more traditional local and national policy issues, the Greens focus their community work and parliamentary activity around the "Four Pillars of the Green Movement":

1. *Ecology*, similar to our own environmental quality and deep ecology emphases;

2. *Social responsibility*, concerns for social justice and for the concerns of working-class people;

3. *Grassroots democracy*, recognizing the need for mass-based community action groups on a variety of issues; and

4. *Nonviolence*, opposition to violence both as it becomes institutionalized in social structures and in the relationships of human beings to one another.

Today, these environmental parties are actively campaigning in each of the 12 countries in the EEC. Hundreds of Green candidates are up for office. Once largely socialist in political orientation (now a tendency of the "Left Greens" in the United States) and demanding the total overhaul of every aspect of the traditional capitalist political economy, the Greens have in the past few years begun to tone down their antiestablishment language. Properly emphasizing the internationalization of the movement, leaders like Daniel Cohn-Bendit of Germany believe that the Greens can take the progressive environmental policies of certain countries and attempt to make these the norms for the entire EEC.

The Green movement has also been increasingly visible in the United States, where it has espoused the same general principles as its European predecessor. The Citizen's party, which was begun in 1980 by Barry Commoner and for several years placed candidates for election in local, state, and national elections, has been the closest functional U.S. approximation to a European Green political party. Although Green principles are advocated as forcefully in the United States as anywhere in the world, it is doubtful that the attempt to gain political office on a Green agenda would ever be as successful in this country as it has been in Europe. Dominated by the two-party system and lacking the proportional-representation entrée, Green-type candidates must understand that election to office is normally impossible. Entering political campaigns for the purpose of educating the public can be useful, but the strategy is inevitably difficult to sustain over extended periods. The demise of the Citizen's party after two ambitious—and relatively successful—national campaigns was due in large part to the fact that registering to vote as a member of the Citizen's party (or any other third-party alternative) makes one automatically ineligible to vote in the primary elections of the major parties—where the final decisions on the major candidates and issues are made. To act on a political principle in this case means to remove oneself from the final electoral process. Notwithstanding this dilemma, what Charlene Spretnak recently called "the greening of America" is now well under way, albeit in different form than that found in the parliamentary democracies.[9]

The Labor–Health–Environmental Connection

Coalition building may yet prove to be the key to any future successes in environmental activism. Single-issue organizing may work for very short-range, tactical efforts, but no major organizing effort has ever succeeded without the identification of common concerns and issues within different groupings. As I often tell students, when one is working on issues that relate to any of the negative "isms" of the age—classism, racism, sexism, militarism—one is also working on the others. One of the more important economic and political linkages for the U.S. environmental movement in the last decade of the twentieth century will be the labor–public-health–environmental connection. With quality-of-life concerns now affecting the consciousness of everyone (bad drinking water, toxic wastes, radioactivity, air pollution, workplace hazards), the overlapping self-interest of these communities is clear.

Simple but powerful (and slightly true) myths about labor and about environmentalists have been peddled for years by both sides. Environmentalists are indifferent to the welfare of working people; they are more concerned for birds and animals and flowers than for people. Workers are indifferent to nature; they would cut down every tree and dam every river as long as jobs were provided. Beyond the simplistic mythologies are some very real issues. Environmentalists *have* often called for policies that have a negative impact on employment in the short run: energy conservation, air and water quality controls, sustainable resource-use practices, limits to economic growth and development. And official labor *has* on occasion called for precisely the opposite policies.

The short-range conflicts between working people and environmentalists thus have a real basis in fact and history. Often coming from more privileged classes, the ecology-minded sometimes forget the survival imperatives that inevitably motivate most U.S. workers. The pragmatics of keeping a job and supporting a family when real wages are static or declining are more real to most people than the environmental ideologies of John Muir or E. F. Schumacher. But things are changing. Worker–environmentalist lobbies are springing up around the country. The old insistence by official labor (whose leadership so commonly takes positions identical to that of industry) that environmental laws would mean plant closing and job losses has been proven wrong. In the first decade after NEPA—although there were in fact 128 plant closings cited by industry sources as having been occasioned in part by new environmental regulations—the major reason cited for closures was the obsolescense of plant and equipment. And while 24,000 workers lost their jobs through these closures, more than 1 million new jobs were created during the decade by federal and state expenditures for environmental programs.[10]

Estimating the overall job impact of environmental legislation, a 1979 Data Resources, Incorporated (DRI) study indicated that overall employment was expected to be higher through 1986 than it would have been without the new regulations. "The decrease in the unemployment rate ranges from 0.1% to 0.4%, ending up at 0.2% in 1986. In 1979, DRI estimates that the unemployment rate will be 0.2% lower with the programs . . . and will range . . . to 0.4% lower from now through 1986."[11]

In addition to being exposed to the generalized public-health threats from contaminated drinking water, toxic wastes, and bad air, working people are the most direct recipients of environmental degradation both in the workplace and the home. They more commonly live in environmentally impacted areas. They are more regularly exposed to heavy chemical contamination in the workplace. Inadvertently, they too often bring contaminants home, thus also polluting the household environment. During the past 50 years, more than 2 million chemical compounds have been introduced into the workplace. Few have ever been tested for their effects on either worker or public health. In 1980, the National Institute of Occupational Safety and Health (NIOSH)—the government's official testing bureau for workplace chemical hazards (being the research arm of the Occupational Safety and Health Administration, or OSHA)—estimated it would take at least 100 years to set standards for the workplace toxins now being used. NIOSH also estimated that 25 percent of the total U.S. workforce is regularly exposed to illness-causing substances; that 390,000 people contract serious occupational diseases every year, with at least 100,000 job-related deaths annually; and that at least 50 percent of all cancers are caused or complicated by occupational factors. And all of this was during the pre-Reagan era. Since then, under Reagan–Bush policies, standards have been lowered; NIOSH has been effectively disbanded, and industry told to "voluntarily comply" with EPA regulations, since government would effectively no longer be involved in enforcement procedures. The mutuality of concern and interests among workers, the health community, and environmentalists is clear and may provide the basis for the most powerful pro-ecology coalition yet seen in this country.[12]

A Concluding Unscientific Postscript

The Gaia connections may now be a bit easier to follow. A healthy and restored ecology requires from human beings both a revised economics and a new ecoethic. Perhaps more than anything else, this will take sound organizational skills, clear first principles, and a bit of hope and optimism about the future and our role in defining what that future should be. This will not be easy. A bit of review may be in order.

Almost 20 years ago, an environmentalist friend of mine delivered a lecture that cataloged the many environmental sins of Homo sapiens and then concluded with the statement, "If I could push the button to destroy the human species, I would do so because of what man has done to nature." Over the years, other doomsaying prophets have reiterated this message. And indeed our problems are many. Some of the causes are clear.

In his now classic book *Design with Nature,* environmental planner Ian McHarg critiques the radically anthropocentric perspectives of the Western religious tradition, and declares that Christianity,

> in its insistence upon domination and subjugation of nature, encourages the most exploitative and destructive instincts in man rather than those that are deferential and creative. Indeed, if one seeks license for those who would increase radioactivity, create canals and harbors with atomic bombs, carry poisons without constraint, or give consent to the bulldozer mentality, there could be no better injunction than this biblical creation text. Here can be found the injunction to conquer nature—the enemy, the threat to Jehovah.[13]

Indeed, religions *have* generally insisted on the dominance and subjugation of nature to human end goals, encouraging exploitative and destructive instincts. The entire biosphere—plants and animals, the many wonders of the creation—is viewed as nothing more than the stage setting for our little drama of the human species. Purpose and end goals are commonly defined solely in terms of the nature of humankind. Caught up in such perverse priorities, science and technology accelerate the drift toward a new and terminal holocaust. And we doom ourselves to irrelevance unless we come to see and understand the political nature of biology—indeed of all science—in third-century America.

David Ehrenfeld in *The Arrogance of Humanism* made his own list of humanity's sins: inappropriate technologies, inadequate economic systems, our many misuses of freedom, turning resources into commodities, pollution, inept bureaucracies, destructive political leaders, dependence on capital rather than labor, and the limited viewpoints of both socialism and capitalism. Moreover, we have lost many things as a result of our mistakes: wilderness, species and communities, cultivated lands, human skills, natural resources, human and environmental health. Ehrenfeld pleads with us "for a gentler and more humble approach to the environment."[14]

As this book has hopefully demonstrated, humanity's arrogant exploitation of the environment and its resources has indeed resulted in enormous dangers to the future of our species and all others. The ravaging of ourselves and our Earth, and the mining of our brains, for purposes antithetical to human or animal survival are consistent with the dominant economic and ideological assumptions of the past two centuries of human history.

Our priorities have become totally confused. Human labor and Earth's bounties have alike become commodities. We thus become alienated from ourselves, from our neighbors, and from the world in which we live. Things have meaning only in terms of their exchange value. Individuals (both human and animal) become means to those ends determined appropriate by political economies and their respective ideologies. Trees, water, animals, minerals become natural resources, instrumentalities for certain economically defined "greater" ends. Regardless of the social order, human beings become human resources, exploited as any other resource by those with political and economic power.

Nonetheless, we hope. We do not necessarily expect that everything we hope for will in fact come to pass. But we hope. And the basis for our hope can be found in the emergence of a new and redemptive model for a biological ethic—an ecoethic—as the ecological model for our future. It is then only reasonable for ecoethicists to pose a set of standards to the governments and economic leaders of the world and some principles as a basis of unity for people seeking to effect positive change.

Knowing that science does what it is told to do by those who control the purse strings, we affirm that the control of science should be subject in part to the collective and representative will of the citizenry—lay and expert alike—in the attempt to answer problems deemed important by them, rather than by those who control and profit from the operative technological ideologies of the era.

We hope for and work for distributive justice within societies and among the peoples of the world. We claim the rights of people to live meaningful and unexploited lives. We condemn war, and we work for the total abolition of chemical, biological, and nuclear weapons.

We believe that nonhuman life forms have intrinsic value as well as being instruments of use to humankind. Knowing that if we are to safeguard our own liberties, we must struggle for the minimization of suffering in all areas of life implies for us a new kind of ethic for everyday existence. We demand respect for the biosphere itself, including all of its animal and plant life. We oppose all political and economic systems that indiscriminately exploit either human or other natural systems.

Perhaps we can only call attention to some of these ethical dilemmas of the age through helping people understand and analyze the magnitude of the problems we face. That has been the primary intention of this little book. If we do only that, but do it in conscience and with clear intention, it will be a very good thing. Beyond that, if we think carefully and struggle diligently—organizing ourselves for action—some of these problems can be resolved and that which we hope for actually come to pass. What we all most desperately need are new relationships in and understandings of power that can enable us to live in humanly supportive and affirming social situations, refusing to submit any longer to the intentions of those who seek to program our political and biological futures. As we have hopefully learned, one changes power only by confronting it.

Above all, we must not give up hope on our species. Albert Camus in his novel *The Plague* describes the importance of both realistic optimism about the future and unremitting struggle against all forms of ethical contamination. Were he writing today, he would most surely include in his call for struggle the demand that we work for a real science of the people and for the rights of all God's creatures. His words suggest the importance not only of discerning the Gaia connections—ecology, ecoethics, and economics—but of acting on them.

> Many fledgling moralists in those days were going about our town proclaiming there was nothing to be done to fight the plague and that we should simply bow to the inevitable. But . . . our conclusion was always the same, the certitude that a fight must be put up, in this way or that, and that there must be no bowing down. The essential thing was to save the greatest number of persons from dying. . . . And to do this there was only one resource: to fight the plague. There was nothing admirable about this attitude; it was simply logical.[15]

Notes

1. Alan S. Miller, "Reagan Era Environmentalism," *RAIN* (Spring 1981), pp. 4–7.

2. Daniel Faber and James O'Connor, "The Struggle for Nature: Environmental Crises and the Crisis of Environmentalism in the United States," unpublished paper, 1989, p. 1.

3. See the April 21, 1980, press release of the Council on Environmental Quality, Executive Office of the President.

4. For a good review of this Earth Day history, see Richard Neuhaus, *In Defense of People* (New York: Macmillan, 1971), esp. pp. 69–91.

5. Ibid., p. 322.

6. Murray Bookchin, "An Open Letter to the Ecology Movement," *RAIN* (April 1980), p. 5.

7. Daniel Berman, "We Need a Socialist Ecology?" *Zeta Magazine* (April 1989), p. 4.

8. Note the strategies for "non-reformist reforms" outlined in Andre Gorz, *A Strategy for Labor* (Boston: Beacon Press, 1967).

9. The best overall analysis of the history of the European Greens and the prospects for "greening America" will be found in Charlene Spretnak and Fritjof Capra, *Green Politics: The Global Promise* (Santa Fe, N.M.: Bear, 1986). Note also Charles A. Reich, *The Greening of America: How the Youth Revolution Is Going to Make America Livable* (New York: Random House, 1970).

10. Statistics from the EPA report, *Economic Dislocation Early Warning System,* May 9, 1979.

11. The most thorough study of the "jobs versus the environment" issue is the January/February 1979 report to the EPA by Data Resources, Incorporated, *The Management Impact of Federal Pollution Control Programs.*

12. Richard Kazis and Richard Grossman, *Fear at Work: Job Blackmail, Labor, and the Environment* (New York: Pilgrim Press, 1982).

13. Ian L. McHarg, *Design with Nature* (Garden City, N.Y.: Natural History Press, 1969), p. 24.

14. David Ehrenfeld, *The Arrogance of Humanism* (London: Oxford University Press, 1978).

15. Albert Camus, *The Plague* (New York: Random House, 1948), p. 122.

The Influence Coming into Play:
THE SEVEN OF PENTACLES

Under a sky the color of pea soup
she is looking at her work growing away there
actively, thickly like grapevines or pole beans
as things grow in the real world, slowly enough.
If you tend them properly, if you mulch, if you water,
if you provide birds that eat insects a home and winter food,
if the sun shines and you pick off caterpillars,
if the praying mantis comes and the ladybugs and the bees,
then the plants flourish, but at their own internal clock.

Connections are made slowly, sometimes they grow underground.
You cannot tell always by looking what is happening.
More than half a tree is spread out in the soil under your feet.
Penetrate quietly as the earthworm that blows no trumpet.
Fight persistently as the creeper that brings down the tree.
Spread like the squash plant that overruns the garden.
Gnaw in the dark and use the sun to make sugar.

Weave real connections, create real nodes, build real houses.
Live a life you can endure: make love that *is* loving.
Keep tangling and interweaving and taking more in,
a thicket and bramble wilderness to the outside but to us
interconnected with rabbit runs and burrows and lairs.

Live as if you liked yourself, and it may happen:
reach out, keep reaching out, keep bringing in.
This is how we are going to live for a long time: not always,
for every gardener knows that after the digging, after the
planting,
after the long season of tending and growth, the harvest comes.

Marge Piercy
To Be of Use
New York: Doubleday, 1973, p. 49.
Reprinted with permission.

Supplementary Reading List

In addition to the books and articles referred to in the notes at the end of each chapter, the following books are recommended as supplementary reading on chapter topics.

Chapter 1: Environmental Ethics

Berger, John J. *Restoring the Earth*. New York: A. A. Knopf, 1985.

Birch, Charles, and John Cobb, Jr. *The Liberation of Life: From the Cell to the Community*. Cambridge, U.K.: Cambridge University Press, 1981.

Callicott, J. Baird. Editor. *Companion to a Sand County Almanac: Interpretive and Critical Essays*. (Madison: University of Wisconsin Press, 1987.

————. *In Defense of the Land Ethic: Essays in Environmental Philosophy*. Albany: State University of New York Press, 1989.

Capra, Fritjof. *The Turning Point: Science, Society, and the Rising Culture*. New York: Simon and Schuster, 1982.

Devall, Bill, and George Sessions. *Deep Ecology: Living as if Nature Mattered*. Layton, Utah: Gibbs M. Smith Publishers, 1985.

Goldfarb, Theodore D. Editor. *Clashing Views on Controversial Environmental Issues*. Guilford Conn.: Dushkin Publishing Group, 1989.

Gunn, Alastair S., and P. Arne Vesiland. *Environmental Ethics for Engineers*. Chelsea, Mich.: Lewis Publishers, 1989.

Hargrove, Eugene C. *Foundations of Environmental Ethics*. Englewood Cliffs, N.J.: Prentice-Hall, 1989.

Joranson, P. N., and Ken Butigan. Editors. *Cry of the Environment: Rebuilding the Christian Creation Tradition*. Santa Fe, N.M.: Bear, 1984.

Merchant, Carolyn. *The Death of Nature: Women, Ecology, and the Scientific Revolution*. New York: Harper and Row, 1980.

————. *Ecological Revolutions: Nature, Gender, and Science in New England*. Chapel Hill: University of North Carolina Press, 1989.

Piel, Jonathan. Editor. *Managing Planet Earth*. New York: W.H. Freeman, 1990.

Regan, Tom. Editor. *Earthbound: New Introductory Essays in Environmental Ethics.* Philadelphia: Temple University Press, 1984.

Rolston, Holmes III. *Environmental Ethics: Duties to and Values in the Natural World.* Philadelphia: Temple University Press, 1988.

Sagoff, Mark. *The Economy of the Earth: Philosophy, Law, and the Environment.* New York: Harper and Row, 1986.

Stone, Christopher D. *Environmental Ethics.* New York: Harper and Row, 1986.

Worster, Donald. *Nature's Economy.* New York: Anchor Books, 1979.

Chapter 2: Theories of Justice

Ehrenfeld, David. *The Arrogance of Humanism.* London: Oxford University Press, 1978.

Fletcher, Joseph. *Situation Ethics.* Philadelphia: Westminster Press, 1966.

Kant, Immanuel. *Groundwork of the Metaphysics of Morals.* Translated by H. H. Paton. New York: Harper Torchbooks, 1964.

Mill, John S. *Utilitarianism.* Edited by M. Warnock. New York: New American Library, 1962.

Plato. "The Dialogues" and "The Republic." In *Great Books of the Western World,* Volume 7. Chicago: Encyclopaedia Britannica, 1952.

Ramsey, Paul. *Ethics at the Edges of Life.* New Haven, Conn.: Yale University Press, 1975.

Rawls, John. *A Theory of Justice.* Cambridge, Mass.: Belknap Press, 1971.

Regan, Tom. Editor. *Matters of Life and Death: New Introductory Essays in Moral Philosophy.* New York: Random House, 1986.

Wolff, R. P. *Understanding Rawls.* Princeton, N.J.: Princeton University Press, 1977.

Chapter 3: World Order Imperatives

Heilbroner, Robert. *An Inquiry into the Human Prospect.* New York: W.W. Norton, 1974.

Laszlo, Ervin. *A Strategy for the Future: The Systems Approach to World Order.* New York: George Braziller, 1974.

Limerick, Patricia M. *The Legacy of Conquest: The Unbroken Past of the American West.* New York: W.W. Norton, 1987.

Meadows, Donella H., Dennis L. Meadows, Jorgen Randers, and William Behrens. *The Limits to Growth.* New York: Universe Books, 1972.

Mesarovic, Mihaljo, and Eduard Pestel. *Mankind at the Turning Point.* New York: E.P. Dutton, 1974.

Reisner, Marc. *Cadillac Desert. The American West and Its Disappearing Water.* New York: Viking Penguin, 1986.

Tingbergen, Jan. *RIO: Reshaping the International Order.* New York: E.P. Dutton, 1976.

Chapter 4: The Moral Demand for the Biological Steady State

Daly, Herman E. "The Economic and Moral Necessity for Limiting Economic Growth." In L. Shinn, Editor, *Faith and Science in an Unjust World.* Philadelphia: Fortress Press, 1980.

———. "Entropy, Growth, and the Political Economy of Scarcity." in *Steady State Economics: The Economics of Biophysical Equilibrium and Moral Growth.* San Francisco: W. H. Freeman, 1977.

Georgescu-Roegen, Nicholas. *Analytical Economics.* Cambridge, Mass.: Harvard University Press, 1966.

Hardin, Garrett. "The Tragedy of the Commons." *Science* 162 (1968), pp. 1243–48.

Lovins, Amory B. "Energy Strategy: The Road Not Taken." *Foreign Affairs* 55 (1976), pp. 65–97.

Malthus, Thomas. *Essay on the Principle of Population*, Volume 2. New York: E.P. Dutton, 1961.

Ophuls, William. *Ecology and the Politics of Scarcity.* San Francisco, W.H. Freeman, 1977.

Rifkin, Jeremy. *Entropy: Into the Greenhouse World,* Revised Edition. New York: Bantam Books, 1989.

Chapter 5: Economics as if Nature Mattered

Capitalism, Nature, Socialism: A Journal of Socialist Ecology, 1803 Mission Street, Santa Cruz, CA 95060.

Heilbroner, Robert L. *Marxism: For and Against.* New York: W.W. Norton, 1980.

Heilbroner, Robert L., and Lester Thurow. *Five Economic Challenges.* Englewood Cliffs, N.J.: Prentice-Hall, 1981.

Hunt, E. K., and H. J. Sherman. *Economics: An Introduction to Traditional and Radical Views.* New York: Harper and Row, 1978.

Pirages, Dennis. *Global Ecopolitics.* North Sciute, Mass.: Duxbury Press, 1978.

Zarsky, Lyuba, Samuel Bowles, and Susan Ells. Editors. *Economic Report of the People.* Boston: South End Press, 1986.

Chapter 6: Bioethical Limits to Scientific Inquiry

Broad, William, and Nicholas Wade. *Betrayers of the Truth: Fraud and Deceit in the Halls of Science.* New York: Simon and Schuster, 1982.

Capra, Fritjof. *The Tao of Physics: An Exploration of the Parallels between Modern Physics and Eastern Mysticism.* Berkeley: Shambhala, 1975.

Churchman, C. West. *The Systems Approach and Its Enemies.* New York: Basic Books, 1979.

De Tocqueville, Alexis. *Democracy in America.* New York: Schocken Books, 1961.

Easlea, Brian. *Liberation and the Aims of Science.* London: Sussex University Press, 1973.

Heilbroner, Robert. *An Inquiry into the Human Prospect: Updated for the 80's.* New York: W.W. Norton, 1980.

Kuhn, Thomas. *The Structure of Scientific Revolution.* Chicago: University of Chicago Press, 1962.

Miller, Alan S. *A Planet to Choose: Value Studies in Political Ecology.* New York: Pilgrim Press, 1978.

Rifkin, Jeremy. *Algeny: A New Word—A New World.* New York: Penguin Books, 1984.

Sale, Kirkpatrick. *Human Scale.* New York: Coward, McGann, and Geoghegan, 1980.

Schumacher, E. F. *Small Is Beautiful: Economics as if People Mattered.* New York: Harper and Row, 1973.

Shinn, Rogert L. Editor. *Faith and Science in an Unjust World,* Volumes 1, 2, 3. Philadelphia: Fortress Press, 1980.

Teich, A. H. Editor. *Technology and Man's Future.* New York: St. Martin's Press, 1977.

Chapters 7 and 8: Genetic Engineering and Genetic Counseling

Fletcher, Joseph. *The Ethics of Genetic Control.* New York: Anchor Press, 1974.

Harsanyi, J., and Hulton, M. *Genetic Prophecy.* New York: Rawson-Wade, 1981.

Lappe, Marc. *Broken Code: The Exploitation of DNA.* San Francisco: Sierra Club Books, 1984.

———. *Genetic Politics.* New York: Simon and Schuster, 1979.

Mappes, T. A., and J. S. Zembatty. *Biomedical Ethics.* New York: McGraw-Hill, 1981.

Nelkin, Dorothy, and Laurence Tancredi. *Dangerous Diagnostics: The Social Power of Biological Information.* New York: Basic Books, 1989.

Norwood, J. A. *At Highest Risk: Hazards to the Unborn.* New York: McGraw-Hill, 1980.

Packard, Vance. *The People Shapers.* Boston: Little, Brown, 1977.

Ramsey, Paul. *The Ethics of Fetal Research.* New Haven, Conn.: Yale University Press, 1975.

Chapter 9 and 10: Bioethics

Ackerman, T. F., and Carson Strong. *A Casebook of Medical Ethics.* New York: Oxford University Press, 1989.

Beauchamp, Thomas L., and LeRoy Walters. *Contemporary Issues in Bioethics,* 3rd Edition. Belmont, Calif.: Wadsworth Publishing, 1989.

Brody, Baruch A., and H. Tristan Engelhardt, Jr. *Bioethics: Readings and Cases.* Englewood Cliffs, N.J.: Prentice-Hall, 1987.

Hull, Richard T. *Ethical Issues in the New Reproductive Technologies.* Belmont, Calif.: Wadsworth Publishing, 1990.

Mappes, Thomas E., and Jane S. Zembatty. *Biomedical Ethics,* 2nd Edition. New York: McGraw-Hill, 1986.

Pellagrino, Edmund D., and David C. Thomasma. *A Philosophical Basis of Medical Practice.* New York: Oxford University Press, 1981.

Reich, Warren T. Editor. *Encyclopedia of Bioethics.* New York: Free Press, 1978.

Sagan, Leonard A. *The Health of Nations: The Cause of Sickness and Well-being.* New York: Basic Books, 1987.

Veatch, Robert. *Case Studies in Medical Ethics.* Cambridge, Mass.: Harvard University Press, 1977.

———. *Cross Cultural Perspectives in Medical Ethics.* Boston: Jones and Bartlett, 1989.

———. *Medical Ethics.* Boston: Jones and Bart, 1989.

Chapter 11: The Selfish Gene

Boyd, Robert, and Peter J. Richerson. *Culture and the Evolutionary Process.* Chicago: University of Chicago Press, 1986.

Caplan, A. L. *The Sociobiology Debate.* New York: Harper and Row, 1978.

Dawkins, Richard. *The Selfish Gene.* Oxford, U.K.: Oxford University Press, 1976.

Gould, Stephen Jay. *Ever since Darwin.* New York: W.W. Norton, 1977.

————. *Hen's Teeth and Horse's Toes.* New York: W.W. Norton, 1983.

————. *The Panda's Thumb.* New York: W.W. Norton, 1980.

Kass, Leon R. *Toward a More Natural Science: Biology and Human Affairs.* New York: Free Press, 1985.

Keiffer, George H. *Bioethics: A Textbook of Issues.* New York: Addison-Wesley, 1979.

Levins, Richard, and Richard Lewontin. *The Dialectical Biologist.* Cambridge, Mass.: Harvard University Press, 1985.

Lewontin, Richard C. "The Corpse in the Elevator." *New York Review of Books.* January 20, 1983.

Singer, Peter. *The Expanding Circle: Ethics and Sociobiology.* New York: Meridian Press, 1981.

Stebbins, G. Ledyard. *Darwin to DNA, Molecules to Humanity.* San Francisco: W.H. Freeman, 1982.

Taylor, Gordon R. *The Great Evolution Mystery.* New York: Harper and Row, 1983.

Wilson, Edward O. *On Human Nature.* Cambridge, Mass.: Harvard University's Belknap Press, 1978.

————. *Sociobiology: The Abridged Edition.* Cambridge, Mass.: Harvard University's Belknap Press, 1980.

Chapter 13: Ecoethics and Modern War

Abbot, Walter M., S.J. Editor. *The Documents of Vatican II.* New York: Guild Press, 1966.

Aristophanes. "The Peace." In *Great Books of the Western World,* Volume 5. Chicago: Encyclopaedia Britannica, 1952.

Aristotle. "The Politics." In *Great Books of the Western World,* Volume 9. Chicago: Encyclopaedia Britannica, 1952.

Augustine. "The City of God." In *Great Books of the Western World,* Volume 18. Chicago: Encyclopaedia Britannica, 1952.

Broad, William. *The Star Warriors.* New York: Simon and Schuster, 1985.

Cohen, Avner, and Steven Lee. Editors. *Nuclear Weapons and the Future of Humanity.* Totowa, N.J.: Rowman and Allenheld Publishers, 1986.

Dyson, Freeman. *Weapons and Hope*. New York: Harper and Row, 1984.

Falk, Richard A. *Law, Morality, and War in the Contemporary World*. Princeton, N.J.: F.A. Praeger, 1963.

Freedman, Lawrence. *The Evolution of Nuclear Strategy*. New York: St. Martin's Press, 1984.

Holloway, David. *The Soviet Union and the Arms Race*. New Haven, Conn.: Yale University Press, 1984.

Jervis, Robert. *The Illogic of American Nuclear Strategy*. Ithaca, N.Y.: Cornell University Press, 1984.

Johnson, James T. *Just War Tradition and the Restraint of War*. Princeton, N.J.: Princeton University Press, 1981.

Kidron, Michael, and Dan Smith. *The War Atlas: Armed Conflict—Armed Peace*. New York: Simon and Schuster, 1983.

Lackey, Douglas P. *Moral Principles and Nuclear Weapons*. Totowa, N.J.: Rowman and Allenheld Publishers, 1984.

Locke, John. *Concerning Civil Government*. In *Great Books of the Western World*, Volume 35. Chicago: Encyclopaedia Britannica, 1952. Originally published in 1689.

Niebuhr, Reinhold. *Christian Realism and Political Problems*. New York: Scribner's, 1953.

———. *Moral Man and Immoral Society*. New York: Charles Scribner's Sons, 1960. Originally published in 1932.

Nimroody, Rosy. *Star Wars: The Economic Fallout*. Cambridge, Mass.: Ballinger, 1988.

Ramsey, Paul. *The Just War: Force and Political Responsibility*. New York: Charles Scribner's Sons, 1968.

———. *War and the Christian Conscience: How Shall Modern War Be Conducted Justly?* Durham, N.C.: Duke University Press, 1961.

Schell, Jonathan. *The Abolition*. New York: A.A. Knopf, 1984.

———. *The Fate of the Earth*. New York: A.A. Knopf, 1981.

Solomon, Frederick, and Robert Q. Marston. *The Medical Implications of Nuclear War*. Washington, D.C.: National Academy Press, 1986.

Walzer, Michael. *Just and Unjust Wars: A Moral Argument with Historical Illustrations*. New York: Basic Books, 1977.

Chapter 14: All God's Creatures

Ehrlich, Anne, and Paul Ehrlich. *Extinction: The Causes and Consequences of the Disappearance of Species*. New York: Random House, 1981.

Godlovitch, R., and J. Harper. *Animals, Men, and Morals.* New York: Grove Press, 1971.

Gorman, James. "Burden of the Beasts." *Discover* (February 1981).

Hartshorne, Charles. "Subhuman Rights." *Environmental Ethics* 1 (Spring 1979).

Lasch, Christopher. *The Culture of Narcissism.* New York: W.W. Norton, 1979.

Regan, Tom. *All That Dwell Therein: Essays on Animal Rights and Environmental Ethics.* Berkeley: University of California Press, 1982.

Regan, Tom, and Peter Singer. *Animal Rights and Human Obligations.* Englewood Cliffs, N.J.: Prentice-Hall, 1989.

Singer, Peter. *Animal Liberation: A New Ethic for Our Treatment of Animals.* New York: Avon Books, 1975.

Solomon, Robert C. "Has Not an Animal Organs, Dimensions, Senses, Affections, Passions?" *Psychology Today* (March 1982).

Index

About the Author

ALAN S. MILLER is a member of the faculties in Conservation and Resource Studies and Peace and Conflict Studies at the University of California, Berkeley. Teaching on the Berkeley campus since 1973, he is the author of numerous articles and books including *Global Stakes: The Linkages of Peace* (Wellington, N.Z.: Pacific Institute of Resource Management, 1986 and 1988), and *A Planet to Choose: Value Studies in Political Ecology* (New York: Pilgrim Press, 1978). Twice nominated for Berkeley's distinguished teaching award, Dr. Miller teaches courses in Global Environmental Issues, Environmental Philosophy, Bioethics, Nuclear Safety, and World Order and the Environment. He has been a parish minister and director of an ecumenical higher education agency, a community organizer, and an editor with Pacific News Service in San Francisco. A native of Minneapolis, Minnesota, he and Barbara Jones Miller are the parents of five children.